Cyberterrorism and Military Preparedness: An International Prospective

Cyberterrorism and Military Preparedness: An International Prospective

Retd. Major Randhir Pal

SWASTIK

SWASTIK PUBLICATIONS

DELHI-110094 (INDIA)

SWASTIK PUBLICATIONS
31 Gali No. 1, A Block, Pocket 5, CRP Water Tank,
Sonia Vihar, Delhi-110094
Cell: 9968482939, 9899462604
e-mail: swastik_books@yahoo.com

Cyberterrorism and Military Preparedness:
An International Prospective

First Published 2012

ISBN:- 978-93-81084-11-3

PRINTED IN INDIA

Published by Indra Mani Pandey for Swastik Publications, Delhi and Printed at Deepak Offset Press, Delhi-32

PREFACE

The use of information systems, electronic networks, and the entire information technology environment changed dramatically in last decade expanding and linking all social sectors. Those advances brought significant benefits to individual citizens and to the financial, industrial, business, academic, and service sectors. Yet, the reliable and safe operation of the myriad of technological solutions, information systems, and support infrastructure requires that far-reaching concerns about security issues are effectively addressed by governments, business concerns, organizations, and individual users who develop, own, provide, manage, service, and use those information systems, resources, and networks. The distinction between cybercrime on one side and cyberterrorism and cyberwarfare on the other is of significant import as the ways and means to detect and fight each are radically different. Equating a terrorist that bombs civilian targets with criminals and thus being on a par with smugglers, drug traffickers, Internet pornographers, and others, generally limits protective interventions to mostly reactive and defensive measures. As is the case with the determined and often suicidal terrorist, his or her characterization as a "criminal" and the use of traditional law enforcement interventions is utterly inadequate to deal with individuals and organizations that are highly organized and trained paramilitary units conducting offensive campaigns against nations and civilian organizations and populations that they consider to be at war.

Thirty-three countries, including the United States, have signed the Council of Europe's Convention on Cybercrime of November 2001. The Convention's goal is to combat cybercrime by harmonising national laws, improving investigative abilities and boosting international co-operation. Supporters argue that the Convention will enhance deterrence, while critics counter that it will have little effect without the participation of countries in which cybercriminals operate freely. Others warn that it will endanger privacy and civil liberties. This invaluable book addresses the issues of fighting cybercrime and evaluates measures undertaken by various governments to prevent these attacks from happening. America, Russia, Korea, Netherlands, Japan, Israel and France, are specifically discussed.

Enormous efficiencies have been gained over the past twenty-five years as a result of the introduction of computers and telecommunications technologies. The use of these systems and networks translates into a major concentration and centralization of information resources, however, this consolidation creates a major vulnerability to a host of attacks and exploitations. Cyber Warfare and Cyber Terrorism reviews related problems, issues, and presentations of the newest research in this field. Cyber Warfare and Cyber Terrorism provides an overview with basic definitions of cyber terrorism and information warfare, along with recommendations on how to handle these attacks. It presents detailed discussion on primary target facilities, deliverables, external penetration, starting points for preparations against attacks, and planning security systems. Enormous efficiencies have been gained over the past twenty-five years as a result of the introduction of computers and tele-communications technologies. The use of these systems and networks translates into a major concentration and centralization of information resources, however, this consolidation creates a major vulnerability to a host of attacks and exploitations. Cyber Warfare and Cyber Terrorism reviews related problems, issues, and presentations of the newest research in this field. Cyber Warfare and Cyber Terrorism provides an overview with basic definitions of cyber terrorism and information warfare, along with recommendations on how to handle these attacks. It presents detailed discussion on primary target facilities, deliverables, external penetration, starting points for preparations against attacks, and planning security systems.

The book gives a solid introduction to cyber warfare and cyber terrorism in the 21st Century and the military precautions. It is a must-have for information technology specialists, information security specialists and military personals who want a first hand briefing on developments related to cyber warfare and cyber terrorism attacks.

Author

CONTENTS

1

Terrorism and the Internet: New Threats Posed by Cyberterrorism and Terrorist Use of the Internet

Introduction

Although it is known that terrorists already routinely use the Internet for purposes such as spreading propaganda or conducting internal communication, the threat that results from this use is heavily debated. Especially the question whether a cyberterrorist attack is imminent or if it is only a purely fictitious scenario is subject to many discussions. One reason for these differences in opinion is a lack of exact terminology. Already for the term "terrorism", more than 100 different definitions with more than 20 definitional elements have been identified.

Consequently, current interpretations of "cyberterrorism" range from very narrow to very broad. A more narrow view is often worded close to common terrorism definitions and might include only politically motivated attacks against information systems and only if they result in violence against noncombatant targets (Pollitt 1998). Broader approaches often include other forms of terrorist use of the Internet and therefore might define cyberterrorism as almost any use of information technology by terrorists. To complicate matters even more, additional terminology is being introduced into the discussion, *e.g.*, "digital Pearl Harbor", "electronic Waterloo", "Cyber war", or "electronic Chernobyl". These terms, however, focus mainly on the effects of possible future attacks by terrorists. Therefore, they rather cloud the discussion about a precise terminology on cyberterrorism or a terrorist use of the Internet.

This chapter is divided into three parts that depict the problematic areas that are currently under discussion. Part one will deal with what is usually considered as "real" cyberterrorism: attacks that are carried out via the Internet and that are aimed either at other IT systems or at real-world property and human lives. Part two will then cover issues that might not be considered as cyber terrorism in a narrow sense, but rather a use of the Internet for terrorist purposes. Finally, part three will cover uses of the Internet that might commonly be regarded as conventional or even harmless. A look in more detail will reveal, however, that even the everyday use of the Internet can offer some specific advantages for terrorists.

This chapter will not go into further details of the problems of defining cyberterrorism or a terrorist use of the Internet. Instead, it will give–as outlined above–an assessment of the risks and thus the threat of terrorists who can use the Internet for their purposes. The underlying term "terrorism" is for this reason understood in a broad sense to allow an expanded view of the risks and chances.

Furthermore, to allow a realistic risk analysis, it is not sufficient to look only at cases of terrorist involvement that have officially been confirmed. Often, the facts of such cases will be kept confidential, *e.g.*, because they affect issues of national security. Therefore, this analysis is based on cybercrime and cyberterrorism literature as well as on specialised security reports, case studies, and news reports. Only such a broad approach allows the inclusion of occurrences of the past and also gives consideration to possible future threats.

Attacks via the Internet

Attacks that are launched over the Internet are commonly known as integral parts of what is commonly called "cyber crime". Formerly, perpetrators in this area were often young hackers, keen on experimenting with security-related issues and curious about technology. In the meantime, however, this situation has changed. Instead of experimenting youngsters, highly organised groups that use attacks as a source of income, businesses that conduct industrial espionage, and states engaging in electronic warfare can be observed. The only group of actors that seem to be missing are the terrorists who rarely admit to computer-related aggression. Nevertheless, this is no reason for an all-clear. The events in Estonia in 2007, for example, have shown that even whole countries can be put at risk without the use of a single conventional weapon. This will not go unnoticed by terrorists. A more thorough look at the motivation of terrorists for attacks over the Internet is therefore of the essence before looking at the concrete possibilities for terrorist attacks.

Motivation

Some authors claim that, to date, not a single instance of cyberterrorism has been recorded (Sieber 2004). According to informal sources, however, many attacks have already taken place, but are kept confidential due to the security threat to important infrastructures that would evolve from details becoming publicly known. Whatever the case may be, it is undeniable that the threat of terrorist action over the Internet is realistic. Already this fact can and is abused by terrorists as a form of psychological warfare: cyber-fear is generated by the fact that what a computer attack *could* do is too often associated with what will actually happen (Weimann 2006).

General Motivation

Beyond the potential for psychological warfare, five main issues are relevant for a general motivation to commit crimes over the Internet:

Location Independence: Attacks in the Internet are not bound to a definite physical place. Although it is necessary to visit the locality of a conventional attack, *e.g.*, to "case" the target or place the bomb, cyber terrorists do not have to be physically present at the place of their deed. This is a great advantage over conventional attacks where the danger of being suspected during the preparation phase or even detected immediately before the commitment of the crime is omnipresent. For any cyber crime, it is sufficient to be connected to the Internet from any place on earth. This can be a static connection, *e.g.*, at home or at an internet café, or a mobile connection, *e.g.*, over a cellular telephone. Often, it is assumed that many countries that host terrorist groups are not well enough equipped with Internet connections to pose a real threat. However, this is true only with regard to the current status.

The Internet penetration rates of North America, Australia, or Europe are still clearly above those of Africa, for example. The increase of Internet users within the last years, however, was extremely fast, in some countries, even close to 5,000% within the last 7 years. Especially the number of Internet cafés that can be used for rates affordable even to the poor has rapidly increased in most major cities during the last years. This allows large parts of the population (and the terrorists among them as well) to access the Internet without any further control.

Speed

Attackers are hardly dependent on their own connection speed for attacks that are launched over the Internet. Instead, they can use the bandwidth and speed of third parties, *e.g.*, to launch distributed denial-of-service (DDoS) attacks. The party's own connection speed is needed only to distribute commands to the systems attached or to receive feedback about the successes. In both cases, even slow, low-band-width connections are sufficient.

The aspect of independency is true also for those attacks that act without human interaction, *e.g.* viruses or worms. These programs–once released by their creators–act on their own. The speed of their spreading is determined solely by the connection speed of the victims that help them to spread. This could be observed, for example, by the speed in which the Sapphire, the Melissa, or the I-Love-You- Worms spread during 1999 and 2003. None of them was dependent on the link-up of their creators.

Finally, the possibility to create and test malicious computer programs can be used to prepare action for future events. This makes it possible to react in a seemingly spontaneous manner to incidents, even though the preparation took place long before ("cyber revenge").

Anonymity

The anonymity of perpetrators is often alleged as a core feature of Internet-based communication. It is necessary to remember, however, that an IP address at least is transmitted with every step taken on the Internet. This can be used to get evidence of the person who initiated certain actions over the Internet. In many cybercrime cases, this can successfully be used to arrest the real perpetrator who thought that just by using the Internet he would remain anonymous.

Technologically knowledgeable people, however, have ways of hiding their identity and camouflaging their trail to an extent that makes a prosecution hard or–in some cases–impossible (Brunst 2009). The IP address of a user of an Internet café, for example, is transmitted as it is in any other case. If the owner of the establishment is not obliged or fails to register their users, however, the lead will end at the Internet Café without any further possibility to identify the culprit. Similar problems arise with wireless networks (WLAN) that–if not especially protected by the possessor–can be used to access the Internet by almost anybody within the range of the access point.

Apart from these purely organisational means, a number of additional–more technical ways–of hiding the identity on the Internet can be used. Perpetrators, for example, use proxy servers, anonymity networks, or they simply route their traffic over hacked computers of innocent users. In any of these cases, the trace cannot be followed to the computer of the perpetrator, who then cannot normally be identified either.

Internationality

The Internet connects countries regardless of their physical borders or diplomatic or political relations. Nation states, however, are still acting according to their national sovereignty, not as an operator or supervisor of a globally active network. This is actively being taken advantage of by criminals. The aspect of internationality therefore has to be seen in close context with the anonymity and independency of place.

Examples of this technique are manifold. Especially in the area of controversial contents, it can be observed that perpetrators actively seek countries with more liberal free-speech laws to host their contents. Because content that is made available on the Internet, *e.g.* on the World Wide Web, is accessible from all over the world, the physical places of someone offering information and of a person accessing these data can easily differ. Other examples concern attacks that are routed through different computers to hide the traces. Often, the routing is deliberately chosen to pass through countries that do not cooperate either in criminal matters or at least in cybercrime matters.

Alternatively, the routing can pass through countries where it is known that the technical capabilities of investigating cybercrime are not developed far enough to successfully gather evidence–a particular problem when considering internationally operating terrorists.

Cost-Benefit Ratio

When choosing targets and weapons, terrorists are often bound to a rigorous cost-benefit analysis of their own definition. Actions that bear a great risk of being detected too early or that will not achieve high visibility (and therefore fear in the population) have to be disregarded in favour of more "efficient" instruments. Attacks committed over the Internet–at least in general–have an extremely positive cost-benefit ratio. On the one hand, such attacks require only minimal initial investment. Computers are cheap and nowadays, in many areas of the world, are already part of daily life.

Furthermore, an up-to-date computer model is not required. Because speed does not play an important role a computer of the last product line or even the generation before will be sufficient. Even some of the newer mobile phones can be used for simple Internet access. If these options are–for any reason–not available, Internet cafés that are found in any major city can also be used to cheaply access the Internet. The information that is needed to find relevant security holes and technical possibilities for exploitation is also available cost free.

On the other hand, even small attacks against targets lead to high costs for their owners. Constant updating, state-of-the-art equipment, and permanent monitoring is required to protect systems even against the so-called script kiddies. Therefore, costs for personnel, machinery, and software constantly put pressure on the owners of publicly accessible computer services. The Internet can therefore be seen as a form of "force multiplier". This military term means that the striking power potential of a unit is increased without increasing the personnel at the same time (White 1990). Especially for smaller terrorist groups this is true, because the Internet allows them to create harm much larger than possible with their conventional capabilities.

Furthermore, the Internet can be used by them to create the illusion of greater size and power as well as having more followers than is truly the case. This, in turn, will lead their opponents to defensive measures that are far-reaching (and therefore, again, more costly) then objectively necessary.

Specific Terrorist Motivation

These five main areas of motivation are valid for terrorists as well as for ordinary cyber criminals. Differences can, however, be observed with regard to the underlying agenda (Brunst 2008). Terrorists aim primarily at the generation of fear, the creation of economic confusion, or a discrimination of the political opponent. Apart from these main motives, the generation of monetary income or the gathering of information (either for conventional or for electronic attacks) can also be objectives. To conduct actions over the Internet is only one way to achieve these goals.

The problematic issue relating to the terrorist intention behind action on the Internet is, however, that it is often undetectable. If, for example, a hacking attack with the aim of shutting down important systems at an airport is successful, terrorists will probably have an interest in making this publicly known to arouse fear in the population. In this case, it is easy to determine terrorists because the source of a cybercrime act and also the underlying agenda is clear.

If, however, a hacking attack is committed in the hope of gaining information on the automobile route of an important person, this might be kept secret so as not to endanger future plans for a bomb assassination of that person (Brunst 2008). In this case, it is unknown that the act was committed by terrorists. Additionally, even if this fact would emerge, the specific intention of the perpetrators, *i.e. why* the hacking attack occurred (*e.g.*, test of technical capabilities, preparation of conventional attack or allotted victim), would still be unknown. Therefore, from a purely objective perspective, in many cases the distinction between ordinary cybercrime and cyberterrorism is hard to make.

Attacks

Any attack with a computer–maybe with the unlikely exception of physical attacks with computer hardware–is aimed at another computer system. However, with respect to the terrorist intention and the outcome of cyber attacks, a distinction should be made between attacks that are actually aimed "only" at other computer systems and those that are intended to harm human lives.

Attacks Aimed at other IT Systems

Attacks that are aimed at other IT systems can serve different intentions. Often, a first aim will be to get access to the computer system. This can be achieved either with technical means or with the help of deceiving users and administrators. If such an attack is successful, data that is stored or otherwise handled through this computer can be changed or secretly copied from the machine. In many cases, however, terrorists will not even try to gain access to the computer. Instead, it might be sufficient–as with a conventional attack–to hinder the system from functioning correctly. The use of either denial-of-service (DoS) attacks or even conventional attacks on computer infrastructure can be a successful means to achieve these goals. Finally, a combination of classic conventional and new electronic attacks is regarded as a main threat by many experts.

Illegal Access ("Hacking")

Hacking, *i.e.* the illegal access to computer systems and data, is the scenario where problems, action, and results of terrorists and other cyber criminals probably differs the least. In general, a differentiation between illegal access by only technical means and access with human help can be made. An example of purely technical access would be the use of a computer program that uses software flaws that have been identified to gain access to a system (so-called exploit). Some exploits have already been available for a long time and will work only if a system administrator was not able to keep their computer up-to-date. Other exploits, however, are not known to the public or even the software manufacturers. These "zero-day exploits" or "less than zero-day exploits" can be acquired on the black market and will give access to systems, even if the administrator installed all possible security fixes that were available from the software company that developed the product (Wilson 2005).

The second category refers to access with human help. This can be achieved, for example, in the form of so-called social engineering, *i.e.* deceiving the user to give passwords or other protected information. Other ways to gain access with human help include the infiltration of dedicated personnel or the bribing of existing staff members. In general, the choice of the right technique (or a combination thereof) depends on the individual circumstances. Therefore, successful attacks against protected targets often require technical and social skills.

According to a study of the *Center for the Study of Terrorism and Irregular Warfare* , the capabilities that are needed for successful attacks can be divided into three groups (Nelson et al. 1999):

- ***Simple–unstructured:*** The capability to conduct basic hacks against individual systems using tools created by someone else. The organisation possesses little target analysis, command and control or learning capability.
- ***Advanced–structured:*** The capability to conduct more sophisticated attacks against multiple systems or networks and possibly, to modify or create basic hacking tools. The organisation possesses an elementary target analysis capability and command and control structure for sequential attacks from a single location. Some learning ability–can assimilate some new technologies and train personnel.
- ***Complex–coordinated:*** The capability for coordinated attacks capable of causing mass-disruption. Ability to analyse vulnerabilities, penetrate integrated, heterogeneous defences (including cryptography) and create attack tools. Strong ability to conduct target analysis and high confidence in results. Strong command and control structure capable of employing multiple, simultaneous attacks from different locations. Strong organisational learning capacity–can keep up with latest technology, train personnel, diffuse knowledge throughout the organisation, make necessary doctrinal and organisational changes to enhance capabilities.

Already attacks of the lowest level, *i.e.* "simple–unstructured" can–under some circumstances–be sufficient to successfully gain access to a computer system. However, these forms of attack will only work if it is sufficient to attack *any* system. In this case, a computer system can be sought that is vulnerable to a certain form of attack, *e.g.*, where a certain version of a software product is installed. If it is necessary to attack a *given* target, however, the efforts to successfully attack are incomparably higher. In this case, it might be necessary to acquire certain specialised tools, like the above-mentioned "zero-day exploits".

Attacks of the highest level, *i.e.* "complex–coordinated", will require a high degree of innovation and technical effort. In exchange, they allow access even to systems that are extraordinary well protected. An example for a successful combination of *social engineering* and an individually developed malicious program was shown in the year 2006 by a security company. To gain access to the systems of their client (who hired them to test their computer security), the company prepared USB sticks with a custom-designed, newly developed Trojan horse program that could not be detected by virus scanners. Twenty of these sticks were "lost" on the premises of the client. Of these, 15 sticks were found by employees–and promptly connected to the company network where the Trojan started to collect passwords and other valuable information and e-mailed this data back to the offenders (Weimann 2005). Of course, such an attack would be a powerful way for a terrorist organisation to initiate counterespionage.

The assessment as to what extent hacking terrorists are realistic threats differs immensely. In many countries the information about actual incidents is classified and hard to verify. According to experts, however, terrorist groups had considered the integration of hacking into their repertoire already by the end of the 1990s. Today, at least some terrorists are known to possess considerable hacking skill.

Apart from the actual skills, the time that is needed to educate a group on relevant hacking skills is also under debate. Members of the US *Naval Postgraduate School* , for example, estimated in 1999 that it would take from 2 to 4 years to acquire the skills necessary to launch "advanced–structured" attacks. For "complex–coordinated" attacks a time-frame of 6–10 years is expected. Because access to the

Internet and therefore the amount of freely available information has enormously increased since 1999, however, it has to be doubtful that those figures can still be regarded as realistic.

Furthermore, terrorists do not have to rely on their knowledge alone. Experts assume that it is a realistic option for professional hackers to be hired by terrorist groups–in some cases without knowing about the true expectations of their customer (Borland 1998). On the other hand, most terrorist organisations have worked in conspiratorial and close environments where weapons, attacks, and personnel were chosen and tested carefully and put to use only if no risk was to be expected. Therefore, a final assessment whether terrorists would use this form of "outsourcing" remains speculative.

Data Alteration

After a successful hacking attack, a perpetrator has many options on what to do with the system. A comprehensible first reaction would be to delete information or shut down the system. However, this technique would not be successful (at least not for any length of time), because administrators would immediately notice the failure and could reconstruct the system from backup files or switch to reserve systems. The amount of damage that would result from such an attack would therefore not be too high. However, in some areas, *e.g.*, certain industrial production facilities or in medical environments, even short outages could have disastrous consequences.

Defacements

Alterations that are visible to a large audience are often considered to be better, because they can demonstrate the technical capabilities and create fear of what other systems could fall foul of future attacks. An example of an attack that is widely recognizable is a so-called defacement that often takes place after a hacker has gained access to a web server. In this case, a page on the web server, often the prominent entry page, is altered. Often insults (*e.g.*, to the technical incapability of the system administrators) are put on the page together with hints as to the identity of the perpetrator (*e.g.*, the name of a hacking group). By leaving this form of "digital business card", the perpetrator can keep record of their successful break-in and therefore of their technical capabilities. While other forms of cyber crime often remain in the dark, defacements are clearly meant to be seen by a large audience. A large-scale series of defacements could be interesting for terrorists, especially if servers that belong to security agencies, the military, or other important services are concerned.

This has already been observed. In the year 2001, for example, the group "Pentaguard" demonstrated its capabilities when it simultaneously defaced a multitude of government and military websites in the UK, Australia, and the United States. This attack was later evaluated as one of the "largest, most systematic defacements of worldwide government servers on the Web" (Leyden 2001). In another case, pro-Palestinian hackers used a coordinated attack to break into 80 Israel-related sites and deface them. Even al-Qaeda used the technique of defacement to demonstrate its technological as well as its conventional dangerousness when it deposited images of the hijacked (and later beheaded) Paul Marshall Johnson, Jr. on the hacked website of the Silicon Valley Landsurveying, Inc.

Other forms of Data Alteration

Other forms of data alterations are discussed mainly as theoretical threats. Unlike the defacements that were discussed above, other alterations are usually not as obvious and therefore hard to recognize. This enables them to result in great damage. Targets that are discussed in the literature as exceptionally disastrous are, for example, databases with social security numbers, data sets of banks and other financial institutions, or collections with military and classified information. Unnoticed attacks on any of these databases could have disastrous effects on the economy of a country and result in a continuing lack of trust of the people in their systems and institutions if changes were not to be detected (and repaired) within a short period of time (Berinato 2002).

Some authors claim that activities such as a manipulation of large and central databases would exceed the capabilities of terrorist groups that are often not composed of long-time experienced hackers. Planning games such as "Eligible Receiver" and current information regarding recent attacks have shown, however, that even top-secret military computers and research laboratories that are handling nuclear materials are not immune against all possible forms of electronic attacks. For a realistic risk assessment, at least the possibility that terrorists are considering or evaluating such attacks has to be taken into account.

Data Espionage

For terrorist groups, the acquisition of information about their opponent is as important as for any other organisation. If, for example, it becomes known that communication channels between members of the group are being monitored or that plans for a future operation have leaked to government agencies, appropriate action needs to be taken. Because most of today's communication structure is computer based, data espionage is on the rise throughout.

Commonly, the clandestine exploration and obtaining of protected digital information was originally particularly known between states that try to acquire security relevant information from other states to gain tactical advantages. However, in the meantime, industrial espionage has also become an important factor for many economies. With regard to electronic espionage that is directed against digital information, the boundaries between the activities of individual hackers, organised groups, and state-sponsored fractions become increasingly blurred. In a case that took place in 1999 and that was later named "Moonlight Maze", for example, hackers allegedly were able to get access for a period of more than 1 year to computer networks at the US Energy Department nuclear weapons and research labs, at the National Aeronautics and Space Administration, and at numerous university research facilities and defence contractors.

Although no classified computers were known to have been breached, even the unclassified networks are said to contain confidential and sensitive data that could potentially be valuable to any foreign government or terrorist group. Experts therefore claimed that the value of the information that was gathered was "in the tens of millions–perhaps hundreds of millions–of dollars".

Although evidence indicated in the beginning that the attacks of "Moonlight Maze" originated from Russian computers and that the attacks were state sponsored (Drogin 1999), this was later refuted by government officials. As in many cases, in the end, it remained unclear as to what extent which kind of information had been accessed. In addition, it could not be determined if the computer that was really used to attack was the computer of the actual attacker, if the attacker was acting on their own or on behalf of a government, or if the computer was only a hacked computer that was used to camouflage the traces to the real offender.

Almost the same is true for a series of attacks that started in 2003 and were named "Titan Rain" by the US government. Although evidence indicated, according to experts, that it would be "unlikely to come from any other source than the Chinese military" (AFP News Agency 2005) , the exact source of the attack, the amount of data that was acquired, and the precise nature (*i.e.* state-sponsored, corporate espionage, or random hacker attacks) remain unclear.

Apart from cases where data espionage is handled either by technical means as described above or by ways of social engineering, terrorist organisations can also try to get access to sensitive information by legal means. One example concerns the Japanese Metropolitan Police Department, which hired a company for the development of a software system for the tracking of their (also partly unmarked) cars. It later turned out that a part of the software was developed by members of the Aum Shinrikyo cult–the same group that was responsible for the gassing of the Tokyo subway in 1995. This was possible because the software developers were engaged as subcontractors, thus enabling personnel clearance to be circumvented. As it turned out later, members of the cult had developed not only this piece of software, but they were engaged in activities for at least 80 firms and 10 government agencies.

Another case concerned the company Ptech in Boston. The firm was, among others, working for the US Air Force, NATO, the US Congress, and it was developing counterterrorism software for the FBI. Accordingly, the company had access to sensitive military and similar sensitive security relevant information. According to news reports, Yassin Al Qadi, a Saudi millionaire with alleged connections to Osama Bin Laden and al-Qaeda, had invested several millions of dollars into the company. Therefore, the US government feared that security-relevant information could have leaked to the terrorist organisation, and they raided the company premises in 2002.

Denial-of-Service Attacks

Denial-of-service (DoS) attacks are targeted at the unavailability of a system or service and have a long tradition in computer crime. Modi operandi range from a crude cutting of power cables to complex exploitations of security weaknesses. Since the last couple of years, individual attacks have been replaced by DDoS attacks. So-called bot-nets, with hundreds or even thousands of Trojan horse-infected computers, are commanded by individuals to send massive requests to single targets.

These computers are often not able to handle the enormous amount of traffic and are no longer able to send answers to either the computers of the bot-net or to other–legitimate–requests. Computers that are under the attack of a bot-net therefore seem to be unreachable. An impressive example of the use of bot-nets was the "Estonian Cyberwar" that took place in 2007. During a longer period of time, Estonian government, news, and banking sites were under massive attacks by bot-nets. At the same time, coordinated hacking and defacement attacks took place. According to Estonian Defence Minister Aaviksoo, more than one million computers worldwide were engaged in the attacks. Because most of the attacks originated from Russia and some evidence indicated that the coordination of the attacks was of a quality unseen before, it was assumed that the Russian government was involved in the attack. Later, however, these charges had to be dropped, because it was not possible to determine whether the attacking computers were the origin of the attack or if they were only used to disguise the real perpetrators.

DDoS attacks do not necessarily have to be launched only with technical means. To call attention to the involvement of the German airline Lufthansa in the deportation of illegal alien residents, supporters of an online demonstration were asked to open the web page of the company at the same date and time. More than 13,000 people followed the call. In return, the Lufthansa server was unable to reply to the sudden peak of requests, and the web page became unavailable to customers during this time frame (OLG Frankfurt a.M. 2006). This technique is also known as "swarming", "virtual blockade", or "virtual sit-in" and it shows that even technically non-adept organisations can use the power of distributed attacks against targets on the Internet. Instead of launching a DDoS attack by themselves or motivating followers to engage in such activities, terrorist organisations can also "outsource" activities. Prices for attacks range from approximately 150–400 US dollars, depending on the target and the duration of the attack. Some bot-net operators even offer discounts for multiple orders.

In the past, it could be observed that groups were actively using DDoS attacks to push their goals. For example, six different Hizbollah sites, the Hamas site, and other Palestinian information sites were brought down by a so-called FloodNet attack of pro-Israeli hackers. The service virtually "flooded" the respective servers with pings resulting in the unavailability of the servers for all other requests. Even after a relaunch with a slightly different spelling, the sites were still unreachable because the hackers immediately adjusted the attack to the new names.

Conventional Attacks on IT Infrastructure

Terrorists are free in the choice of their weapons and their targets. It is only the expected success, the necessary effort, and the possible consequences that guide terrorists. Because IT infrastructure and especially the use of the Internet have become essential parts of the everyday life of most individual and corporate users, conventional attacks might also be considered as an option by terrorists. Three examples show possible scenarios.

The domain name system (DNS), for example, is essential for many services that use the Internet. It is necessary to translate a human-readable domain name into the IP address (*e.g.*, 194.94.219.193) that is needed by the computer to contact the appropriate server. If an attacker was able to disrupt DNS services, large parts of the Internet would be unusable. The attempt to hamper the functioning of the 13 root-DNS servers in 2002 was therefore evaluated by some authors as an attack against the "heart of the Internet" (Weimann 2004a). However, the consequences of these attacks were hardly noticeable due to built-in safeguards of the DNS systems: no slowdowns or even outages were caused. The same is true for a recent attack that took place in February 2007: even though the aggression lasted for almost 12 hours, the influence was hardly noticeable (ICANN 2007). If, however, terrorists were able to find a way to successfully disrupt the functioning of the DNS–even for a limited region–the consequences would be noticeable immediately by all of the affected users.

This, on the one hand, could result in dramatic consequences for the economy that is largely dependent on the Internet as a main connector to their customers and other businesses. On the other hand, a destruction of Internet communication could also be used in connection with conventional attacks. The incidents in Estonia, for example, have shown what happens if a whole population is no longer able to access independent information about recent incidents, because Internet connections are not available. Therefore, a terrorist organisation could be interested in launching a conventional attack and blocking all (apart from traditional media) access to independent information from the Internet, thereby raising the amount of panic and the feeling of helplessness within the population.

A second approach to attack IT infrastructure with conventional means could target the intercontinental connections. For example, many transcontinental data connections rely on transatlantic cable connections between Europe and the United States. Whereas European cable ends are widely spread between many different countries, they are often bundled on the American side and could therefore be an interesting target. The effects of such an attack could be observed when cables between the United States and China were damaged accidentally (Brunst 2008).

According to a survey after this mishap, 97% of the Chinese users reported problems accessing foreign web pages; 57% claimed that their life and work was being affected by the damage (Persson 2006). If committed intentionally by terrorists, economic effects, in particular, could be the consequence. Furthermore, the psychological side within the population at large (terrorists being able to "shut down" the Internet) would be interesting. Even though the structure of the Internet is spread widely and between many different systems, important connection points between different networks exist, so-called peeringpoints that could pose as possible targets for a third approach.

The German peeringpoint DE-CIX in Frankfurt, for example, is said to handle 80% of the German and 35% of European Internet traffic (according to Force10 Networks 2007). The London Internet Exchange, LINX, is the world's largest Internet peeringpoint and was in the centre of a planned assault in the year 2006. However, Scotland Yard was able to arrest the suspects beforehand so that no damage was done. An MI5 website is reported to have said in this context that "without these services, the UK could suffer serious consequences, including severe economic damage, grave social disruption, or even large-scale loss of life" (Leppard 2007).

Hybrid Attacks

Although the attacks mentioned above are either pure electronic or pure conventional, many authors see a particular danger in hybrid attacks. Hybrid attacks are aggressions that use the advantages of both the virtual and the real world, *e.g.*, to increase the number of casualties. This, for example, could be the case if perpetrators were able to manipulate the communication systems of police and ambulances to hinder an effective coordination of rescue teams in the event of a conventional bomb attack. Reality has already shown that such a scenario is not total science fiction. For example, a hacker from Toborg, Sweden was able to partially manipulate the "911" emergency call system in Florida, United States. It is unknown, however, if this was the intention of the hacker or only a coincidence.

Apart from these attacks that are aimed at the lives of people, other hybrid attacks are being discussed that focus on severe economic consequences. These could occur if the perpetrators were able to launch a successful assault against national financial networks (such as Fedwire or Fednet) or against transfer networks (such as SWIFT). It is estimated that such an attack could weak havoc on the entire global economy (Wilson 2005).

Attacks against Human Lives

Even more dangerous than attacks that are targeted purely against other IT systems are those that target human lives. To understand the concept of such attacks, it is necessary to first describe the technical background for such attacks. Afterwards, a distinction is necessary between scenarios that target immediate death or bodily harm of the victims and those that try to achieve a long-term success.

Technical Background

Often, attacks against computer systems are considered less dangerous than conventional attacks with bombs, because damages to computers are said to "only" lead to economic losses. At first glance, it seems almost impossible that human lives could be endangered by mere electronic attacks. However, the convergence between a "real", *i.e.* physical, and a "virtual", purely electronic, world is constantly rising. Therefore, computers are no longer exclusively used to "crunch numbers" and store huge amounts of data. Instead, a new type of computing services has quietly evolved without which production facilities for food, pharmaceutical products, electricity, traffic management systems (especially for trains and airplanes), and many other military and civil establishments would be unthinkable today. So-called supervisory control and data acquisition (SCADA) systems are used to measure and control other systems.

Often, SCADA systems are either directly connected to the Internet or they are connected to internal networks that are themselves connected to the Internet. According to informal sources, 17% of SCADA malfunctions are caused by a direct Internet access to the SCADA system. The reason for this is often the wish that systems should be ubiquitously accessible so that data and systems can be controlled remotely (Collin 1997). In the long run, owners hope to save costs if they are able to reduce personnel on site and consolidate at a central location. As a result, many connection lines that carry sensitive data exist on the ground, in the air, or in the water. All of these could pose as targets for terrorist attacks. Furthermore, a successful attack against only one site can reveal access and possibilities for manipulations at many different localities.

Because many of the control systems are based on standard Windows and UNIX operating systems (Bachfeld 2003) , some hackers claim that it would take them only about a week to get into most of the existing control systems (Lenzner and Vardi 2004). The effect that SCADA systems that are connected to the Internet can have on a population could be observed in 2003 when 21 power plants were brought down, and other critically important institutions in the United States (including Edwards Air Force Base, the test centre for B-2 and B-1 bombers) were also affected. Following the incident it was discussed whether these breakdowns were the result of the W32. Lovsan worm that was using the same port to exploit a weakness on individual personal computers being used by the plants to communicate with each other (Bachfeld 2003). The collision resulted in a large power-down in the United States and Eastern Canada. It is therefore an important task to determine which parts of a national infrastructure have to be regarded as "critical", *i.e.* a successful attack would have a serious impact on a nation. By the mid-1990s, the US *President's Commission on Critical Infrastructure Protection* determined eight areas of critical infrastructure that were considered as vulnerable and potential targets for attacks (Embar-Seddon 2002).

Attacks with an Immediate Outcome

Most of the attacks that are aimed at critical infrastructure have an effect that is immediately noticeable. Additionally, none of the scenarios that are described below have–as far as it is known to the public–taken place yet. Nevertheless, many authors see them as realistic possibilities that could be taken into consideration by terrorists, because their outcome is more direct and visible than most of the pure attacks on IT infrastructure described above. Furthermore, they almost guarantee what is important to generate fear within a population: extensive news coverage with impressive picture material. As such, mainly three scenarios are discussed in the literature: attacks on hydroelectric dams; tampering with control systems, especially for railways or air traffic; and taking over control of power plants.

Attacks on Hydroelectric Dams

Probably the most discussed scenario of cyberterrorism with an immediate danger for human lives is an attack on a hydroelectric dam. A perpetrator could gain access to a control system and remotely open the floodgates, thereby endangering the areas and inhabitants behind the gates. The consequences of (accidentally) damaged dams could be observed in the past, *e.g.*, when, in 1975, the Banqiao and Shimantan dams on tributaries of Hang He (Yellow) river in China failed. Dozens of lower dams were damaged and at least 85,000 people died (Gleick 2006). Today, security measures at most dams probably would prevent such extreme results.

However, if terrorists were able to control a dam, *e.g.*, by hacking into the SCADA system controlling it, a deliberate opening of the floodgates could put hundreds or even thousands of people at risk. The danger of dams connected to SCADA systems could be observed especially in two scenarios. In the first scenario, an individual was able to break into the computer system that runs Arizona's Roosevelt Dam. Although some details of the attack are being disputed, the fact alone that the Roosevelt dam was compromised is sufficient to show the danger of a terrorist attack. The second case concerns a case that took place in the year 2000 in Queensland, Australia. There, the culprit was able to manipulate the control system of the sewage treatment facilities over a period of 2 months, letting hundreds of thousands of gallons of putrid sludge ooze into parks and rivers. According to an employee of the Australian Environmental Protection Agency "marine life died, the creek water turned black and the stench was unbearable for residents". In the concrete case, the motive of the perpetrator was not to generate fear in the public.

The damage was caused "only" to bargain for a consulting contract to fix the problems he had caused. However, the case also shows the potential a terrorist would have for bio-related terrorism, *i.e.* causing illness or death not only in people, but also in animals or plants.

Attacks on Traffic Control Systems

In the attacks of 9/11, the hijackers impressively and horrifically showed the amount of damage that they could do with airplanes under their control. It is easy to imagine the possibilities and the fear that would be created if terrorists were able to gain control over airplanes or airport control systems without actually being on board. In 1997, for example, a juvenile was able to access the communication systems of Worcester, MA airport. The action disrupted the telephone service to the Federal Aviation Administration Tower at the airport, the Airport Fire Department, and other related services such as airport security, the weather service, and various private airfreight companies. Furthermore, the main radio transmitter and the circuit that enables aircraft to send an electronic signal to activate the runway lights on approach were disabled. Fortunately, no accidents were caused by the attack. The incident, however, shows the vulnerability of modern transportation systems. Therefore, not only airports and airplanes (which are usually quite well protected), but also train systems are the focus of the discussion. In a worst-case scenario, colliding trains or airplanes could possibly cost hundreds of lives (Giacomello 2004 ; Weimann 2005).

Attacks on Power Plants

The scenario that probably causes the most fear is a manipulation of power plants, especially of nuclear power plants. A similar danger is expected from intrusions into military missile control centres. Although these premises should count as areas with the highest protection and control density, authors still see a possibility for terrorist attempts (Foltz 2004). Furthermore, the massive breakdown of nuclear power plants in 2003 that was described above clearly shows that even these systems are vulnerable to cyber attacks.

Attacks with a Long-term Effect

Some scenarios that are discussed in the literature do not result in a one-time catastrophe. Instead, they aim at a long-lasting panic, fear within the population, and a continuing distrust in local economies. As such, they pose tempting targets for terrorist groups. One of the cases that are being discussed as a theoretical threat is the manipulation of the production line for breakfast cereals or for baby food. If, for example, a terrorist was able to manipulate the production process and change to proportion of ingredients, this could prove dangerous for the customers, *e.g.,* if the portion of iron in baby food was increased to a hazardous amount (Collin 1997). The same effect could be induced if terrorists changed the doses or composition of pharmaceutical products and medicine.

Other areas that are being discussed concern the manipulation of weapons production processes, where a manipulation could lead to useless ammunition or attacks on the economical stability of a country by way of secret manipulations on bank, currency, and transfer systems.

Risk Assessment

The scenarios that are discussed last, *i.e.* attacks with a long-term effect are probably the ones that have to be feared the least. The production chain of a food company, for example, is usually constantly monitored. A manipulation would therefore often be detected already at an early stage. In addition, a sudden increase in the use of different ingredients would likely draw attention. Finally, a manipulation of the composition of certain food products will most likely alter the taste of the product so that again either quality control or customers will detect the change. Other areas that were mentioned (*e.g.*, weapons or medication production sites) are often high-risk areas, where security measures are high, and production computers are seldom linked to public networks.

The same seems–at first glance–to be true for many of the attacks that would lead to an immediate outcome. Often, the sites affected by attacks–especially military ones–are "air-gapped", meaning that they are completely physically, electrically, and electromagnetically isolated (Brunst 2008). In these cases, a remote launch of, for example, a military missile would simply be impossible. Furthermore, many of the situations described rely on a failure of all accompanying security measures at the same time.

Especially air traffic controllers and pilots are trained regarding "situational awareness", however, and use computers only as an aid. For a successful attack, it would therefore be necessary to manipulate not only the control system, but also pilots and/or controllers (Pollitt 1998).

There are, however, no grounds for a complete all-clear: One reason is that it is not reasonable or sufficient to distinguish exclusively between "computer-only" and "human-only" scenarios. Many organisations will, for example, have the funds to buy or otherwise introduce an insider.

This can happen either in the form of active participation or in the form of gathering otherwise protected information. With such help, many security measures can be dangerously compromised. The cases of the Japanese Metropolitan Police Department or the company Ptech that were describedabove show that even vettings can be successfully circumvented. Another problematic area is the increasing use of connectivity and remote controlling even in high-risk areas. For example, new weapons are being developed by the military that rely on remote control, *e.g.*, semi-autonomous military robots. Many of these products rely on civilian technology and established operating systems, thereby opening additional loopholes for security risks.

Finally, terrorists can use the fact that often, due to a lack of technical knowledge, members of the press or even politicians will draw wrong conclusions from facts that have become known to the public. For example, it is widely known that computers are used within missile launching premises. Computers have security weaknesses that can be exploited. Therefore, the deduction that missile centres are vulnerable to cyber attacks suggests itself. However, this conclusion might be wrong, if systems are in fact air-gapped as described above.

This is, in turn, used by terrorists who do not necessarily rely on attacks being successful. An important aspect of terrorist attacks on the Internet is rather the creation of fear and uncertainty and the expectation that terrorists *could* at any time strike at any target they chose. In this context, attacks against IT infrastructure can be of great help. The pure number of vulnerabilities that have become known and the number of targets that can be chosen offer a wide range of possible actions for cyber criminals as well as for terrorists. Any successful attack against "prominent" targets, *e.g.*, government or intelligence websites, can be used to increase the level of anxiousness regarding more serious attacks.

The real danger that evolves from cybercrime attacks could be seen already in 1999, when the United States conducted an exercise named "Eligible Receiver". Hackers of the NSA acted as a so-called red team and attacked computer systems of the CIA, FBI, Defense Intelligence Agency, National Reconnaissance Office, Defense Information Systems Agency, Department of State, Department of Justice, and civilian establishments of relevant infrastructures during a 5-day period.

Although many details of the exercise remained secret, it has become known that the red team relied solely on techniques and software that was freely available over the Internet. The group was able to enter protected networks, render systems inaccessible with the help of DoS and DDoS attacks, forge e-mails and gain root level access to 36 government networks. Even the take-over of resources of the US Pacific Fleet, control of electric power systems, and the emergency number "911" in nine larger American cities was allegedly possible.

Often, those who claim that cyberterrorism is not a real threat state also that terrorists lack the necessary skills for an electronic attack. The current generation of young terrorists, however, has–at least partly–grown up in a digital world. Computers seized from al-Qaeda, for example, show that they are becoming increasingly familiar with hacker tools that are freely available over the Interne. Furthermore, know-how, personnel, and outsourced services can be acquired on the free market, making it possible even for incapable groups to enter the new world of cyber attacks. The Islamic fundamentalist group "Harkat-ul-Ansar", for example, attempted to buy cyber attack software from hackers as early as late 1998 (Wilson 2005).

Finally, many nation states have started to invest into cyber forces to increase their powers also in this relatively new sector. This, in turn, opens new possibilities for state-sponsored terrorism. The threat of future terrorist attacks that involve specific use of the Internet therefore has to be taken very seriously.

Dissemination of Terrorist Contents

With the establishment of the WWW, the Internet has created the possibility for everyone to disseminate information without costs– and largely without any control regarding the content. Terrorists are using the Internet therefore not only to launch attacks, but also to fight a "war of ideas" (Giacomello 2004).

Terrorist Websites

For a terrorist organisation, it is extremely important to communicate their views, aims, and ambitions. Although in former times this was extremely difficult, the Internet now offers possibilities to easily communicate and possibly influence the media and the public at large (Brunst 2008). Therefore, it is no wonder that today almost every underground organisation has its own website (Weimann 2004b, 2006) and the number is still steadily rising. In 1999, only a few of the 30, according to the US Department of State, deemed foreign terrorist organisations were able to operate a website. By 2005, this number had increased to more than 4,500 terrorist-related websites. The number of Internet-related items that carry terrorist contents (*i.e.* including forums, blogs, *etc.*) is even higher. According to some sources, in 2007, there were approximately 50,000 sites with extremist and terrorist content.

Terrorist websites can be used for a number of purposes. For example, it is possible to target special audiences, *e.g.,* the media, followers, or–with cartoon-style design and children stories–even young kids. Contents can be presented as mere text-written viewpoints or–often with the help of fresh graphics, sound, or video files–as a glorification of recent acts or as an incitement to future acts (Brunst 2008). Although it is difficult to assess how many people are paying attention to these websites, it is said that the most popular terrorist sites are able to attract tens of thousands of visitors every month (Conway 2002). The difficulty of judging an organisation only by its website (often as its only "official" organ) can also be abused. For example, a terrorist organisation with an impressive website can easily claim to be bigger and to have more followers than it actually has (Embar-Seddon 2002).

Another issue of popular terrorist websites is that governments will often try to shut them down when they becomes too popular. However, the censorship resistance of the Internet in many cases prohibits these efforts. For this reason, many websites are not stored in the country of their organisation. Instead, they are hosted on servers in countries that have a more liberal freedom-of-speech approach. Several websites of al-Qaeda, for example, were physically stored in the United States and Canada (Brunst 2008). The same is true also for other organisations that chose to be hosted outside of their country.

Threats and Propaganda

As already mentioned above, terrorist websites are not restricted to presenting only their own viewpoints. Instead, they can also be used to threaten the enemy or to spread propaganda. Especially if threats are presented with the help of multimedia technology, this gets the attention of the press and the public. For this reason, computer games have been developed, *e.g.*, one named "Quest for Bush" that lets followers kill US President Bush (Vargas 2006). Other multimedia threats can literally burn images into the memories of the viewing audience. The assassination of Daniel Pearl, for example, showed the impact of psychological warfare that was conducted by these new means. Since then, the use of multimedia has rapidly increased. Whereas the al-Qaeda media arm As-Sahab issued only six audio or video web messages in 2002, this number increased to an impressive 97 multimedia messages in 2007.

To improve the presentation of their viewpoints, threats, propaganda, or incitements to terrorism, terrorists have even begun to record their attacks. For the best results, they are often filmed simultaneously from different angles so that the material can be better used for the distribution to the media, websites, and the production of DVDs (Kristof 2005). This kind of material is often used to (directly or indirectly) influence public opinion. In the past, only a few well-established organisations were able to produce newspapers, magazines, or TV shows. The Internet makes it now possible for virtually anyone to launch their own periodicals. Al-Qaeda therefore was able, for example, to start its own TV program "voice of the caliphate", which is available on the Internet. In the program, a hooded newsreader with a gun and a copy of the Koran on his desk, reads the latest headlines from the world of the Islamist jihad.

Additional multimedia items were often sent out by the "Global Islamic Media Front" (GIMF). This kind of information can normally be easily recognised as terrorist material. Other information, however, might be disguised as seemingly neutral material in the hope that less critical members of the press take up the news and report about them. Because the Internet has become a major source for stories, background information, and also for photographic and similar material, this hope cannot be dismissed. By attractively presenting viewpoints and opinions, terrorist organisations can at least increase their chances of introducing these opinions into mass media products.

Financing

Online advertising and similar ways of gaining monetary income with Internet services has become a profitable business model for many. For terrorists and terrorists groups, this is not as easy, especially if explicit terrorist content is contained on a website. Nevertheless, some organisations have started to use their site not only to disseminate information, but also to use their site as a source of income for financing and fundraising. Some websites, for example, are used–apart from their original purpose–to sell CDs, DVDs, T-shirts, badges, flags, or book. Another way to finance terrorist activities is to give instructions on how to donate money. This can be done, for example, by giving necessary information (*e.g.*, bank account details for transfers) or by implementing possibilities to enter credit card information for automatic withdrawals.

Since the websites terrorist organisations are often at the center of surveillance by security agencies, hundreds of support websites commonly appear and disappear. Each website provides links to other supporter websites so that a visitor who once has found an entry point into the terrorist web can easily find other and similar sites. In some cases, even specialised web rings are founded. Yahoo!, for example, hosted dozens of sites in the "Jihad Web Ring", a coalition of 55 Jihad-related sites. If, at any point, users give personal information, terrorists are also able to gather user demographics. This can happen, for example, if a user fills out online questionnaires, order forms, or enters relevant e-mail lists. Users that are identified as potential sympathisers can then be e-mailed and asked to make donations over other (*e.g.*, more secret) channels (Weimann 2006). Because this first contact is made electronically and over a distance, users might engage more easily into this "clean" form of terrorist support, which also can function as a gateway into closer ties between terrorist organisations and their future supporters.

Conventional Use of the Internet

A commonly underestimated threat is the conventional use of the Internet. While the access to "dangerous" sources, *e.g.*, terrorist websites or relevant message boards, could–at least potentially–be constantly monitored and taken as an initial point for action, this is not possible with everyday services such as search engines, common websites, or e-mail traffic. However, a closer look reveals that even seemingly harmless sites offer information that is, on the one hand, valuable and important for terrorists and, on the other hand, uncontrollable. By way of example, the use of individual communication between terrorists and the planning and supporting of conventional attacks will be highlighted below.

Individual Communication

Although conventional methods for individual communication are still widely available, *e.g.*, telephone or letters, they have individual disadvantages over the possibilities that the Internet offers. A telephone conversation, for example, requires both parties to be present simultaneously at their point of communication. Additionally, contents are transmitted unencrypted so that government agencies can listen if the parties are already under surveillance (or if they are affected by strategic large-scale surveillance measures). A letter, on the other hand, offers the possibility for asynchronous communication and easy encryption, but it takes longer to transmit. Additionally, like the telephone, it requires both parties to be present at certain points, *e.g.*, at a mailbox for the sender or at the destination address for the recipient.

The Internet, however, allows both parties to communicate asynchronously, *e.g.*, by e-mail. This service does not require much bandwidth, making it possible to send and retrieve information even over older mobile phones or in areas where Internet connections are limited. Additionally, messages can be stored and retrieved at any given point in time; terrorists neither have to be online all the time, nor do they have to entrust third parties with the task of accepting personal messages for them. Therefore, e-mail allows terrorists to communicate independently of a specific and pre-determined place. Furthermore, many companies offer e-mail services free of charge so that several different e-mail accounts can be used simultaneously.

The organisers of the 9/11 attacks, for example, had operated in such a way and opened multiple accounts on largely anonymous e-mail services, such as "Hotmail" (Conway 2002). If, for any reason, a synchronous communication is preferred, the Internet offers many different opportunities as well. Internet Relay Chat (IRC), for example, allows for a conversation between two or more persons who are online at the same time. The service is text-based, fast–and largely unsupervised. Even voice-based systems, like Skype, can be used.

The biggest advantage of Internet-based communication, however, is that all messages are digital right from the start. Therefore, many publicly available encryption programs can be used. These are accessible as open source so that terrorists can check themselves for hidden backdoors or other unwanted "features". Nevertheless, terrorist groups have started to compile their own software products for encrypted communication. The software "Secrets of the Mujahideen"– currently available as version 2.0–is advertised as "the first Islamic program for secure communications through networks with the highest technical level of encoding" (Sedarat 2008). The use of such specialised and often easy-to-use applications drastically increases the protection of terrorist's messages between each other. This, in turn, makes it hard or–if used correctly–impossible for government agencies to successfully monitor communication, resulting in a lack of information.

Planning and Supporting

It seems surprising that most of the information needed for a conventional attack is not protected, but freely available. This can, for example, be a picture of an important manager that is available on a company's website or the favourite nightclub of his teenage daughter that can be taken from her profile on facebook.com. According to a terrorist manual, public sources can therefore provide up to 80% of all required information on an opponent (Weimann 2004b).

An example that is often cited is the satellite maps that are provided, for example by Google, Microsoft, or NASA. In former times, images of that quality were available only to experts, now they are a common good and accessible to anybody. It is therefore of no surprise that terrorists have started to use these services for their own purposes. According to UK army intelligence sources, for example, during a raid in 2007, printouts from Google Earth were found. They showed buildings inside the British bases in Basra in detail and vulnerable areas "such as tented accommodation, lavatory blocks and where lightly armoured Land Rovers are parked" (Harding 2007). Due to some additional evidence, officials believed that this information was used to prepare attacks on the premises.

According to some authors, terrorist organisations have even started to use databases to gather, sort, and evaluate the details of potential targets in the United States (Weimann 2004b). Actual findings on terrorists' computers have shown that publicly available information of all kinds are indeed being downloaded and used for planning purposes. It can therefore be assumed that information that is freely available on the Internet is indeed significantly strengthening the operational capabilities of terrorist groups. Terrorists, however, are not only taking information from the Internet. They use the net also to store information and make it available for others. Some authors therefore claim that the Web has become "an open university for jihad". This "university" offers information such as the "Mujahadeens Poisons Handbook" that contains various "recipes" for homemade poisons and poisonous gases (Weimann 2004b, 2006). Similar information is compiled in other collections, such as the "Terrorist's Handbook", the "Anarchist Cookbook", the "Encyclopedia of Jihad", the "Sabotage Handbook", and the famous "How to Make Bombs". Today, many collections are amended by extra information, *e.g.*, on hostage taking, guerrilla tactics, or special kinds of bombs (Brunst 2008).

In this chapter, different risks of terrorists using the Internet have been assessed. Although a large cyber attack that was verifiably committed by terrorists has–up until now–not taken place, this is no reason to underestimate the risks and potential of future scenarios. Already the brief outline of the conventional use of the Internet by terrorists has shown that terrorists are not unfamiliar with the Internet. On the contrary, it is known that the Internet is constantly used for their purposes already today, *e.g.*, to prepare conventional attacks, to communicate, or to disseminate their respective contents.

The general characteristics of the Internet indicate furthermore that digital attacks are a likely scenario. Chances are high that such incidents will be directed against other IT systems, especially if connected to real-world machinery, and result in an immediate outcome rather than long-term effects. The attacks and aggressions that have been launched in the past by common cyber criminals, statesponsored, or (presumably) governmental groups have partly demonstrated the potential of such assaults. Especially the two last-mentioned groups have to be considered as extremely dangerous, because they have the ability to use monetary and technical resources to which common criminals seldom have access.

The actions that have been taken on a political and legal level to counter cyberterrorism have, for a long time, been rather reluctant. In the end, it was probably the attacks on Estonia in 2007 that showed governments around the world and the public at large what knowledgeable aggressors can do to a whole nation solely by digital means. International organisations such as NATO therefore now take cyber attacks "as seriously as the risk of a missile strike" and see cyberterrorism as a chief threat (Johnson 2008). Especially if a nation with offensive cyber capabilities is willing to support perpetrators, the risks and potential damages will additionally increase. The convergence of terrorism and the cyber world therefore creates a new threat that has to be taken very seriously.

2

Threats and Effects of Cyberterrorism

Cyberterrorism can have a serious large-scale influence on significant numbers of people. It can weaken countries' economy greatly, thereby stripping it of its resources and making it more vulnerable to military attack. Cyberterror can also affect internet-based businesses. Like brick and mortar retailers and service providers, most websites that produce income (whether by advertising, monetary exchange for goods or paid services) could stand to lose money in the event of downtime created by cyber criminals. As internet-businesses have increasing economic importance to countries, what is normally cybercrime becomes more political and therefore "terror" related.

Cyberterrorism causes a lot of financial damage. They usually affect huge numbers of people. Cyberterrorism is a very serious crime as it can cause problems to many people at any one time. It has crippling effects on the economy. By crippling a country's economy, a cyber terrorist can also potentially weaken the country for a military attack to be successful. In the wake of the recent terror attacks on Mumbai, Cyber Society of India (CYSI) said that the country is equally vulnerable to cyber terrorism, as it is to physical terrorism. Urging the government to take proactive measures to prevent any possible cyber attacks, Cyber Security Group (CSG) of CYSI in a recent report, submitted to the ministry of telecom and IT, makes recommendations under four broad areas. These areas include management, technology, governance and legal aspects.

In its emphasis on e-security of money transactions, CSG calls for expanding the legal purview of IT Act to include Electronic

Payment and Settlement Act envisaging protection of wider gamut of work involved in e-money, issuance, control, management of supply logistics, settlement and denotification *etc.* CSG wants IT Act on electronic notary to include who authenticates documents, and how this can be done. CSG suggests that mandatory e-notary authentication of e-documents akin to public notary procedure can be simplified and made hassle-free by introducing e-notary counters having e-notaries and e-forms where a user at such counters can avail online e-forms that can be notarised and transmitted back by an e-notary upon submission.

Among the host of recommendations to be incorporated under the IT Act, CSG called for introduction of a single universal ID in India provisionally functioning under federated ID management till universal ID department is created and put in place. To make e-commerce transactions truly functional, e-images of the documents should be made valid through a legislation, it said. On digital rights management area, there is a need to create a counter mechanism against breaches of copyright law to take care of description, identification, trading, protection, monitoring and tracking of all forms of rights usages over both tangible and intangible digital matter, it added. On electronic archives, and info management, the IT Act should address the issue of life cycle management of e-archives and its term of validity and strengthening due diligence in retention of e-documents and e-shares complete transaction management, CSG said.

On mobile devices and remote access, CSG said the IT Act should mull over establishing standards for mobile devices that access devices of questionable security under compulsions of business. Due diligence combined with education and remote access policy should be put in place, it added. On security certification, CSG wanted the IT Act to stress on common standards across countries and cyber space particularly in case of biometerics where common standards can be adopted.

Computing professionals all over the world need to be aware of possible areas of weakness to such terrorism, in order to better protect their computer systems and possibly help put an end to terrorist activity. An important part of any profession is promoting the good name of that profession, but cyber-terrorist continue to give the computing profession a bad reputation. Thus, it is important for computing professionals to understand cyber-terrorism for the benefit of themselves, their profession, and society as a whole.

The resources to launch a cyber attack are commonplace in the world; a computer and a connection to the Internet are all that is really needed to wreak havoc. Adding to the problem is that the public and private sectors are relatively ignorant of just how much their lives depend on computers as well as the vulnerability of those computers. Another problem with cyber crime is that the crime must be solved, (*i.e.* who were the perpetrators and where were they when they attacked you) before it can be decided who has the actual authority to investigate the crime. The board recommends that critical systems should be isolated from outside connection or protected by adequate firewalls, use best practices for password control and protection, and use protected action logs.

Most other government organisations have also formed some type of group to deal with cyber-terrorists. The CIA created its own group, the Information Warfare Center, staffed with 1,000 people and a 24-hour response team. The FBI investigates hackers and similar cases. The Secret Service pursues banking, fraud and wiretapping cases. The Air Force created its own group, Electronic Security Engineering Teams, ESETs. Teams of two to three members go to random Air Force sites and try to gain control of their computers. The teams have had a success rate of 30% in gaining complete control of the systems.

How can I Protect Myself?

Currently there are no foolproof ways to protect a system. The completely secure system can never be accessed by anyone. Most of the militaries classified information is kept on machines with no outside connection, as a form of prevention of cyber terrorism. Apart from such isolation, the most common method of protection is encryption. The wide spread use of encryption is inhibited by the governments ban on its exportation, so intercontinental communication is left relatively insecure.

Others promote the use of firewalls to screen all communications to a system, including e-mail messages, which may carry logic bombs.

Firewall is a relatively generic term for methods of filtering access to a network. They may come in the form of a computer, router other communications device or in the form of a network configuration. Firewalls serve to define the services and access that are permitted to each user. One method is to screen user requests to check if they come from a previously defined domain or Internet Protocol (IP) address. Another method is to prohibit Telnet access into the system.

Here are few key things to remember to protect yourself from cyber-terrorism:

1. All accounts should have passwords and the passwords should be unusual, difficult to guess.
2. Change the network configuration when defects become know.
3. Check with venders for upgrades and patches.
4. Audit systems and check logs to help in detecting and tracing an intruder.
5. If you are ever unsure about the safety of a site, or receive suspicious email from an unkown address, don't access it. It could be trouble.

Some Relevant Ethical Issues

The ethical issues involved in cyber-terrorism are manifold. Any sort of crime or ethical violation can occur using a computer. Extortion of banks takes money from the banks, as well as their customers. The bank's, on the other hand, which many times refuse to admit to their inadequate defenses violate the public trust that the bank will be secure.

The illegal altering medical records is unethical, as it can quickly and easily cause harm to another. Spreading disinformation is unethical in its lack of regard for the truth, as well as for the safety of and consequences on others who believe the misinformation. Altering, destroying, or stealing others data is a violation of their privacy. The ordinary hacker is guilty of lack of regard for the privacy of the peoples systems that he or she would enter. Hacking-for-hire is additionally illicit because they openly sell their services to break into others systems.

Statistics on Cyber-terrorism

Who is at Risk of an Attack?

Most feel that military installations, power plants, air traffic control centers, banks and telecommunication networks themselves are the most likely targets. Other targets include police, medical, fire and rescue systems, which could be hurt, along with Wall Street, water systems, *etc.*

Who are the Terrorists?

The graphic below shows that amateur hackers are by far the biggest threat on the Internet at the current time. They are responsible for about 90% of all hacking activity.

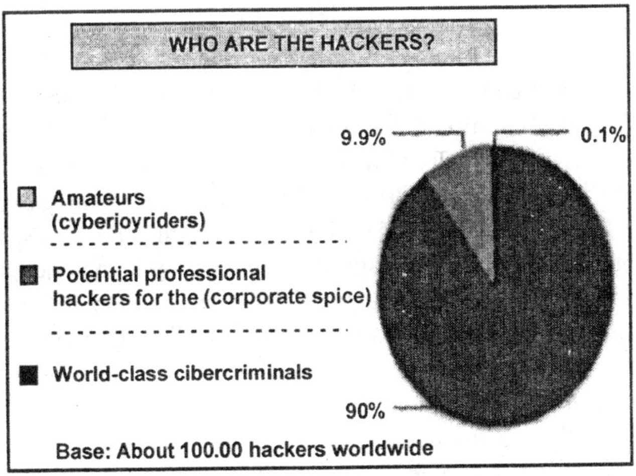

Source: IBM Global Security Analysis Lab, Yorktown Heights, N.Y.

Cyber terrorism does not have to come from the average hacker or even online terrorists. The Govt. carried out a series of its own attacks on itself, in order to test its own defenses against online-based attacks. The Defense Information Security Agency (DISA) found that 88% of the 3000 defense computer systems that were attacked were "easily penetrable". Of the systems that were illegally entered, 96% of the entries were not detected. Of the 4% that were detected, only 5% of them were reported or investigated.

How Common is Unauthorised System Entry?

A survey conducted by the Science Applications International Corp. in 1996 found that 40 major corporations reported losing over $800 million to computer break-ins. An FBI survey of 428 government, corporate and university sites found that over 40% reported having been broken into at least once in the last year. One third said that they had been broken into over the Internet. Another survey found that the Pentagon's systems that contain sensitive, but unclassified information, had been accessed via networks illegally 250,000 times and only 150 of the intrusions were detected. The FBI estimates that U.S. businesses loose $138 million every year to hackers. According to the CIA in the past three years government systems have been illegally entered 250,000.

Costs of Cyberterrorism

According to a source in Great Britain, terrorists have gained at least up to 400 million pounds from 1993 to 1995 by threatening institutions. Over the three years, there were 40 reported threats made to banks in the U.S. and Britain. In January of 1993, three separate incidents took place in London. During the sixth, a brokerage house paid out 10 million pounds after receiving a threat and one of their machines crashed. On the fourteenth incident, a blue-chip bank paid blackmailers 12.5 million pounds after receiving threats. Another brokerage house paid out 10 million pounds on the twenty-ninth incident. Some terrorists just take money, rather than resorting to blackmail. A Russian hacker, for example, tapped into Citibank's funds transfer system and took $10 million.

Cyber terrorism takes many forms. One of the more popular is to threaten a large bank. The terrorists hack into the system and then leave an encrypted message for senior directors, which threatens the bank. In essence, the message says that if they do not pay a set amount of money, then the terrorists will use anything from logic bombs to electromagnetic pulses and high-emission radio frequency guns to destroy the banks files. What adds to the difficulty to catch the criminals is that the criminals may be in another country. A second difficulty is that most banks would rather pay the money than have the public know how vulnerable they are. Here are some examples of cyber-terrorism in its many forms:

1. Cyber-terrorists often commit acts of terrorism simply for personal gain. Such a group, known as the Chaos Computer Club, was discovered in 1997. They had created an Active X Control for the Internet that can trick the Quicken accounting program into removing money from a user's bank account. This could easily be used to steal money from users all over the world that have the Quicken software installed on their computer. This type of file is only one of thousands of types of viruses that can do everything from simply annoy users, to disable large networks, which can have disastrous, even life and death, results.
2. Cyber-terrorists are many times interested in gaining publicity in any possible way. For example, information warfare techniques like Trojan horse viruses and network worms are often used to not only do damage to computing resources, but also as a way for the designer of the viruses to "show off." This is a serious ethical issue because many people are affected by these cases. For one, the viruses can consume system resources until networks become useless, costing companies lots of time and money. Also, depending on the type of work done on the affected computers, the damage to the beneficiaries of that work could be lethal. Even if the person never meant to harm someone with their virus, it could have unpredictable effects that could have terrible results.
3. In one of its more unusual forms, cyber-terrorism can be used for an assassination. In one case, a mob boss was shot but survived the shooting. That night while he was in the hospital, the assassins hacked into the hospital computer and changed his medication so that he would be given a lethal injection. He was dead a few hours later. They then changed the medication order back to its correct form, after it had been incorrectly administered, to cover their tracks so that the nurse would be blamed for the accident. There are many ethical issues involved in a case like this. Most obviously, a man was killed by the hackers' actions. Also, the life of the nurse was

probably ruined, along with the reputation of the hospital and all its employees. Thus, there are often more stakeholders in a terrorist situation that the immediate recipient of the terrorism.

4. Terrorism can also come in the form of disinformation. Terrorists can many times say what they please without fear of reprisal from authorities or of accountability for what they say. In a recent incident, the rumour that a group of people were stealing people's kidneys for sale was spread via the Internet. The rumor panicked thousands of people. This is an ethical issue similar to screaming 'Fire' in a crowded theater. In case like this, the number of people affected is unlimited. Thousands of people were scared by this and could have suffered emotionally.
5. Minor attacks come in the form of "data diddling", where information in the computer is changed. This may involve changing medical or financial records or stealing of passwords. Hackers may even prevent users who should have access from gaining access to the machine. Ethical issues in this case include things like invasion of privacy and ownership conflicts. It could be even more serious if, for instance, the person who needed access to the machine was trying to save someone's life in a hospital and couldn't access the machine. The patient could die waiting for help because the computer wouldn't allow the necessary access for the doctor to save his or her life.

The term cyberterrorism is becoming increasingly common in the popular culture, yet a solid definition of the word seems hard to come by. While the phrase is loosely defined, there is a large amount of subjectivity in what exactly constitutes cyberterrorism. In the aftermath of the September 11th attacks, this is somewhat disconcerting.

Action

In traditional scenarios, terrorist scenarios typically are violent or involve threats of violence. While there have been many studies of violence in the physical world, more research is called for in terms of 'violence' as a virtual phenomenon. Violence in virtual environments is a relatively new field, with many unanswered questions. These open issues include the psychological effects of traditional real-world violence portrayed in virtual environments, possible behavior modification resulting from violence in virtual environments, physical trauma from virtual violence and the use of virtual violence in military training (Stone, 1993; Whiteback, 1993). However, despite the prevalence of traditional violence portrayed in virtual environments, 'cyberviolence' is still very much an unknown quantity.

Tool

There are an almost uncountable number of ways that the terrorist can use the computer as a tool. Facilitating identity theft, computer viruses, hacking, use of malware, destruction or manipulation of data all fall under this category. These uses of the computer, when combined with 'computer as target' form the 'traditional' picture of cyberterrorism.

Target

There are a large number of potential targets that involve, either directly or indirectly, computers. Consider, for example, the impact of Personal Identity Theft. While the incidence of identity theft is comparatively low, the impact of theft upon the unfortunate soul whose ID is stolen can be large: terrorists could use the stolen identity to mask their work, carrying out certain operations under their target's name, not their own. This would help evade detection by authorities, as well as potentially acting as a 'signal' that an identity or operation had been compromised.

The Internet, especially the essentially useless authentication provided by email, provides the perfect breeding ground for identity theft. Another interesting twist on this scenario is that of 'virtual' identity theft. For example, many users have multiple online personalities or profiles. Conceptually, there may be reasons why a terrorist would benefit from stealing a user's online identity. Attacks could be as trivial as exploiting tkrust relationships with other users when logged in as the stolen identity, to planting of Trojans *etc.*, via 'trusted' email.

Similarly, the rise of online stock trading and stock message boards has created an environment in which it is possible to deliberately manipulate a stock price (perhaps via a stolen identity). A terrorist could use such techniques as a funding source, or even attempt to move the markets towards chaos. Thus, a well organised virtual attack upon a bank or corporation's stock rather than the bank or corporation itself, could in fact prove to be highly effective. In my opinion all of the attacks mentioned above are more likely to be successful when carried out against individual users or corporations rather than governments. However, governmental control currently relies heavily on the stability of the overall economy; thus economic destabilisation is a viable attack against a government as well as the attacked third-party entity.

Using the terrorism matrix, effective solutions for computer as 'target' can be conceptualised and designed — but these will be useless overall unless problems (technical, social, legal) arising from the interaction of computer with every cell of the terrorism matrix is addressed. If I can buy a ticket for an unknown 'friend' in Bulgaria to fly to London and blow up the London Eye, antivirus software on the computer controlling the London Eye is of little relevance.

Affiliation

It is possible for a person to read all about a given cause and chat with proponents of the cause without ever leaving the safety of his or her own home. New recruits can thus become affiliated with a terrorist group, commit to carrying out given actions, all without ever actually coming into contact with another human being. At the same time, these loose affiliations can complicate investigations and confuse media reports. Additionally, the introduction of computing technology facilitates alliances between groups with similar agendas; this type of affiliation can result in strengthening of the individual organisations as they can immediately acquire access to the information resources of their allies.

Motivation

Political, social, and economic changes are the motivations present in real-world terrorism. Combining a dependence on Internet-connected systems for banking and Ecommerce with the ability of anyone with a desire and readily available tool to disrupt these areas, results in a situation that is all too clear: unless steps are taken to significantly reduce risks, disaster is inevitable. Even with the best risk reduction, there are still likely to be problems.

Pure Cyberterrorism

The concept of 'pure' cyberterrorism — that is, terrorism activities that are carried out entirely (or primarily)—in the virtual world is an interesting one. The Internet provides many different ways of anonymously meeting with 'like minded' individuals in a (comparatively) safe way. Furthe-rmore, a successful cyberterrorism event could require no more prerequisite than knowledge—something that is essentially free to the owner once acquired, and an asset that can be used over and over again.

Thus, it would be possible that such an environment could facilitate the creation of entirely new terrorist groups —no monies would be required for actions, and members could organize themselves quickly and easily in the anonymity of cyberspace. This is very different from certain examples given above, where the computer can aid the task of the terrorist, but 'real' resources are still required to execute the plan. It is this pure cyberterrorism that most writers mean when they discuss the dangers posed by the cyberterrorist, and this compartmentalisation poses a significant barrier to our ability to protect ourselves.

The New Terrorism

New terrorist organisations are highly funded, technologically articulate groups capable of inflicting devastating damage to a wide range of targets. While most published work in the computer industry has focused on the impact of the computer as target (pure cyberterrorism) it is our belief that the real danger posed by the synthesis of computers and terrorism is not only the insertion of computer as target in the terrorism matrix, but in many of the other areas, too. The current narrowness of focus poses a significant risk to US infrastructure. By being too concerned about one particular part of the matrix, we are apt to let our guard down in areas which may be more critical. A forward-looking approach to terrorism that involves computers is highly contextual in its basis. Traditional antiterrorism defenses must be deployed, but these countermeasures must fully take into account many of the virtual factors that we have outlined here.

If the events of September 11th teach us one thing, it is that we should always consider the 'big picture' of the overall terrorist threat, rather than view one aspect in isolation. The 'cyber' aspects of the puzzle must be woven throughout the picture, not simply confined to one cell. To view a problem with too narrow a perspective is to invite anarchy into our lives.

Computers—The Weapons of the Cyberterrorist

Following on from the discussions above, it becomes obvious that the most likely 'weapon' of the cyberterrorist is the computer. Thus, one might ask, are we arguing that one should restrict access to computers, just as access to explosives is restricted? Not quite, but close. We believe that the stockpile of connected computers needs to be protected. There are many laws that define how one should protect a firearm from illegal/dangerous use. The mandatory use of trigger locks, though controversial, has been put forward to prevent danger should the gun end up in the wrong hands.

Similarly, powerful explosives like C4 are not simply sold over the counter at the corner store. Explosives and guns are certainly not entirely analogous to computers. A better analogy might stem from the concept of an 'attractive nuisance'. For example, a homeowner shares some responsibility for injury caused by a pool on his property —it is deemed an attractive nuisance, and as such, the innocent should be prevented from simply being attracted and harmed.

Thus, there are many instances of laws which already discuss damage done by/to a third party from the intentional/unintentional misuse of a piece of corporate/personal property. The application of these laws or the definition of 'misuse' with respect to computers seems unclear. However, there is a need for clear laws and standards which require operators of large networks of Internet-connected computers to exercise appropriate due diligence in their upkeep and security. To this end, we believe that there is an urgent need for definition of a minimum standard of security for computer networks.

The definition of such a standard has far reaching implications not only for the usability of America's technology foundation, but the security of corporations and indeed of the nation itself. By formalising an industry best practice guideline, companies will have a clear understanding of what must be carried out. Clearly, such a guideline is a moving target, but its inception would allow the structuring of a valid and robust posture against both terrorist threats and other hostile entities. Such a set of minimum standards would have to be easily and affordably supported by the security/application vendors themselves, rather than relying on individual users needs/requirements to drive the best practice guidelines.

This is not exactly a novel concept. International standards have been developed in other areas where safety and security are a concern. Consider the airline industry. There are international guidelines for airport safety; in cases where these standards are not met, consequences range from warnings to prohibited travel. The needs for such changes, and how a due diligence standard could be created are subjects of future research. However, it seems clear that such standards are urgently needed.

Future Research

Certainly there are many unanswered questions. Most people, governments included, consider cyberterrorism primarily as the premeditated, politically motivated attack against information, computer systems, computer programs, and data by sub national groups or clandestine agents. However, as we have seen, the real impact of the computer on the terrorism matrix is considerably wider. By limiting our understanding of cyberterrorism to the traditional 'computer as target' viewpoint, we leave our nation open to attacks that rely on the computer for other aspects of the operation.

Even when considering the purely virtual impact of cyberterrorism, the approach is not adequately thought out. For example, consider an act that incorporated a desire for political change with the release of an otherwise benign computer virus within which an antigovernment message is embedded. Given the lack of physical boundaries in the virtual community, does a group's physical location have any bearing on whether or not they may be considered a subnational group? What is a 'national group' in cyberspace anyway? Which government agency deals with *that?* What constitutes combatant targets in virtual environments? Consider the 1998 response by the Pentagon to civilian target computers as a response to Floodnet protests (McKay, 1998). Is the system that automatically strikes back considered combatant? Are its owners moved from 'noncombatant' to 'combatant' based on an auto-response? Is the response perhaps engaging in 'violence'?

Some claim "terrorists and activists have bombed more than 600 computer facilities". What specific components may be considered an element of a cyber system; what differentiates these incidents from conventional terrorism? Physical property, civil disorder and economic harm are easily understood in the physical world; however, are there virtual equivalents that could lead to a broadening of the concept of cyberterrorism?

Defending against the New Terrorism

Defending against terrorism where a computer or the Internet plays an important part in the terrorism matrix is very similar to defending against terrorism that does not. The regular practices (deterrence, law, defense, negotiations, diplomacy, *etc.*) are still effective, except that the scope of certain elements is expanded. For example, traditional strikes against military bases, targeting of key leaders, and collective punishment have been effective in traditional terrorism (Whitelaw, 1998) and certainly have potential for dealing with some aspects of cyberterrorism. These techniques are often presented, and can be to be updated to include their 'virtual' counterparts. It should be noted, however, that differences in international law and culture could make this process a complex task.

Deterrence

Governments can use their coercive capacity to make terrorism too costly for those who seek to use it. They can do this by military strikes against terrorist bases, assassinations of key leaders, collective punishment, or other methods. There are several drawbacks to this approach, however. On the one hand, it can lead to unacceptable human rights violations. In addition, groups may not come to government attention until movements are so well developed that efforts to contain them through deterrent methods are insufficient.

Criminal Justice

Governments can treat terrorism primarily as a crime and therefore pursue the extradition, prosecution, and incarceration of suspects. One drawback to this approach is that the prosecution of terrorists in a court of law can compromise government efforts to gather intelligence on terrorist organisations. In addition, criminal justice efforts (like deterrent efforts) are deployed mostly after terrorists have struck, meaning that significant damage and loss of life may have already occurred.

Enhanced Defence

Governments can make targets harder to attack, and they can use intelligence capabilities to gain advance knowledge of when attacks may take place. As targets are hardened, however, some terrorist groups may shift their sights to softer targets. An example is the targeting of US embassies in Kenya and Tanzania in August 1998 by truck bombs. Although the attacks are believed to have been coordinated by individuals with Middle Eastern ties, targets in Africa were chosen because of their relatively lax security compared with targets in the Middle East.

Negotiations

Governments can elect to enter into negotiations with terrorist groups and make concessions in exchange for the groups' renunciation of violence. While governments are often reluctant to do so at the beginning of terror campaigns, negotiations may be the only way to resolve some long-standing disputes. For example, data gathering and monitoring operations of terrorist communications has typically applied to signal intelligence and fieldwork. In a virtual environment, the ability to gather information from various sources is eminently achievable in a somewhat automated manner. Specific groups can be watched easily, and computers are comparatively simple to 'bug'. All contacts that a particular user interacts with could then be tracked, and the network of communication mapped. Furthermore, much of this surveillance can be carried out over the very same network that the terrorists intend to use to facilitate their plot.

This extension, however, must be carried out with care. Consider, for example, the original US export regulations on the export of 'strong encryption' (ITAR). Under such regulations, certain encryption products were classified as munitions. While ITAR has since been replaced, the revamped 'Export Administration Regulations' (DOC, 2002), while somewhat more relaxed, continue to blacklist several countries from receiving encryption products, despite the fact that strong encryption technology is freely available via the Internet. While this law seems to be aimed at preventing the use of strong encryption by other potentially hostile governments and terrorist entities, strong encryption algorithms and implementations remain trivially available to pretty much anyone.

This classification of knowledge as munitions seems to be the ultimate (and flawed) extension of traditional anti-terrorist tactics into the virtual realm. Clearly, it is not sufficient to quickly draw analogies that are not, in fact, correct. A far better approach is to carefully consider the impact of the computer in the different cells of the terrorism matrix.

For example, banning the export of encryption from just America is akin to banning the sale of C4 only on weekdays — the asset would be hardly even an inconvenience to the would be terrorist. A far better solution is to consider the safeguard in the context of the virtual world. When examined in this aspect, for example, it is reasonably clear that the original classification of encryption products as munitions is not likely to be effective. Similarly, while the use of export grade encryption can (and has) resulted in the ability of officials to read some terrorist communiqués, a restrictive "export to here, not here" ban is unlikely to succeed in any meaningful way.

A forward-looking approach to terrorism that involves computers is therefore highly contextual in its basis. Traditional antiterrorism defenses must be deployed, but these countermeasures must fully take into account the virtual factors that we have outlined already. The Internet was developed primarily as an unregulated, open architecture. Not only are we observing a predictable backlash to the 'corporatisation' of the network, where the tools of destruction can easily be placed in the hands of the dissatisfied or malevolent people, we must also deal with the fact that the infrastructure is ideally suited to criminal activities. Some of these activities are being promoted as cyberterrorism; however, the loose use of the term is actually undermining the defense capabilities of the very corporations and governments who are at risk.

Events can be analysed in terms of their critical factors, and only if these factors all exist can the event legitimately be called terrorism. However, that does not mean if all these factors do not exist that a corporation is 'safe'. Unfortunately, corporations are built around the premise that people will do the right thing. The fact, as we have seen, is that this is not necessarily the case. We do not use the term 'ice pick terrorism' to define bombings of ice-pick factories, nor would we use it to define terrorism carried out with ice picks. Thus, we question the use of the term cyberterrorism to describe just any sort of threat or crime carried out with or against computers in general. At the same time, those who do insist on treating only 'pure cyberterrorism' as cyberterrorism are completely missing the true threat posed by the addition of acts in the virtual world to the terrorists' playbook. Finally, the nascent danger in the term cyberterrorism is that cyberterrorism will somehow be dealt with separately to regular terrorism. This artificial fragmentation of our defenses is likely to provide the terrorist with a significant advantage in any campaign against a nation state, and is to be avoided at all costs.

This brings us to the final point of this study: turning the tables on terrorism. As we have shown, computers can play an enormous role in terrorism. At the same time they can provide perhaps our biggest defense against terrorism if used to our advantage. However, just like as we need to understand the integration of computers with terrorism, we must examine how computers can assist in defense broadly. This begins with the re-examination of basic beliefs about 'cyberterrorism' which must take place within academia, industry, government and defense sectors.

This re-examination is, however, only the first step in combating terrorism. Information at each level of analysis must be shared, collated and redistributed across federal, state and local government boundaries, as well as amongst industry and academia, and in some cases, the private citizenry. Obviously, this type of endeavour is information technology intensive.

In the United States alone there are over 87 000 different jurisdictions (HLS, 2002); combined with information from industry, academia and the private citizenry, this amount will increase many times over. Fortunately, one of the things computers are good at is processing information. By developing an information technology architecture that would sort, correlate and facilitate the most effective use of that information, information could be shared in a timely manner amongst these groups, some of which historically have had little, if any, communication.

Additionally, a well-designed technical solution can circumvent some of the cultural problems inherent in cross-sector information sharing, by eliminating the need for the actual data to do the correlation. Some technologies have been developed which would appear to lend themselves particularly well to this sort of implementation, but practical tests are required before any conclusion can be reached (Legion, 2002). Aside from the role of computers in defense, we must attempt to re-educate policy makers, defusing the latent danger of vertical 'cyberterrorism' defenses and replacing them with a well-rounded, integrated approach to a problem that is extremely broad. From a corporate and governmental perspective this requires a careful examination of the 'messaging' that is broadcast. How do we portray the fusion of computers with terrorism? Can the messaging be made more productive so that we can shape the mindset of our audience to one that is synergistic with a broad view of cyberterrorism?

Finally, it is impossible to neglect to mention the fact that the rapid increase in connectivity and the ultimate frailty of our national IT infrastructure coupled with the astonishing homogeneity of our computing base is a matter of grave concern. Continued focus must be put on increasing the public demand for computer security as well as the corporate aware-ness of the issue: whereas security flaws in widely used applications were once perceived as personal risks, we must begin to recognize the potentially global consequences of such issues in balance with the more general problems posed by the integration of computing with terrorism. The lack of understanding of cyberterrorism, and the overall insecurity of America's networks have allowed a situation to develop which is not in the best interests of the country or computer users. The need to protect computing resources, making the job of a cyberterrorist more difficult is obvious. However, this can only be accomplished by re-examining commonly held beliefs about the very nature of computer systems and of cyberterrorism itself.

3

Cyber Crime in the International Sphere and Impending Dangers

Cyberterrorism is the convergence of terrorism and cyberspace. It is generally understood to mean unlawful attacks and threats of attack against computers, networks, and the information stored therein when done to intimidate or coerce a government or its people in furtherance of political or social objectives. Further, to qualify as cyberterrorism, an attack should result in violence against persons or property, or at least cause enough harm to generate fear. Attacks that lead to death or bodily injury, explosions, plane crashes, water contamination, or severe economic loss would be examples. Serious attacks against critical infrastructures could be acts of cyberterrorism, depending on their impact. Attacks that disrupt nonessential services or that are mainly a costly nuisance would not.

Cyberspace is constantly under assault. Cyber spies, thieves, saboteurs, and thrill seekers break into computer systems, steal personal data and trade secrets, vandalize Web sites, disrupt service, sabotage data and systems, launch computer viruses and worms, conduct fraudulent transactions, and harass individuals and companies. These attacks are facilitated with increasingly powerful and easy-to-use software tools, which are readily available for free from thousands of Web sites on the Internet.

Many of the attacks are serious and costly. The recent ILOVEYOU virus and variants, for example, was estimated to have hit tens of millions of users and cost billions of dollars in damage. The February denial-of-service attacks against Yahoo, CNN, eBay, and other e-commerce Web sites was estimated to have caused over a billion in losses. It also shook the confidence of business and individuals in e-commerce.

Some attacks are conducted in furtherance of political and social objectives, as the following examples illustrate:

- In 1996, a computer hacker allegedly associated with the White Supremacist movement temporarily disabled a Massachusetts ISP and damaged part of the ISP's record keeping system. The ISP had attempted to stop the hacker from sending out worldwide racist messages under the ISP's name. The hacker signed off with the threat, "you have yet to see true electronic terrorism. This is a promise."
- In 1998, Spanish protestors bombarded the Institute for Global Communications (IGC) with thousands of bogus e-mail messages. E-mail was tied up and undeliverable to the ISP's users, and support lines were tied up with people who couldn't get their mail. The protestors also spammed IGC staff and member accounts, clogged their Web page with bogus credit card orders, and threatened to employ the same tactics against organisations using IGC services. They demanded that IGC stop hosting the Webs site for the Euskal Herria Journal, a New York-based publication supporting Basque independence. Protestors said IGC supported terrorism because a section on the Web pages contained materials on the terrorist group ETA, which claimed responsibility for assassinations of Spanish political and security officials, and attacks on military installations. IGC finally relented and pulled the site because of the "mail bombings."
- In 1998, ethnic Tamil guerrillas swamped Sri Lankan embassies with 800 e-mails a day over a two-week period. The messages read "We are the Internet Black Tigers and we're doing this to disrupt your comm-unications." Intelligence authorities characterised it as the first known attack by terrorists against a country's computer systems.
- During the Kosovo conflict in 1999, NATO computers were blasted with e-mail bombs and hit with denial-of-service

attacks by hacktivists protesting the NATO bombings. In addition, businesses, public organisations, and academic institutes received highly politicised virus-laden e-mails from a range of Eastern European countries, according to reports. Web defacements were also common. After the Chinese Embassy was accidentally bombed in Belgrade, Chinese hacktivists posted messages such as "We won't stop attacking until the war stops!" on U.S. government Web sites.

- Since December 1997, the Electronic Disturbance Theater (EDT) has been conducting Web sit-ins against various sites in support of the Mexican Zapatistas. At a designated time, thousands of protestors point their browsers to a target site using software that floods the target with rapid and repeated download requests. EDT's software has also been used by animal rights groups against organisations said to abuse animals. Electrohippies, another group of hacktivists, conducted Web sit-ins against the WTO when they met in Seattle in late 1999. These sit-ins all require mass participation to have much effect, and thus are more suited to use by activists than by terrorists.

While the above incidents were motivated by political and social reasons, whether they were sufficiently harmful or frightening to be classified as cyberterrorism is a judgement call. To the best of my knowledge, no attack so far has led to violence or injury to persons, although some may have intimidated their victims. Both EDT and the Electrohippies view their operations as acts of civil disobedience, analogous to street protests and physical sit-ins, not as acts of violence or terrorism. This is an important distinction. Most activists, whether participating in the Million Mom's March or a Web sit-in, are not terrorists.

To understand the potential threat of cyberterrorism, two factors must be considered: first, whether there are targets that are vulnerable to attack that could lead to violence or severe harm, and second, whether there are actors with the capability and motivation to carry them out. Looking first at vulnerabilities, several studies have shown that critical infrastructures are potentially vulnerable to cyberterrorist attack. Eligible Receiver, a "no notice" exercise conducted by the

Department of Defense in 1997 with support from NSA red teams, found the power grid and emergency 911 systems had weaknesses that could be exploited by an adversary using only publicly available tools on the Internet. Although neither of these systems were actually attacked, study members concluded that service on these systems could be disrupted. Also in 1997, the President's Commission on Critical Infrastructure Protection issued its report warning that through mutual dependencies and interconnectedness, critical infrastructures could be vulnerable in new ways, and that vulnerabilities were steadily increasing, while the costs of attack were decreasing.

Although many of the weaknesses in computerised systems can be corrected, it is effectively impossible to eliminate all of them. Even if the technology itself offers good security, it is frequently configured or used in ways that make it open to attack. In addition, there is always the possibility of insiders, acting alone or in concert with other terrorists, misusing their access capabilities. According to Russia's Interior Ministry Col. Konstantin Machabeli, the state-run gas monopoly, Gazprom, was hit by hackers who collaborated with a Gazprom insider. The hackers were said to have used a Trojan horse to gain control of the central switchboard which controls gas flows in pipelines, although Gazprom, the world's largest natural gas producer and the largest gas supplier to Western Europe, refuted the report.

Consultants and contractors are frequently in a position where they could cause grave harm. This past March, Japan's Metropolitan Police Department reported that a software system they had procured to track 150 police vehicles, including unmarked cars, had been developed by the Aum Shinryko cult, the same group that gassed the Tokyo subway in 1995, killing 12 people and injuring 6,000 more. At the time of the discovery, the cult had received classified tracking data on 115 vehicles. Further, the cult had developed software for at least 80 Japanese firms and 10 government agencies. They had worked as subcontractors to other firms, making it almost impossible for the organisations to know who was developing the software. As subcontractors, the cult could have installed Trojan horses to launch or facilitate cyberterrorist attacks at a later date. Fearing a Trojan horse of their own, last February, the State Department sent an urgent cable to about 170 embassies asking them to remove software, which they belatedly realised had been written by citizens of the former Soviet Union. If we take as given that critical infrastructures are vulnerable to a cyberterrorist attack, then the question becomes whether there are actors with the capability and motivation to carry out such an operation. While many hackers have the knowledge, skills, and tools to attack computer systems, they generally lack the motivation to cause violence or severe economic or social harm. Conversely, terrorists who are motivated to cause violence seem to lack the capability or motivation to cause that degree of damage in cyberspace.

Terrorists do use cyberspace to facilitate traditional forms of terrorism such as bombings. They put up Web sites to spread their messages and recruit supporters, and they use the Internet to communicate and coordinate action. However, there are few indications that they are pursuing cyberterrorism, either alone or in conjunction with acts of physical violence. In February 1998, Clark Staten, executive director of the Emergency Response and Research Institute in Chicago, testified before the Senate Judiciary Committee Subcommittee on Technology, Terrorism, and Government Information that it was believed that "members of some Islamic extremist organisations have been attempting to develop a 'hacker network' to support their computer activities and even engage in offensive information warfare attacks in the future."

And in November, the *Detroit News* reported that a member of the militant Indian separatist group Harkat-ul-Ansar had tried to buy military software from hackers who had stolen it from Department of Defense computers they had penetrated. The Provisional Irish Republican Army employed the services of contract hackers to penetrate computers in order to acquire home addresses of law enforcement and intelligence officers, but the data was used to draw up plans to kill the officers in a single "night of the long knives" if the British government did not meet terms for a new cease-fire. As this case illustrates, terrorists may use hacking as a way of acquiring intelligence in support of physical violence, even if they do not use it to wreak havoc in cyberspace.

In August 1999, the Center for the Study of Terrorism and Irregular Warfare at the Naval Postgraduate School in Monterey,

California, issued a report titled "Cyberterror: Prospects and Implications." Their objective was to articulate the demand side of terrorism. Specifically, they assessed the prospects of terrorist organisations pursuing cyberterrorism. They concluded that the barrier to entry for anything beyond annoying hacks is quite high, and that terrorists generally lack the wherewithal and human capital needed to mount a meaningful operation. Cyberterrorism, they argued, was a thing of the future, although it might be pursued as an ancillary tool.

The Monterey group defined three levels of cyberterror capability:

- ***Simple-Unstructured:*** The capability to conduct basic hacks against individual systems using tools created by someone else. The organisation possesses little target analysis, command and control, or learning capability.
- ***Advanced-Structured:*** The capability to conduct more sophisticated attacks against multiple systems or networks and possibly, to modify or create basic hacking tools. The organisation possesses an elementary target analysis, command and control, and learning capability.
- ***Complex-Coordinated:*** The capability for a coordinated attacks capable of causing mass-disruption against integrated, heterogeneous defenses (including cryptography). Ability to create sophisticated hacking tools. Highly capable target analysis, command and control, and organisation learning capability.

They estimated that it would take a group starting from scratch 2-4 years to reach the advanced-structured level and 6-10 years to reach the complex-coordinated level, although some groups might get there in just a few years or turn to outsourcing or sponsorship to extend their capability. The study examined five terrorist group types: religious, New Age, ethno-nationalist separatist, revolutionary, and far-right extremists. They determined that only the religious groups are likely to seek the most damaging capability level, as it is consistent with their indiscriminate application of violence. New Age or single issue terrorists, such as the Animal Liberation Front, pose the most immediate threat, however, such groups are likely to accept disruption as a substitute for destruction. Both the revolutionary and ethnonationalist separatists are likely to seek an advanced-structured capability. The far-right extremists are likely to settle for a simple-unstructured capability, as cyberterror offers neither the intimacy nor cathartic effects that are central to the psychology of far-right terror. The study also determined that hacker groups are psychologically and organisationally ill-suited to cyberterrorism, and that it would be against their interests to cause mass disruption of the information infrastructure.

Thus, at this time, cyberterrorism does not seem to pose an imminent threat. This could change. For a terrorist, it would have some advantages over physical methods. It could be conducted remotely and anonymously, and it would not require the handling of explosives or a suicide mission. It would likely garner extensive media coverage, as journalists and the public alike are fascinated by practically any kind of computer attack. Indeed cyberterrorism could be immensely appealing precisely because of the tremendous attention given to it by the government and media. Cyberterrorism also has its drawbacks. Systems are complex, so it may be harder to control an attack and achieve a desired level of damage than using physical weapons. Unless people are injured, there is also less drama and emotional appeal. Further, terrorists may be disinclined to try new methods unless they see their old ones as inadequate, particularly when the new methods require considerable knowledge and skill to use effectively. Terrorists generally stick with tired and true methods. Novelty and sophistication of attack may be much less important than assurance that a mission will be operationally successful. Indeed, the risk of operational failure could be a deterrent to terrorists. For now, the truck bomb poses a much greater threat than the logic bomb.

Logic Bomb

A logic bomb is a piece of code intentionally inserted into a software system that will set off a malicious function when specified conditions are met. For example, a programmer may hide a piece of code that starts deleting files (such as the salary database), should they ever leave the company. Software that is inherently malicious, such as viruses and worms, often contain logic bombs that execute a certain payload at a pre-defined time or when some other condition is met.

This technique can be used by a virus or worm to gain momentum and spread before being noticed. Many viruses attack their host systems on specific dates, such as Friday the 13th or April Fool's Day. Trojans that activate on certain dates are often called "time bombs". To be considered a logic bomb, the payload should be unwanted and unknown to the user of the software. As an example, trial programs with code that disables certain functionality after a set time are not normally regarded as logic bombs.

Time Bomb (Software)

In computer software, a time bomb refers to a computer program that has been written so that it will stop functioning after a predetermined date or time is reached. The term "time bomb" does not refer to a program that stops functi-oning a specific number of days after it is installed; instead, the term "trialware" applies. Time bombs are commonly used in beta (pre-release) software when the manufacturer of the software does not want the beta version being used after the final release date. One example of time bomb software would be Microsoft's Windows Vista Beta 2, which was programmed to expire on May 31, 2007. The time limits on time bomb software are not usually as heavily enforced as they are on trial software, since time bomb software does not usually implement secure clock functions.

The next generation of terrorists will grow up in a digital world, with ever more powerful and easy-to-use hacking tools at their disposal. They might see greater potential for cyberterrorism than the terrorists of today, and their level of knowledge and skill relating to hacking will be greater. Hackers and insiders might be recruited by terrorists or become self-recruiting cyberterrorists, the Timothy McVeigh's of cyberspace. Some might be moved to action by cyber policy issues, making cyberspace an attractive venue for carrying out an attack. Cyberterrorism could also become more attractive as the real and virtual worlds become more closely coupled, with a greater number of physical devices attached to the Internet. Some of these may be remotely controlled. Terrorists, for example, might target robots used in telesurgery. Unless these systems are carefully secured, conducting an operation that physically harms someone may be easy as penetrating a Web site is today.

The violent pursuit of political goals using exclusively electronic methods is likely to be at least a few years into the future. However, the more general threat of cybercrime is very much a part of the digital landscape today. In addition to cyberattacks against digital data and systems, many people are being terrorised on the Internet today with threats of physical violence. On-line stalking, death threats, and hate messages are abundant. The Florida teen who threatened violence at Columbine High School in an electronic chat room is but one example. These crimes are serious and must be addressed. In so doing, we will be in a better position to prevent and respond to cyberterrorism if and when the threat becomes more serious.

4

Internet and Terrorism

In today's world, where computers and communications systems are linked, it can truly be said that "everything depends on software." It is bad enough that this has proven irresistably seductive to pranksters. The potential damage which can be inflicted on our infrastructure— systems such as air traffic control, power, telecommunications, and the like, by a malicious person sitting at a keyboard on the other side of the planet, is mindboggling. So significant, in fact, that considerable attention is being given around the world to its military applications.

Offensive Content

Content of every conceivable variety may be found in cyberspace. Erotica, racist propaganda, information relating to the manufacture of drugs and explosives, and instructions on how to commit suicide, now lie at one's fingertips. How to protect children and those who are easily offended, while allowing the emerging medium of the internet to flourish, has become a challenge to most governments, and to many parents, in the developed world.

The Protection of Intellectual Property

Possibilities for forgery, plaigarism, and other offences against intellectual property have been significantly enhanced by the advent of digital technology. Piracy has become a growth industry, so much so, that it may strain the capacity of governments to control it. Here again, a fundamental policy question is whether state enforcement is preferable to self-help on the part of the individual. Are private precautions and private remedies sufficient in most cases? Private legal solutions are likely to be more effective within jurisdictions than across them. One would not expect Microsoft, for example, to receive a great deal of comfort from the legal process of the People's Republic of China. Organisations with access to considerable resources, may, however, pursue telecommunications offenders across the globe. A recent example involves the protracted litigation being taken by the Church of Scientology in respect of alleged copyright infringements on the Internet. In a series of actions taken in various jurisdictions in the United States as well as in the Netherlands, the church has sought interim orders restraining the publication of materials on the Internet which are said to infringe its copyright. Such remedies do not come cheaply, however, and one of the problems of private remedies is that they are only available to those who are able to afford them.

Commercial Crime

It seems only a matter of time before most commerce will be electronic. Then, to invoke the ghost of Willie Sutton, that's where the money will be. The proliferation of electronic funds transfer systems will enhance the risk that such transactions may be intercepted and diverted. How to facilitate commerce in the digital age, and how to obtain a competitive advantage, while ensuring the security and integrity which is essential for commerce to flourish, has become the question of the hour.

The above forms of illegality are not necessarily mutually exclusive, and need not occur in isolation. Just as an armed robber might steal an automobile to facilitate a quick getaway, so too can one steal telecommunications services and use them for purposes of vandalism, fraud, or in furtherance of a criminal conspiracy.

International Legal Controls

The global nature of information technology enables criminal activity to be truly transnational. That is, a person sitting in Spain can disable a computer in Singapore, or disseminate child pornography in Swaziland. Additional problems arise from the difficulty of exercising national sovereignty over capital and information flows. Jurisdictional issues may arise from transborder online transmission.

If an online financial newsletter originating in Albania contains fraudulent speculation about the prospects of a company whose shares are traded on the Australian Stock Exchange, where has the offence occurred?

The globalisation of crime poses further problems, as the cost of investigating and prosecuting transnational crime may be prohibitive in all but the most serious cases. Sovereign governments are finding it difficult to exercise control over online behaviour at home, not to mention abroad. A resident of Chicago who falls victim to a telemarketing scam originating in Albania, for example, can expect little assistance from law enforcement agencies in either jurisdiction. As a result, regulation by territorially-based rules may prove to be inappropriate for some types of offences. Of equal concern is the lack of international consensus on what constitutes criminal behaviour. What is treasonous in Tibet, or blasphe-mous in Bangladesh, is protected in Philadelphia. New international arrangements are being crafted to address these issues. Will they be adequate to meet the challenge?

Local Legal Controls

Even without a transnational dimension, tasks facing law enforcement in the digital age are formidable. Emerging technologies of encryption may reduce the extent to which criminal communications are vulnerable to interception. Will this require new technologies, new laws, or rather increased reliance on labour intensive undercover investigations? The collection of electronic evidence is still a novel experience for many law enforcement officers. Proof of possession of illegal materials or of criminal intent may be more difficult to achieve than would be the case with conventional criminal prosecutions.

Ironically, it would appear that some aspects of crime involving high technology will be best addressed by relatively low tech solutions. One thinks, for example, of the use of undercover investigative methods. Meanwhile, there remains the challenge of balancing the public interest as articulated by law enforcement, with the public interest as articulated by advocates of privacy rights. Under what circumstances should service providers disclose subscriber information to law enforcement authorities? Short of this, the very transparency of much traffic on the information superhighway may cause concern to some. Consider, for example, navigational data, the figurative "footprints" which one leaves as one traverses cyberspace. Accessible to commercial institutions, such data have become a powerful marketing tool. One can, for example, receive personalised advertising based on one's previous online usage.

On the brighter side, the information superhighway does have benefits for law enforcement agencies. Although its potential has yet to be realised, the use of technology for general public relations, for the communication of basic information for crime prevention, and for the exchange of information in furtherance of criminal investigation may be expected to increase dramatically in years ahead. Already photographs displayed on the Internet have led to the arrest of fugitives. The activities of pornographers and software pirates (as well as innocent criminologists) may be traced effectively using information available on the Internet.

On-line Crime Prevention

This raises the question about prevention of internet crime, and the extent to which the principles of terrestrial crime prevention may be applied in cyberspace. Opportunity reduction and target hardening, which have become key elements of situational crime prevention, would appear to be as applicable to information systems as to residential dwellings. Whether principles of developmental crime prevention will be similarly generalizable is open to question.

Technological Controls

It does in any event appear that technological solutions will play a significant role in ensuring security and prosperity in cyberspace. I am reminded of the film "The Graduate," now three decades old. The scene in which an older man took the young Dustin Hoffman aside and said, with a view towards pointing him towards a prosperous career, "Son, I have one word for you—Plastics." Today, I would say, "Son, I have two words for you— computer security." Few would argue that this will be one of the growth industries of the next century. In addition to more rigorous management practices and the introduction of more sophisticated password and verification procedures, new technologies such as biometric security devices and anomaly detection computer software help alert users to system weaknesses and enhance the security of computer systems themselves. I look forward to learning more about this during tomorrow afternoon's session.

One topic conspicuous in its absence form this conference is gambling. The challenge of regulating gambling in cyberspace is considerable. In part it will be addressed in the panels dealing with content regulation and commercial criminality.

Technological Leap-frog

First is what might be called technological leap-frog— the ongoing contest between the state and the offender to gain the technological edge. New technologies, most notably those relating to telecommunications, have great impact on both sides of the crime control effort. It is no secret that some of the more sophisticated offenders today are able to afford state of the art technology. Indeed, it has long been said that "Crimes have got all the money and no rules, while Cops have got all the rules and no money." Keeping abreast of developments in technology will remain an ongoing challenge to law enforcement agencies in Australia and around the world. New opportunities for democratic participation in the control of internet crime. New technologies provide new opportunities for citizenship. Opportunities for a citzenry to inform itself are unprecedented. Opportunities to communicate with government are unprecedented.

Perhaps one of the most important developments is the availability of facilities by which a citizen can report suspected illegality to service providers or to authorities. So-called "hotlines" encourage the private monitoring and surveillance of cyberspace, and the reporting of suspicious activity, including consumer fraud, racist propaganda, and child pornography. This can be healthy, as long as it does not degenerate into a field-day for busybodies and an impediment to legitimate communication. Moreover, well meaning amateurs can violate the privacy of innocent citizens and contaminate legitimate criminal investigations. For some time now, we have been encouraged to think in terms of self-reliance and decreased dependence upon the state. Limited resources available to governments now require that careful thought be given to the nature and amount of services which it is appropriate for governments to deliver.

Recall the quote attributed to the former Governor of California "Keep low, move fast, and not carry a lot of cash." What is the relevance of this? The first line of protection against internet crime is self help. Given the limited capacity of governments to control crime in cyberspace, the first line of defence lies in the exercise of prudent behaviour by prospective victims. Just as the first step in the control of burglary is to lock one's doors and windows, so too the basic principles of information security should be honoured. Market forces may also exert controlling influences of their own.

As large organisations begin to appreciate their vulnerability to electronic theft or vandalism, they may be expected to insure against potential losses. It is very much in the interests of insurance companies to require appropriate security precautions on the part of their policyholders. Indeed, decisions to set and to price insurance may well depend upon security practices of prospective insureds. Subcontractors may also be required to have strict IT integrity programs in place as a condition of doing business.

Counterproductive Interventions

The last theme on which I would like to dwell is that of counterproductive interventions, whether they soriginate from public or from private sources. It is an understandable reaction to any perceived social evil to attempt to legislate it away. Early efforts to regulate internet content are illustrative. In some instances, these efforts have been grounded jointly in cynicism and realpolitik. Attempts to prohibit anonymous online communications may discourage legitimate expression such as that involving whistleblowers or human rights advocates residing with the jurisdiction of repressive regimes. Although the rush to regulate, or to criminalize, may have political resonance, it may have downside consequences. "Burning the house to roast the pig" may be an awkward metaphor, but it fits here.

Even private remedies may be excessive. Already one sees criticisms of blocking and filtering software which automatically deny access to breast cancer support groups. The risk, or indeed, the fact, that freedom of speech will be abused by some, is insufficient justification for "pulling the plug" on telecommunications. One must always bear in mind that excessive constraints on freedom of expression and communication may inhibit the realisation of competitive advantage. With over 600 million Internet users worldwide in 2005, today the Internet is recognised as a powerful political instrument. David Resnick has identified three types of Internet politics:

1. ***Politics Within the Net***: This refers to the political life of cyber-communities and other Internet activities that have minimal impact on life off the Net.
2. ***Politics Which Impacts the Net:*** This refers to the host of public policy issues raised by the Internet both as a new form of mass communication and a vehicle for commerce. As quoted in New 2004. Clarke was the White House cyber security chief during the tenures of both Bill Clinton and George W. Bush. He resigned in January 2003.
3. ***Political Uses of the Net:*** This refers to the employment of the Internet by ordinary citizens, political activists, organised interests, governments, and others to achieve political goals having little or nothing to do with the Internet *per se* (*i.e.* to influence political activities offline) (1998, 55-56).

There is considerable overlap amongst the terrorist uses of the Net identified by the different authors. While twenty-two different categories of use are mentioned, often authors are simply using different terms to refer to the same issues. This is clearest in terms of the identity shared by the concepts 'fundraising' and 'finance,' but also relates to the concepts 'information gathering' and 'data mining,' for example. Given such overlaps, the analysis below relies on what have been determined to be the five core terrorist uses of the Internet: information provision, financing, networking, recruitment, and information gathering. Each of the uses identified fits into one of these categories or its sub-categories.

5

Important Areas of Concern Information Provision

This refers to efforts by terrorists to engage in publicity, propaganda and, ultimately, psychological warfare. The Internet, and the advent of the World Wide Web in particular, have significantly increased the opportunities for terrorists to secure publicity. This can take the form of historical information, profiles of leaders, manifestos, *etc.* But terrorists can also use the Internet as a tool of psychological warfare through spreading disinformation, delivering threats, and disseminating horrific images, such as the beheading of American entrepreneur Nick Berg in Iraq and US journalist Daniel Pearl in Pakistan via their Web sites (Weimann 2004a, 5). These functions are clearly improved by the Web's enhanced volume, increased speed of data transmission, low-cost, relatively uncontrolled nature, and global reach.

Until the advent of the Internet, terrorists' hopes of winning publicity for their causes and activities depended on attracting the attention of television, radio, or the print media. As Weimann points out, "these traditional media have 'selection thresholds' (multistage processes of editorial selection) that terrorists often cannot reach" (2004a, 6). The same criteria do not, of course, apply to the terrorists' own websites. The Internet thus offers terrorist groups an unprecedented level of direct control over the content of their messages. It considerably extends their ability to shape how different target audiences perceive them and to manipulate not only their own image, but also the image of their enemies. Although, for many groups, their target audience may be small, an Internet presence is nonetheless expected. Regardless of the number of hits a site receives, a well-designed and well-maintained Web site gives a group an aura of legitimacy.

Financing

This refers to efforts by terrorist groups to raise funds for their activities. Money is terrorism's lifeline; it is "the engine of the armed struggle" (Napoleoni 2004, 1). The immediacy and interactive nature of Internet communication, combined with its highreach properties, opens up a huge potential for increased financial donations as has been demonstrated by a host of non-violent political organisations and civil society actors. Terrorists seek financing both via their Web sites and by using the Internet infrastructure to engage in resource mobilisation using illegal means.

Direct Solicitation Via Terrorist Web Sites

Numerous terrorist groups request funds directly from Web surfers who visit their sites. Such requests may take the form of general statements underlining the organisations need for money, more often than not however requests are more direct urging supporters to donate immediately and supplying either bank account details or an Internet payment option. For example, the IRA's main Web site contains a page on which visitors can make credit card donations (Weimann 2004a, 7). While, at one time, the Ulster Loyalist Information Service, which was affiliated with the Loyalist Volunteer Force (LVF), and accepted funds via PayPal, invited those who were "uncomfortable with making monetary donations" to donate other items, including bulletproof vests.

A second, and related, fundraising method is to profile site visitors by employing user demographics (yielded, for example, from identifying information entered in online questionnaires or order forms) and to contact those whose profiles indicate they are potential financial supporters, a function which may be carried out by proxies, according to Tibbetts (2002, 20). A third way in which groups raise funds is through the establishment of online stores and the sale of items such as books, audio and video tapes, flags, t-shirts, *etc.*

Exploitation of E-commerce Tools and Entities

The Internet facilitates terrorist financing in a number of other ways besides direct solicitation via terrorist Web sites. According to Jean-Francois Ricard, one of France's top anti-terrorism investigators, many Islamist terror plots are financed through credit card fraud (Thomas 2003, 117). Imam Samudra, sentenced to death for his part in the Bali bombing of 2002, has published a prison memoir of some 280 pages, which includes a chapter that acts as a primer on 'carding' (Sipress 2004, A19). According to Dutch experts, there is strong evidence from international law enforcement agencies such as the FBI that at least some terrorist groups are financing their activities via advanced fee fraud, such as Nigerian-style scam e-mails. To date, however, solid evidence for such claims has not entered the public realm (Libbenga 2004). There is ample evidence, however, to support the contention that terroristaffiliated entities and individuals have established Internet-related front businesses as a means of raising money to support their activities. For example, in December 2002, InfoCom, a Texas-based ISP, was indicted along with its individual corporate officers on thirty-three counts relating to its provision of communication services, in-kind support, and funds to terrorist organisations including Hamas and its affiliate the Holy Land Foundation for Relief and Development (HLFRD). InfoCom's capital was donated primarily by Nadia Elashi Marzook, wife of Hamas figurehead Mousa Abu Marzook (Hinnen 2004, 18; Emerson 2002, 11-12 and 16).

Exploitation of Charities and Fronts

Terrorist organisations have a history of exploiting not just businesses, but also charities as undercover fundraising vehicles. This is particularly popular with Islamist terrorist groups, probably because of the injunction that observant Muslims make regular charitable donations. In some cases, terrorist organisations have actually established charities with allegedly humanitarian purposes. Examples of such undertakings include Mercy International, Wafa al-Igatha al-Islamiya, Rabita Trust, Al Rasheed Trust, Global Relief Fund, Benevolence International Foundation, and Help The Needy. Along with advertising in sympathetic communities' press, these 'charities' also advertised on websites and chat rooms with Islamic themes, pointing interested parties to their Internet homepages.

Terrorists have also infiltrated branches of existing charities to raise funds clandestinely. Many such organisations provide the humanitarian services advertised: feeding, clothing, and educating the poor and illiterate, and providing medical care for the sick. However, some such organisations, in addition to pursuing their publicly stated mission of providing humanitarian aid, also pursue a covert agenda of providing material support to militant groups. These organisations' Web-based publicity materials may or may not provide hints as to their secret purposes.

As the LVF and InfoCom examples show, the support sought by and provided to terrorist organisations may not always be in the form of cash. Terrorist groups use the Internet to solicit other fungible goods, to accumulate supplies, and to recruit foot soldiers. In this chapter the term 'financing' has been used in its narrow sense to mean the remittance of money. Nonetheless, it may also be used as shorthand for the accumulation of any of the material resources necessary for terrorists to maintain their organisations and carry out operations.

Networking

This refers to groups' efforts to flatten their organisational structures and act in a more decentralised manner through the use of the Internet, which allows dispersed actors to communicate quickly and coordinate effectively at low cost. The Internet allows not only for intra-group communication, but also inter-group connections. The Web enhances terrorists' capacities to transform their structures and build these links because of the alternative space it provides for communication and discussion and the hypertext nature of the Web, which allows for groups to link to their internal sub-groups and external organisations around the globe from their central Web site.

Transforming Organisational Structures

Rand's John Arquilla, David Ronfeldt, and Michele Zanini have been pointing to the emergence of new forms of terrorist organisation attuned to the information age for some time. They contend, "terrorists will continue to move from hierarchical. For a brief introduction to organisational network analysis, see Arquilla and Ronfeldt 2001b and 2001c, 319- 323. More effort will go into building arrays of transnationally internetted groups than into building stand alone groups" (Arquilla *et al*1999, 41). This type of organisational structure is qualitatively different from traditional hierarchical designs. Terrorists are ever more likely to be organised to act in a more fully networked, decentralised, 'all-channel' manner. Ideally, there is no single, central leadership, command, or headquarters.

Within the network as a whole there is little or no hierarchy and there may be multiple leaders depending upon the size of the group. In other words, there is no specific heart or head that can be targeted. To realize its potential, such a network must utilize the latest information and communications technologies. The Internet is becoming an integral component of such organisations, according to the Rand analysts (Arquilla *et al* 1999, 48-53; Arquilla and Ronfeldt 2001a).

Planning and Coordination

"Many terrorist groups share a common goal with mainstream organisations and institutions: the search for greater efficiency through the Internet" (Margulies 2004, 2). Several reasons have been put forward to explain why modern IT systems, especially the Internet, are so useful for terrorists in establishing and maintaining networks. As already discussed, new technologies enable quicker, cheaper, and more secure information flows.

In addition, the integration of computing with communications has substantially increased the variety and complexity of the information that can be shared. (Weimann 2004a, 9). This led Michele Zanini to hypothesize that "the greater the degree of organisational networking in a terrorist group, the higher the likelihood that IT is used to support the network's decision making" (1999, 251). Zanini's hypothesis appears to be borne out by recent events. For example, many of the terrorists indicted by the United States government since 9/11 communicated via e-mail. The indictment of four members of the Armed Islamic Group (Gama'a al-Islamiyya) alleges that computers were used "to transmit, pass and disseminate messages, communications and information between and among IG leaders and members in the United States and elsewhere around the world." Similarly, six individuals indicted in Oregon in 2002 allegedly communicated via e-mail regarding their efforts to travel to Afghanistan to aid al-Qaeda and the Taliban in their fight against the United States (Hinnen 2004, 38).

The Internet has the ability to connect not only members of the same terrorist organisations but also members of different groups. For example, hundreds of so-called 'jihadist' sites exist that express support for terrorism. According to Weimann, these sites and related forums permit terrorists in places as far-flung as Chechnya, Palestine, Indonesia, Afghanistan, Turkey, Iraq, Malaysia, the Philippines, and Lebanon to exchange not only ideas and suggestions, but also practical information about how to build bombs, establish terror cells, and ultimately perpetrate attacks (2004a, 9).

Mitigation of Risk

As terrorist groups come under increasing pressure from law enforcement, they have been forced to evolve and become more decentralised. This is a structure to which the Internet is perfectly suited. The Net offers a way for like-minded people located in Indictment. Denied a physical place to meet and organize, many terrorist groups are alleged to have created virtual communities through chat rooms and Web sites in order to continue spreading their propaganda, teaching, and training. Clearly, "information technology gives terrorist organisations global power and reach without necessarily compromising their invisibility" (Tibbetts 2002, 5). It "puts distance between those planning the attack and their targets...and provides terrorists a place to plan without the risks normally associated with cell or satellite phones" (Thomas 2003, 119).

Recruitment

This refers to groups' efforts to recruit and mobilize sympathisers to more actively support terrorist causes or activities. The Web offers a number of ways for achieving this: it makes information gathering easier for potential recruits by offering more information, more quickly, and in multimedia format; the global reach of the Web allows groups to publicize events to more people; and by increasing the possibilities for interactive communication, new opportunities for assisting groups are offered, along with more chances for contacting the group directly. Finally, through the use of discussion forums, it is also possible for members of the public—whether supporters or detractors of a group—to engage in debate with one another. This may assist the terrorist group in adjusting their position and tactics and, potentially, increasing their levels of support and general appeal (Gibson and Ward 2000, 305-306; Soo Hoo, Goodman and Greenberg 1997, 140; Weimann 2004a, 8).

Online recruitment by terrorist organisations is said to be widespread. Harris et al provide the example of an Iranian site that boasts an application for suicide bombers guaranteeing that the new 'martyr' will take seventy relatives with him into heaven. If the recruit is unsure about joining, or if the group is unsure about the recruit, he is directed to a chat room where he is 'virtually' vetted. If he passes muster, he will be directed to another chat room for further vetting, and finally contacted personally by a group member. This process is said to be aimed at weeding out 'undesirables' and potential infiltrators (2004, 9). It is more typical, however, for terrorist groups to actively solicit for recruits rather than waiting for them to simply present themselves. Weimann suggests that terrorist recruiters may use interactive Internet technology to roam online chat rooms looking for receptive members of the public, particularly young people. Electronic bulletin boards could also serve as vehicles for reaching out to potential recruits (2004a, 8).

Information Gathering

This refers to the capacity of Internet users to access huge volumes of information, which was previously extremely difficult to retrieve as a result of its being stored in widely differing formats and locations. Today, there are literally hundreds of Internet tools that aid in information gathering; these include a range of search engines, millions of subjectspecific email distribution lists, and an almost limitless selection of esoteric chat and discussion groups. One of the major uses of the Internet by terrorist organisations is thought to be information gathering. Unlike the other uses mentioned above terrorists' information gathering activities rely not on the operation of their own Web sites, but on the information contributed by others to "the vast digital library" that is the Internet (Weimann 2004a, 6). There are two major issues to be addressed here. The first may be termed 'data mining' and refers to terrorists using the Internet to collect and assemble information about specific targeting opportunities. The second issue is 'information sharing,' which refers to more general online information collection by terrorists.

Data Mining

In January 2003, US Defence Secretary Donald Rumsfeld warned in a directive sent to military units that too much unclassified, but potentially harmful material was appearing on Department of Defence (DoD) Web sites. Rumsfeld reminded military personnel that an al-Qaeda training manual recovered in Afghanistan states: "Using public sources openly and without resorting to illegal means, it is possible to gather at least eighty percent of information about the enemy." He went on to say, "at more than 700 gigabytes, the DoD Web-based data makes a vast, readily available source of information on DoD plans, programs and activities. One must conclude our enemies access DoD Web sites on a regular basis" (McCullagh 2003).

In addition to information provided by and about the armed forces, the free availability of information on the Internet about the location and operation of nuclear reactors and related facilities was of particular concern to public officials post 9/11. Roy Zimmerman, director of the Nuclear Regulatory Commission's (NRC) Office of Nuclear Security and Incident Response, said the 9/11 attacks highlighted the need to safeguard sensitive information. In the days immediately after the attacks, the NRC took their Web site entirely off line. When it was restored weeks later, it had been purged of more than 1,000 sensitive documents. Initially, the agency decided to withhold documents if "the release would provide clear and significant benefit to a terrorist in planning an attack."

Later, the NRC tightened the restriction, opting to exclude information "that could be useful or could reasonably be useful to a terrorist." According to Zimmerman, "it is currently unlikely that the information on our Web site would provide significant advantage to assist a terrorist" (Ahlers 2004). The measures taken by the NRC were not exceptional. According to a report produced by OMB Watch, 6 since 9/11 thousands of documents and tremendous amounts of data have been removed from US government sites. The difficulty, however, is that much of the same information remains available on private sector Web sites (McCullagh 2003; Bass and Moulton 2002). Patrick Tibbetts points to the Animated Software Company's Web site which has off-topic documents containing locations, status, security procedures and other technical information concerning dozens of U.S. nuclear reactors, while the Virtual Nuclear Tourist site contains similar information. The latter site is particularly detailed on specific security measures that may be implemented at various nuclear plants worldwide (Tibbetts 2002, 15).

Many people view such information as a potential gold mine for terrorists. Their fears appear well founded given the capture of al-Qaeda computer expert Muhammad Naeem Noor Khan in Pakistan in July 2004, which yielded a computer filled with photographs and floor diagrams of buildings in the U.S. that terrorists may have been planning to attack (Jehl and Johnston 2004; Verton and Mearian 2004). The Australian press 6 OMB Watch is a watchdog group based in Washington DC. The government of New South Wales was said to be considering restricting the range of information available on their Web sites as a result (ABC 2004). Terrorists can also use the Internet to learn about antiterrorism measures. Gabriel Weimann suggests that a simple strategy like conducting word searches of online newspapers and journals could allow a terrorist to study the means designed to counter attacks, or the vulnerabilities of these measures (2004b, 15).

Sharing Information

Policymakers, law enforcement agencies, and others are also concerned about the proliferation of 'how to' Web pages devoted to explaining, for example, the technical intricacies of making homemade bombs. Many such devices may be constructed using lethal combinations of otherwise innocuous materials; today, there are hundreds of freely available online manuals containing such information. As early as April 1997, the US Department of Justice had concluded that the availability of this information played a significant role in facilitating terrorist and other criminal acts (US Department of Justice 1997, 15-16). As an example, Jessica Stern points to *Bacteriological Warfare: A Major Threat to North America* (1995), which is described on the Internet as a book for helping readers survive a biological weapons attack and is subtitled 'What Your Family Can Do Before and After.' However, it also describes the reproduction and growth of biological agents and includes a chapter entitled 'Bacteria Likely To Be Used By the Terrorist.' The text is available for download, in various edited and condensed formats, from a number of sites while hard copies of the book are available for purchase over the Internet from sites such as Barnesandnoble.com for as little as $13 (Stern 1999, 51). More recently, an Al Qaeda laptop found in Afghanistan had been used to visit the Web site of the French Anonymous Society (FAS) on several occasions.

The FAS site publishes a two-volume *Sabotage Handbook* that contains sections on planning an assassination and anti-surveillance methods amongst others (Thomas 2003, 115; Weimann 2004a, 9). A much larger manual, nicknamed *The Encyclopedia of Jihad* and prepared by al Qaeda, runs to thousands of pages; distributed via the Web, it offers detailed instructions on how to establish an underground organisation and execute terror attacks (Weimann 2004a, 9).

This kind of information is sought out not just by sophisticated terrorist organisations but also by disaffected individuals prepared to use terrorist tactics to advance their idiosyncratic agendas. In 1999, for instance, right-wing extremist David Copeland planted nail bombs in three different areas of London: multiracial Brixton, the largely Bangladeshi community of Brick Lane, and the gay quarter in Soho. Over the course of three weeks, he killed three people and injured 139. At his trial, he revealed that he had learned his deadly techniques from the Internet by downloading copies of *The Terrorist's Handbook* and *How to Make Bombs: Book Two.* Both titles are still easily accessible (Weimann 2004a, 10).

The Open Source Threat?

The threat posed by the easy availability of bomb-making and other 'dangerous information' is a source of heated debate. Patrick Tibbetts warns against underestimating the feasibility of such threats. He points out that captured Al Qaeda materials include not only information compiled on 'home-grown explosives,' but also indicate that this group are actively pursuing data and technical expertise necessary to pursue CBRN weapons programs. According to Ken Katzman, a terrorism analyst for the Congressional Research Service, much of the material in these captured documents was probably downloaded from the Internet (Tibbetts 2002, 17). As a result, many have called for laws restricting the publication of bomb-making instructions on the Internet, while others have pointed out that this material is already easily accessible in bookstores and libraries (ADL 1998).

In fact, much of this information has been available in print media since at least the late 1960s, with the publication of William Powell's *The Anarchist Cookbook* and other, similar titles. Jessica Stern has observed: "In 1982, the year of the first widely reported incident of tampering with pharmaceuticals, the Tylenol case, only a few poisoning manuals were available, and they were relatively hard to find" (1999, 50). This is doubtless true; they were hard to find, but they *were* available. As Stern herself concedes, currently how-to manuals on producing chemical and biological agents are not just available on the Internet, but are advertised in paramilitary journals sold in magazine shops all over the United States (Stern 1999, 51). According to a US government report, over fifty publications describing the fabrication of explosives and destructive devices are listed in the Library of Congress and are available to any member of the public, as well as being easily available commercially (US Department of Justice 1997, 5). Ken Shirriff sums up this point well:

Despite assertions to the contrary (Weimann 2004a 9), the infamous *Anarchist Cookbook* (1971) is not available online, although it is easily purchased from bookstores or from Amazon.com. The anonymous authors of Web sites claiming to post the *Cookbook* and similar texts often include a disclaimer that the processes described should not be carried out. This is because many of the 'recipes' have a poor reputation for reliability and safety. Perhaps the most likely 'recipes' to be of use to terrorists are those related to hacking tools and activities. Such information is also likely to be considerably more accurate than bomb making information, for example; this is because the Internet is both the domain and tool of hackers. In testimony before the US House Armed Services Committee in 2003, Purdue University professor and information assurance expert, Eugene Spafford said bulletin boards and discussion lists teach hacking techniques to anyone: "We have perhaps a virtual worldwide training camp," he testified (Spafford 2003, 31). Terrorists have been known to exploit this resource. Imam Samudra's instructions regarding the use of chat rooms favoured by hackers to obtain information about 'carding' have already been mentioned. The same report mentions that one Kansas bomber got his bomb instructions from the August 1993 *Reader's Digest* (1997, 6-7).

In 1998, Khalid Ibrahim, who identified himself as an Indian national, sought classified and unclassified US government software and information, as well as data from India's Bhabha Atomic Research Center, from hackers communicating via Internet Relay Chat (IRC). Using the online aliases RahulB and Rama3456, Ibrahim began frequenting online cracker hangouts in June 1998. In conversations taken from IRC logs, Ibrahim claimed to be a member of Harkat-ul-Ansar, a militant Kashmiri separatist group (McKay 1998).

Finally, it is important to keep in mind that removal of technical information from public Web sites is no guarantee of safeguarding it. In essence, this effort is akin to 'closing the barn door after the horse has bolted.' Intelligence and technical data obtained by terrorist operatives prior to 9/11 can be archived, stored and distributed surreptitiously irrespective of government or private attempts to squelch its presence on the Internet in 2005. Indeed, these materials can be loaded onto offshore or other international Web servers that cannot be affected by US legislation, rendering any attempt to halt their spread outside the reach of American law enforcement (Tibbetts 2002, 17).

FIGHTING BACK

Use of the Internet is a double-edged sword for terrorists. They are not the only groups 'operating' the Net (Rogers 2002, 191), which can act as a valuable instrumental power source for anti-terrorist forces also. The more terrorist groups use the Internet to move information, money, and recruits around the globe, the more data that is available with which to trail them. Since 9/11 a number of groups have undertaken initiatives to disrupt terrorist use of the Internet, although a small number of such efforts were also undertaken previous to the attacks. Law enforcement agencies have been the chief instigators of such initiatives, but they have been joined in their endeavours by other government agencies as well as concerned individuals and various groups of hacktivists.

The Role of Law Enforcement and Intelligence Agencies

Intelligence Gathering

The bulk of this chapter has been concerned with showing how the Internet can act as a significant source of instrumental power for terrorist groups. Use of the Internet can nonetheless also result in significant undesirable effects for the same groups. First, unless terrorists are extremely careful in their use of the Internet for e-mail communication, general information provision, and other activities, they may unwittingly supply law enforcement agencies with a path direct to their door. Second, by putting their positions and ideological beliefs in the public domain, terrorist groups invite opposing sides to respond to these. The ensuing war of words may rebound on the terrorists as adherents and potential recruits are drawn away (Soo Hoo, Goodman and Greenberg 1997, 140).

Perhaps most importantly, however, the Internet and terrorist Web sites can serve as a provider of open source intelligence for states' intelligence agencies. Although spy agencies are loathe to publicly admit it, it is generally agreed that the Web is playing an ever-growing role in the spy business. According to the 9/11 Commission's *Staff Statement No. 11*, "open sources—the systematic collection of foreign media—has always been a bedrock source of information for intelligence. Open source remains important, including among terrorist groups that use the media and the Internet to communicate leadership guidance" (2004, 9). By the 1990s the US government's Foreign Broadcast Information Service (FBIS) had built a significant translation effort as regards terrorism-related media. Thus many now believe that terrorists' presence on the Internet actually works against them. "A lot of what we know about al-Qaida is gleaned from their websites," according to Steven Aftergood, a scientist at the Federation of American Scientists in Washington, D.C., and director of the nonprofit organisation's Project on Government Secrecy. "They are a greater value as an intelligence source than if they were to disappear" (as quoted in Lasker 2005). For example, Web sites and message boards have been known to function as a kind of early warning system. Two days before the 9/11 attacks, a message appeared on the popular Dubai-based Alsaha.com discussion forum proclaiming that "in the next two days," "a big surprise" would come from the Saudi Arabian region of Asir. The remote province adjacent to Yemen was where most of the nineteen hijackers hailed from (Bradley 2004).

Innovations such as the FBIS, while useful, do not tell the whole story, however. The problem begins with the sheer volume of information floating about in cyberspace. According to the 9/11 Commission's *Staff Statement No. 9*, prior to 9/11 the FBI did not have a sufficient number of translators proficient in Arabic and other relevant languages, which by early 2001 had resulted in a significant backlog of untranslated intelligence intercepts. In addition, prior to 9/11, the FBI's investigative activities were governed by Attorney General Guidelines, first put in place in 1976 and revised in 1995, to guard against the misuse of government power.

The Guidelines limited the investigative methods and techniques available to FBI agents conducting preliminary investigations. In particular, they prohibited the use of publicly available source information, such as that found on the Internet, unless specified criteria were present (2004, 8). These guidelines have since been modified and terrorist Web sites are thought to be under increased surveillance since 9/11, especially by Western intelligence agencies (Verton 2003, 220). This task remains gargantuan, however; information gleaned from the Net must be corroborated and verified before it can be added to the intelligence mix. This requires significant input of operatives and resources. And still intelligence agencies simply cannot monitor the entire Internet all of the time.

Technological Fixes

Given the above, it is unsurprising that many US officials and commentators are recommending that any additional funds that become available to the intelligence agencies be spent on human intelligence capabilities, rather than new technology. Others, however, are convinced that new technologies need to be developed and deployed in the fight against terrorism. They bemoan the fact that prior to 9/11, "Signals intelligence collection against terrorism, while significant, did not have sufficient funding within the NSA.

The NSA's slow transformation meant it could not keep pace with advances in telecommunications" (Staff Statement No. 11 2004, 10). Although DCS-1000—more commonly known as Carnivore—the FBI's e-mail packet-sniffer system has not been employed since 2002, Bureau officials have instead employed commercially available monitoring applications to aid in their investigations. Intelligence agencies are also said to be deploying the classic spy tactic of establishing so-called 'honey pots' with a high-tech twist: in this case, setting up bogus Web sites to attract those people they are seeking to monitor (Warner 2003; Associated Press 2002). Numerous other technological fixes are also in the works.

Other Innovations

It should be clear at this stage that the events of 9/11 impacted intelligence and law enforcement agencies not just in the United States, but around the world. On this side of the Atlantic, MI5 took the unprecedented step of posting an appeal for information about potential terrorists on dissident Arab websites. The message, in Arabic, was placed on sites that the authorities knew were accessed by extremists, including 'Islah.org,' a Saudi Arabian opposition site, and 'Qoqaz.com,' a Chechen site which advocated *jihad.* The message read: The atrocities that took place in the USA on 11 September led to the deaths of about five thousand people, including a large number of Muslims and people of other faiths.

MI5 (the British Security Service) is responsible for countering terrorism to protect all UK citizens of whatever faith or ethnic group. If you think you can help us to prevent future outrages call us in confidence on 020-7930 9000. MI5 were hopeful of eliciting information from persons on the margins of extremist groups or communities who were sufficiently shocked by the events of 9/11 to want to contact the agency. The agency had intended to post the message on a further fifteen sites known to be accessed by radicals, but many of these were shut down by the FBI in the aftermath of the attacks (Gruner and Naik 2001; Norton-Taylor 2001). The events of 9/11prompted numerous states' intelligence agencies to reappraise their online presence. Since 2001, MI5 has substantially enhanced its Web site while in 2004, Israel's Mossad spy agency launched a Web site aimed at recruiting staff.

Other Agencies: Sanitising Government Sites

US government Web sites were vital repositories of information for Internet users in the days and weeks following the 9/11 attacks. The sites became important venues for those both directly and indirectly affected by the events of 9/11, members of the public wishing to donate to the relief efforts, and the various agencies own employees, some of whom were victims of the attacks (or later of the anthrax scares) (Pew 2002, 33-37). While some agencies were uploading information onto the Net, however, others were busy erasing information from their sites. To avoid providing information that might be useful to terrorists planning further attacks, federal agencies, as well as some state and private Web page operators, took large amounts of material off the Internet in the wake of the 9/11 attacks. Some of the erasures were voluntary; others were carried out following requests from US government departments.

As mentioned earlier the Nuclear Regulatory Commission, which regulates American nuclear power plants, closed its Web site down for a period following a request from the Department of Defence that it do so. Although no other agency removed its entire site, pages were erased from the Web sites of the Department of Energy, the Interior Department's Geological Survey, the Federal Energy Regulatory Commission, the Environmental Protection Agency, the Federal Aviation Administration, the Department of Transportation's Office of Pipeline Safety, the National Archives and Records Administration, the NASA Glenn Research Centre, the International Nuclear Safety Centre, the Los Alamos National Laboratory, the Bureau of Transportation Statistics' Geographic Information Service, and the National Imagery and Mapping Agency (Dalglish, Leslie and Taylor 2002, 25; Pew 2002, 8-9; Baker *et al* 2004).

What sorts of information was removed from the sites? The Environmental Protection Agency (EPA) removed thousands of chemical industry risk management plans dealing with hazardous chemical plants from its site. Department of Transportation officials removed pipeline mapping information as well as a study describing risk profiles of various chemicals, while the Bureau of Transportation Statistics removed the National Transportation Atlas Databases and the North American Transportation Atlas, which environmentalists had used to assess the impact of transportation proposals. The Center for Disease Control and Prevention removed a *Report on Chemical Terrorism* that described industry's shortcomings in preparing for a possible terrorist attack (Dalglish, Leslie, and Taylor 2002, 2; Gugliotta 2001, A29; Pew 2002, 8-9; Scheeres 2001). Many of the agencies posted notices that the information had been removed because of its possible usefulness to terrorists.

Hackers and Hacktivists

Hackers also took to the Net in the aftermath of the terror attacks, some to voice their rage, others to applaud the attackers. A group calling themselves the Dispatchers proclaimed that they would destroy Web servers and Internet access in Afghanistan and also target nations that support terrorism. The group proceeded to deface hundreds of Web sites and launch Distributed Denial of Service (DoS) attacks against targets ranging from the Iranian Ministry of the Interior to the Presidential Palace of Afghanistan. Another group, known as Young Intelligent Hackers Against Terror (YIHAT) claimed, in mid-October 2001, to be negotiating with one European and one Asian government to 'legalize' the groups hacking activities in those states. The group's founder, Kim Schmitz, claimed the group breached the systems of two Arabic banks with ties to Osama Bin Laden, although a spokesperson for the bank denied any penetration had occurred. The group, whose stated mission is to impede the flow of money to terrorists, issued a statement on their Web site requesting that corporations make their networks available to group members for the purpose of providing the "electronic equivalent to terrorist training camps." Later, their public Web site was taken offline, apparently in response to attacks from other hackers (Denning 2001, 1; NIPC 2001b).

Not all hacking groups were supportive of the so-called 'hacking war.' On September 2001, the Chaos Computer Club, an organisation of German hackers, called for an end to the protests and for all hackers to cease vigilante actions. They called instead for global communication to resolve the conflict: "we believe in the power of communication, a power that has always prevailed in the end and is a more positive force than hatred" (as quoted in Hauss and Samuel 2002). A well-known group of computer enthusiasts, known as Cyber Angels, who promote responsible behaviour, also spoke out against the hacking war. They sponsored television advertisements in the US urging hackers to help gather information and intelligence on those who were participating in this hacktivism (Hauss and Samuels 2002; NIPC 2001a). In any event, the predicted escalation in hack attacks (ISTS 2001) did not materialize. In the weeks following the attacks, Web page defacements were well publicised, but the overall number and sophistication of these remained rather low. One possible reason for the non-escalation of attacks could be that many hackers—particularly those located in the US—were wary of being negatively associated with the events of 9/11 and curbed their activities as a result.

Since 9/11 a number of Web-based organisations have been established to monitor terrorist Web sites. One of the most well-known of such sites is Internet Haganah,11 selfdescribed as "an internet counterinsurgency." Also prominent is the Washington Dcbased Search for International Terrorist Entities (SITE) Institute that, like Internet Haganah, focuses on Islamic terror groups. Clients of SITE's fee-based intelligence service are said to include the FBI, Office of Homeland Security, and various media organisations. SITE's co-founder and director, Rita Katz, has commented: "It is actually to our benefit to have some of these terror sites up and running by American companies. If the servers are in the US, this is to our advantage when it comes to monitoring activities" (as quoted in Lasker 2005). Aaron Weisburd, who runs Internet Haganah out of his home in Southern Illinois, says his goal is to keep the extremists moving from address to address: "The object isn't to silence them—the object is to keep them moving, keep them talking, force them to make mistakes, so we can gather as much information about them as we can, each step of the way" (as quoted in Lasker 2005).

Researchers are still unclear whether the ability to communicate online worldwide has resulted in an increase or a decrease in terrorist acts. It is agreed, however, that online activities substantially improve the ability of such terrorist groups to raise funds. In Hebrew, 'Haganah' means defense. The most popular terrorist sites draw tens of thousands of visitors each month. Obviously, the Internet is not the only tool that a terrorist group needs to 'succeed.' However, the Net can add new dimensions to existing assets that groups can utilize to achieve their goals as well as providing new and innovative avenues for expression, fundraising, recruitment, *etc.* At the same time, there are also tradeoffs to be made. High levels of visibility increase levels of vulnerability, both to scrutiny and security breaches. The proliferation of official terrorist sites appears to indicate that the payoffs, in terms of publicity and propaganda value, are understood by many groups to be worth the risks.

6

Military Network Security

Is cyberterrorism a real threat or just a distraction from the day-to-day job of maintaining network security? "Our enemies will use our technology against us...the fact that they may be from a Third World country should not in any way suggest to us that they will not understand how to use our technology. They will see the places where we did not think we needed to build in security and they will take advantage of those seams." This extract from a speech made by Richard Clarke, former special advisor for Cyberspace Security to the US president, in the December following the events of September 11th, describes a scenario that probably seemed entirely plausible and inevitable to the audience of the Global Tech Summit given recent events. But two years on and despite the numerous terror attacks in Bali, Turkey and Iraq, the consensus among security experts is that there has never been a recorded act of cyberterrorism pre- or post-September 11th.

Despite no precedence to support the idea of an "electronic Pearl Harbour", governments continue to warn and even legislate around the issue. Just last month Singapore beefed up its Computer Misuse Act, giving police and other security agencies sweeping powers to "foil cyberterrorists before they attack." The controversial Act, which has been criticised by opposition MPs as an "an instrument of oppression itself" allows for pre-emptive action. Anyone who hacks or defaces a Web site may be jailed for up to three years or fined up to $10,000. "Instead of a backpack of explosives, a terrorist can create just as much devastation by sending a carefully engineered packet of data into the computer systems which control the network for essential services, for example the power stations," said Ho Peng Kee, Singapore's senior minister of state for law and home affairs.

Cyberterror or Just Oybercrime?

Although there has never actually been an act of cyberterrorism, there have been plenty of instances of politically motivated hacking incidents that sit outside the realm of simple cybercrime. A report published by the US Institute for Security and Technology Studies at Dartmouth College, in the weeks following September 11th, Cyber Attacks During The War on Terrorism, warned that US retaliation following September 11th was likely to result in "cyberattacks by terrorist groups themselves or by targeted nation states."

The report cited four case studies as evidence of the growing menace of cyberterrorism. The first example, although not a terrorist incident per se, followed the mid-air collision between a US spy plane and a Chinese fighter on 1 April, 2001. The reports author, Michael Vatis, a director at the institute, claims that as a direct result of the incident approximately 1,200 US sites, including the White House, the US Air Force, and the Department of Energy were subject to DDoS attacks or defaced by pro-Chinese images. "Chinese hacker groups, such as the Honker Union of China and the Chinese Red Guest Network Security Technology Alliance, organised a massive and sustained week-long campaign of cyberattacks against American targets," the report states. Although Vatis accepts that it is unclear if the Chinese government sanctioned these attacks, he pointed out that the activities were "highly visible and no arrests were made by Chinese officials, it can be assumed that they were at least tolerated, if not directly supported by Chinese authorities."

Another example cited in the report is the sustained "cyberbattle" running in parallel to the ongoing conflict between Israel and Palestine. In one instance, responding to the kidnapping of three Israeli soldiers in October 2000, pro-Israeli hackers launched a "sustained DDoS attacks against sites of the Palestinian Authority. Pro-Palestinian hackers apparently retaliated by taking down sites belonging to the Israeli Parliament, the Israeli Defence Forces, and the Tel Aviv Stock Exchange, the report claims. While these kinds of events may be regarded as politically motivated hacking, they fall short of being acts of cyberterrorism, according to security experts. The consensus seems to be that a cyberattack only becomes cyberterrorism when there is serious damage to property, loss of life — or it causes "terror" or fear in the target community.

"Despite the heightened sense of civilian unease and government vigilance in developed countries since 11 September, there hasn't been a validated case of 'cyberterrorism' worldwide. Although terrorists undoubtedly are using the Internet to communicate among themselves and as a research tool, their use of the Internet as a delivery vehicle for a significant, digital terrorist attack is a nightmare scenario not grounded in reality. There have been no losses of life or property because of a digital attack," says Gartner analyst Richard Mogull.

Gartner defines cyberterrorism as a "terrorism attack using a digital channel." The FBI defines terrorism as "unlawful or threatened use of force or violence...against persons or property to intimidate or force a government or civilian population to further political or social objectives." Mogull says that although terrorists are using the Internet to communicate among themselves, their use of the Internet as a "delivery vehicle for a significant, digital terrorist attack is a nightmare scenario not grounded in reality." There have been no losses of life or property because of a digital attack, he adds.

Don't Believe the Hype

Speaking at the CeBit technology fair earlier this year, Bruce Schneier, security expert and chief technology officer of network-monitoring company Counterpane Internet Security, said the threat posed by cyberterrorism had been overestimated. "The hype is coming from the US government and I don't know why. If they want to attack they will do it with bombs like they always have," he said. He added that rather than fostering a climate of fear, disrupting the Net and other communications networks would probably just annoy people. Schneier, like Mogull, claims that companies and consumers should concentrate on "real" threats from criminals, viruses, worms and Trojans.

Responding to Schneier's comments, a statement from the UK NISCC agreed that currently terrorists are more likely to mount physical than electronic attacks and generic warnings around cyberterrorism could be less than helpful. "Each company, industry, user will face different threats and have different vulnerabilities. It is for each to identify where the greatest threat is likely to come from and to protect against it," the memo stated. According to Gatner's Mogull, there are real security issues that the IT industry has to face up to before worrying about cyberterrorism, which is still only a potential threat. "We are not doing ourselves any favours in the security industry by focusing on it; there are plenty of other issues we need to face and we have enough vulnerabilities to manage in protecting our critical national infrastructure as it is."

Information and Network Security

Information and network security are crucial to ensuring wide participation in the information society. There is a lack of reliable data on citizens' security and privacy concerns, the impact of these concerns on the diffusion of electronic commerce, and the amount and type of breaches suffered by organisations worldwide. This could be an impediment to the implementation of on-line government services, commerce, health care, *etc.*, for which a safe information infrastructure is a pre-requisite. This report presents the results of two pilot surveys (for citizens and for businesses) held in 2002, which addressed respondents from the European Union, Switzerland and the United States on a number of topics, among others 'Security and Trust'.

This chapter presents one of the main deliverables of the SIBIS project (Statistical Indicators Benchmarking the Information Society), funded by the European Commission under the 'Information Society Technology' Programme (1998-2002). The overall goal of SIBIS is to develop and pilots indicators for monitoring progress towards the Information Society, taking account of the 'e-Europe action lines'. On this basis SIBIS focuses on nine topics of interest, *i.e.* Telecommunications and Access, Internet for RandD, Security and Trust, Education, Work and Skills, Social Inclusion, e-Commerce, e-Government and e- Health.

Within the SIBIS project two surveys (a General Population Survey and a Decision Makers Survey for businesses) were conducted on the nine e-Europe topics between March and May 2002. This report analyses the outcomes with respect to the topic of 'Security and Trust'. The document has two main objectives, *i.e.* to be a support tool for views shared by experts in the area and, at the same time, to define indicators for quantifying some of the most critical indicators related to e-government such as familiarity with it, willingness to use it, experience with its services, *etc*. The report is organised in six chapters and one annex.

The first three chapters are designed to give the reader an idea of the main outcomes (Executive Summary), the context (Introduction) and the indicators developed (Identification of the Indicator Framework and Hierarchy). The core of the report is the analysis of indicators. On the citizens' side, this chapter focuses on issues related to information security and the impact of people's concerns on the development of e-Commerce; it also measures the propensity of citizens to report violations of their on-line privacy and confidentiality and studies the possible impact of doing this anonymously.

On the businesses side, this chapter analyses the incidence of security breaches and their potential consequences for private and public organisations, as well as the source – actual or perceived–of such occurrences. The Annex is a methodological paper that guides the reader into the surveys and the way they were constructed. The main audience should be policy makers, statistical offices at all levels (national, *e.g.*, CBS, Statistisches Bundesamt, Statistics Finland *etc.*, and supranational, *e.g.*, Eurostat, OECD), industry leaders and researchers in the domain and those involved and interested in benchmarking the domain throughout Europe and the world. The questions and the subsequent indicators developed by SIBIS should be considered by those institutions as a valuable input for their yearly surveys. The project includes a series of workshops with such institutions in the countries represented by the SIBIS consortium.

The report should also be of interest to the European Commission (in particular DG INFSO) and to government officials dealing with information security programmes. Within SIBIS, another report (WP2) for each of the nine topics has been developed during 2001. That report was aimed at setting the scene on the topic, defining the gaps in the statistical coverage and suggesting innovative indicators to be developed through the subsequent survey. The current report, although a self-contained document, is an interim report, since a final summary version will be produced by July 2003.

SIBIS is led by Empirica (Bonn, Germany), and includes the following project partners: RAND Europe (Leiden, The Netherlands), Technopolis Ltd. (Brighton, UK), Databank Information and network security are increasingly recognised as vital elements for ensuring wide participation in the Information Society. As new business models are being developed to exploit the positive functionalities provided by these new global communication and information media, concerns about the security and privacy of information infrastructures and services may inhibit their full take-up. These concerns may hamper users' trust towards these new information and communication instruments.

However, in order to tackle these concerns, it is necessary to determine who the stakeholders are: citizens, businesses and governments. Citizens are the first class of stakeholders of the European information society. They are often at the receiving end of the public and commercial online services and tools. Consequently, it is necessary to assess and determine their perspectives and perceptions concerning online security and trust. Businesses are the second class of stakeholders examined by SIBIS. In part businesses have similar concerns and problems as consumers with regard to security. There is, additionally, the issue of guaranteeing privacy on one hand, and wanting to benefit from micro data on customers (purchasing behaviour *etc.*) on the other hand. Whereas collecting such data in order to target customers better and predict market behaviour more accurately is attractive, it may backfire, as potential consumers may want to opt out. This is where governments, the third group of stakeholders, have an explicit role to balance out interests of citizens/consumers with that of businesses. The role of governments is to balance these interests for the general good, adopting necessary regulations and trying to assure the highest degree of security for its citizens on the one hand, and avoiding putting up too high thresholds for businesses on the other.

SIBIS (Statistical Indicators Benchmarking the Information Society) developed and piloted a number of *Security and Trust* indicators, covering perceptions and experiences of citizens and businesses in Europe and the United States. Before SIBIS, data on information security issues was largely absent. By means of two pilot surveys, *i.e.* the GPS (General Population Survey) and the DMS (Decision Makers Survey), SIBIS tried to fill this gap. This report is intended to inform national and supranational statistical agencies, assisting them in their formulation of indicators for measuring the status and progress of the Information Society. It defines indicators for quantifying some of the most critical variables related to computer security (risk, quality of security policies and 'quality' of security breaches). The GPS was conducted on a population of 11,832 persons aged 15 and over, living in private households, while the DMS was carried out on a population of 3,139 establishments belonging to four aggregated industry sectors in seven European Union member states (Finland, France, Germany, Greece, Italy, Spain and the United Kingdom).

7

NETWAR

Because of changes in the context for possible conflict, netwar will no doubt prove most attractive, for the near-term future, to nonstate actors. It is likely to become a policy tool of choice for ethnonationalists, terrorists, and transnational criminal and revolutionary organisations. However, nation-states may increasingly find netwar a useful option, especially when the need to pursue limited aims with limited means arises. Additionally, the rise of a global civil society heralds the possibility that nongovernmental organisations associated with militant social activism will become netwar combatants, deliberately or sometimes inadvertently. Overall, the context of netwar may come to be defined by conflicts between state and nonstate actors, nonstate actors that use states as arenas, or states that use nonstate actors as their proxies.

The information revolution is altering the nature of conflict across the spectrum. We call attention to two developments in particular. First, this revolution is favouring and strengthening network forms of organisation, often giving them an advantage over hierarchical forms. The rise of networks means that power is migrating to nonstate actors, because they are able to organize into sprawling multiorganisational networks (especially "all-channel" networks, in which every node is connected to every other node) more readily than can traditional, hierarchical, state actors. This means that conflicts may increasingly be waged by "networks," perhaps more than by "hierarchies." It also means that whoever masters the network form stands to gain the advantage. Second, as the information revolution deepens, the conduct and outcome of conflicts increasingly depend on information and communications. More than ever before, conflicts revolve around "knowledge" and the use of "soft power." Adversaries are learning to emphasize "information operations" and "perception management"—that is, media-oriented measures that aim to attract or disorient rather than coerce, and that affect how secure a society, a military, or other actor feels about its knowledge of itself and of its adversaries. Psychological disruption may become as important a goal as physical destruction.

These propositions cut across the entire conflict spectrum. Major transformations are thus coming in the nature of adversaries, in the type of threats they may pose, and in how conflicts can be waged. Information-age threats are likely to be more diffuse, dispersed, multidimensional nonlinear, and ambiguous than industrial-age threats. Metaphorically, then, future conflicts may resemble the Oriental game of *Go* more than the Western game of chess. The conflict spectrum will be remolded from end to end by these dynamics.

A Concept and its Brief History

Back in 1992, while first wondering about such propositions and writing about *cyberwar* as a looming mode of military conflict, we thought it would be a good idea to have a parallel concept about information-age conflict at the less military, low-intensity, more social end of the spectrum. The term we coined was *netwar,* largely because it resonated with the surety that the information revolution favoured the rise of network forms of organisation, doctrine, and strategy. Through netwar, numerous dispersed small groups using the latest communications technologies could act conjointly across great distances. We had in mind actors as diverse as transnational terrorists, criminals, and even radical activists. Some were already moving from hierarchical to new information-age network designs.

We fielded the netwar concept in our first journal article, "Cyberwar Is Coming" (1993), then provided a full exposition in our RAND report, *The Advent of Netwar* (1996). Additional insights were advanced in the concluding chapter of our book, *In Athena's Camp* (1997). Elaborations appeared in multiauthored RAND volumes on *The Zapatista "Social Netwar" in Mexico* (Ronfeldt et al., 1998) and *Countering the New Terrorism* (Lesser et al., 1999). Our study *The*

Emergence of Noopolitik: Toward an American Information Strategy (1999) observed that many socially minded nongovernmental organisations (NGOs) were already using netwar strategies to enhance their soft power. Our recent study *Swarming and the Future of Conflict* (2000) is mainly about developing a new military doctrine for wielding "hard" power, but it generally advances our view that swarming is likely to become the dominant approach to conflict across the spectrum, including among netwar actors. While the Zapatista study provided early evidence for this, short opinion pieces on the military war in Kosovo (1999) and the activist "Battle for Seattle"(1999) identified new cases.

As these writings have spread, the netwar concept has struck a chord with a growing number of theorists, futurists, journalists, and practitioners. In forward-looking books, scholars as diverse as Manuel Castells (1997), Chris Hables Gray (1997), and David Brin (1998) have used the concept for discussing trends at the mostly nonmilitary end of the conflict spectrum. For several years, a web site maintained by Jason Wehling carried a wide range of articles about netwar, social activism, and information-age conflict, leading off with a paper he had written about the netwar concept (1995). Meanwhile, interesting flurries of discussion about netwar arose on email lists related to the Zapatista movement in Mexico following the armed uprising in January 1994. Harry Cleaver's writings (*e.g.*, 1995, 1998, 1999) are particularly illuminating. They show that Mexico became a laboratory for the emergence of a new, non-Leninist model of radicalism.

The Zapatista leader, Subcomandante Marcos, even averred in 1999 that netwar described the Zapatista movement, and that *counternetwar* instructed the strategy of its military and paramilitary opponents. For its part, the high command of the Mexican military also espoused admiration for the concept during 2000. Also in 2000, a leader of the International Campaign to Ban Landmines (ICBL), Jody Williams, remarked in a radio interview that she had heard that RAND researchers were developing the netwar concept to help governments control movements like the ICBL. Elsewhere, the concept cropped up in marginal rants and ruminations by militants associated with various left-wing, rightwing, and eclectic religious movements who posted on Usenet discussion groups.

Meanwhile, officials and analysts in U.S. and European government, military, and police circles began showing an interest in the concept. They were finding it difficult to deal with terrorists, criminals, and fanatics associated with militias and extremist single-issue movements, largely because these antagonists were organising into sprawling, loose, "leaderless" networks, overcoming their former isolated postures as stand-alone groups headed by "great men." U.S. and European officials realised that these troublesome trends put a premium on interagency communication and coordination, for everything from intelligence sharing to tactical operations. But this implied a degree of cross-jurisdictional and international networking, especially for intelligence sharing, that is difficult for state hierarchies to accomplish.

The concepts of netwar and counternetwar attracted some interest because they had a potential for motivating officials to build their own networks, as well as hybrids of hierarchies and networks, to deal with the networked organisations, doctrines, and strategies of their information-age adversaries. A special issue of the journal *Studies in Conflict and Terrorism* on "Netwar Across the Spectrum of Conflict" (1999) may have helped heighten awareness of this. Our formulation of the netwar concept has always emphasised the organisational dimension. But we have also pointed out that an organisational network works best when it has the right doctrinal, technological, and social dynamics. In our joint work, we have repeatedly insisted on this. However, writers enamored of the flashy, high-tech aspects of the information revolution have often depicted netwar (and cyberwar) as a term for computerised aggression waged via stand-off attacks in cyberspace—that is, as a trendy synonym for infowar, information operations, "strategic information warfare," Internet war, "hacktivism," cyberterrorism, cybotage, *etc.*

Thus, in some quarters, the Serb hacks of NATO's web site in 1999 were viewed as netwar (or cyberwar). Yet, little was known about the perpetrators and the nature of their organisation; if they amounted to just a few, clever, government-sponsored individuals operating from a site or two, then the netwar dimensions of this case were minimal, and it was just a clever instance of minor cybotage. This case also speaks to another distortion: These Serbs (presumably they were

Serbs) aimed to bring a piece of "the Net" down. Yet, in a full-fledged ethnonationalist, terrorist, criminal, or social netwar, the protagonists may be far more interested in keeping the Net up. They may benefit from using the Internet and other advanced communications services (*e.g.*, fax machines and cellular telephones) for purposes that range from coordinating with each other and seeking recruits, to projecting their identity, broadcasting their messages to target audiences, and gathering intelligence about their opponents.

With respect to Serbia, then, a better case of netwar as we define it was the effort by Serbia's reformist Radio B-92, along with a supportive network of U.S. and European government agencies and NGOs, to broadcast its reportage back into Serbia over the Internet, after B-92's transmitters were shut down by the Milosevic regime in 1998 and again in 1999. For a seminal case of a worldwide netwar, one need look no further than the ICBL. This unusually successful movement consists of a loosely internetted array of NGOs and governments, which rely heavily on the Internet for communications. Through the personage of one of its many leaders, Jody Williams, this netwar won a well-deserved Nobel peace prize.

DEFINING NETWAR

To be precise, the term netwar refers to an emerging mode of conflict (and crime) at societal levels, short of traditional military warfare, in which the protagonists use network forms of organisation and related doctrines, strategies, and technologies attuned to the information age. These protagonists are likely to consist of dispersed organisations, small groups, and individuals who communicate, coordinate, and conduct their campaigns in an internetted manner, often without a precise central command. Thus, netwar differs from modes of conflict and crime in which the protagonists prefer to develop formal, stand-alone, hierarchical organisations, doctrines, and strategies as in past efforts, for example, to build centralised movements along Leninist lines. Thus, for example, netwar is about the Zapatistas more than the Fidelistas, Hamas more than the Palestine Liberation Organisation (PLO), the American Christian Patriot movement more than the Ku Klux Klan, and the Asian Triads more than the Cosa Nostra.

The term netwar is meant to call attention to the prospect that network-based conflict and crime will become major phenomena in the decades ahead. Various actors across the spectrum of conflict and crime are already evolving in this direction. This includes familiar adversaries who are modifying their structures and strategies to take advantage of networked designs—*e.g.*, transnational terrorist groups, black-market proliferators of weapons of mass destruction (WMD), drug and other crime syndicates, fundamentalist and ethnonationalist movements, intellectual-property pirates, and immigration and refugee smugglers. Some urban gangs, back-country militias, and militant single-issue groups in the United States have also been developing netwar-like attributes. The netwar spectrum also includes a new generation of revolutionaries, radicals, and activists who are beginning to create information-age ideologies, in which identities and loyalties may shift from the nation state to the transnational level of "global civil society." New kinds of actors, such as anarchistic and nihilistic leagues of computer-hacking "cyboteurs," may also engage in netwar. Many—if not most—netwar actors will be nonstate, even stateless.

Some may be agents of a state, but others may try to turn states into their agents. Also, a netwar actor may be both subnational and transnational in scope. Odd hybrids and symbioses are likely. Furthermore, some bad actors (*e.g.*, terrorist and criminal groups) may threaten U.S. and other nations' interests, but other actors (*e.g.*, NGO activists in Burma or Mexico) may not—indeed, some actors who at times turn to netwar strategies and tactics, such as the New York–based Committee to Protect Journalists (CPJ), may have salutary liberalising effects. Some actors may aim at destruction, but more may aim mainly at disruption and disorientation. Again, many variations are possible. The full spectrum of netwar proponents may thus seem broad and odd at first glance. But there is an underlying pattern that cuts across all variations: the use of network forms of organisation, doctrine, strategy, and technology attuned to the information age.

More about Organisational Design

In an archetypal netwar, the protagonists are likely to amount to a set of diverse, dispersed "nodes" who share a set of ideas and interests and who are arrayed to act in a fully internetted "all-channel" manner. In the scholarly literature (*e.g.*, Evan, 1972), networks come in basically three types or topologies:

- The chain or line network, as in a smuggling chain where people, goods, or information move along a line of separated contacts, and where end-to-end communication must travel through the intermediate nodes.
- The hub, star, or wheel network, as in a franchise or a cartel where a set of actors are tied to a central (but not hierarchical) node or actor, and must go through that node to communicate and coordinate with each other.

The all-channel or full-matrix network, as in a collaborative network of militant peace groups where everybody is connected to everybody else. Each node in the diagrams may refer to an individual, a group, an organisation, part of a group or organisation, or even a state. The nodes may be large or small, tightly or loosely coupled, and inclusive or exclusive in membership. They may be segmentary or specialised—that is, they may look alike and engage in similar activities, or they may undertake a division of labour based on specialisation. The boundaries of the network, or of any node included in it, may be well-defined, or blurred and porous in relation to the outside environment. Many variations are possible.

Each type may be suited to different conditions and purposes, and all three may be found among netwar-related adversaries—*e.g.*, the chain in smuggling operations; the hub at the core of terrorist and criminal syndicates; and the all-channel type among militant groups that are highly internetted and decentralised. There may also be hybrids of the three types, with different tasks being organised around different types of networks. For example, a netwar actor may have an all-channel council or directorate at its core but use hubs and chains for tactical operations. There may also be hybrids of network and hierarchical forms of organisation. For example, traditional hierarchies may exist inside particular nodes in a network. Some actors may have a hierarchical organisation overall but use network designs for tactical operations; other actors may have an all-channel network design overall but use hierarchical teams for tactical operations. Again, many configurations are possible, and it may be difficult for an analyst to discern exactly what type characterises a particular network.

Of the three network types, the all-channel has been the most difficult to organize and sustain, partly because it may require dense communications. But it is the type that gives the network form its new, high potential for collaborative undertakings and that is gaining new strength from the information revolution. Pictorially, an all-channel netwar actor resembles a geodesic "Bucky ball" (named for Buckminster Fuller); it does not look like a pyramid. The organisational design is flat. Ideally, there is no single, central leadership, command, or headquarters—no precise heart or head that can be targeted. The network as a whole (but not necessarily each node) has little to no hierarchy; there may be multiple leaders. Decision making and operations are decentralised, allowing for local initiative and autonomy. Thus the design may sometimes appear acephalous (headless), and at other times polycephalous (Hydra-headed).

The capacity of this design for effective performance over time may depend on the existence of shared principles, interests, and goals— perhaps an overarching doctrine or ideology—which spans all nodes and to which the members subscribe in a deep way. Such a set of principles, shaped through mutual consultation and consensusbuilding, can enable members to be "all of one mind" even though they are dispersed and devoted to different tasks. It can provide a central ideational and operational coherence that allows for tactical decentralisation. It can set boundaries and provide guidelines for decisions and actions so that the members do not have to resort to a hierarchy because "they know what they have to do."

But when communication is needed, the network's members must be able to disseminate information promptly and as broadly as desired within the network and to outside audiences. In many respects, then, the archetypal netwar design corresponds to what earlier analysts (Gerlach, 1987, p. 115, based on Gerlach and Hine, 1970) called a "segmented, polycentric, ideologically integrated network" (SPIN): By segmentary I mean that it is cellular, composed of many different groups.... By polycentric I mean that it has many different leaders or centers of direction.... By networked I mean that the segments and the leaders are integrated into reticulated systems or networks through various structural, personal, and ideological ties. Networks are usually unbounded and expanding.... This acronym (SPIN) helps us picture this organisation as a fluid, dynamic, expanding one, spinning out into mainstream society.

Caveats about the Role of Technology

Netwar is a result of the rise of network forms of organisation, which in turn is partly a result of the computerised information revolution. To realize its potential, a fully interconnected network requires a capacity for constant, dense information and communications flows, more so than do other forms of organisation (*e.g.*, hierarchies). This capacity is afforded by the latest information and communication technologies—cellular telephones, fax machines, electronic mail (email), web sites, and computer conferencing. Such technologies are highly advantageous for netwar actors whose constituents are geographically dispersed.

But two caveats are in order. First, the new technologies, however enabling for organisational networking, are not absolutely necessary for a netwar actor. Older technologies, like human couriers, and mixes of old and new systems may do the job in some situations. The late Somali warlord, Mohamed Farah Aidid, for example, proved very adept at eluding those seeking to capture him while at the same time retaining full command and control over his forces by means of runners and drum codes. Similarly, the first Chechen War (1994–1996), which the Islamic insurgents won, made wide use of runners and old communications technologies like ham radios for battle management and other command and control functions (Arquilla and Karasik, 1999). So, netwar may be waged in high, low, or no-tech fashion.

Second, netwar is not simply a function of "the Net" (*i.e.*, the Internet); it does not take place only in "cyberspace" or the "infosphere." Some *battles* may occur there, but a *war's* overall conduct and outcome will normally depend mostly on what happens in the "real world"—it will continue to be, even in information-age conflicts, generally more important than what happens in cyberspace or the infosphere. Netwar is not solely about Internet war (just as cyberwar is not just about "strategic information warfare"). Americans have a tendency to view modern conflict as being more about technology than organisation and doctrine. In our view, this is a misleading tendency. For example, social netwar is more about a doctrinal leader like Subcomandante Marcos than about a lone, wild computer hacker like Kevin Mitnick.

A Capacity for Swarming, and the Blurring of Offense and Defense

This distinctive, often ad-hoc design has unusual strengths, for both offense and defense. On the offense, networks tend to be adaptable, flexible, and versatile *vis-a-vis* opportunities and challenges. This may be particularly the case where a set of actors can engage in *swarming.* Little analytic attention has been given to swarming, which is quite different from traditional mass- and maneuveroriented approaches to conflict. Yet swarming may become the key mode of conflict in the information age (Arquilla and Ronfeldt, 2000, and Edwards, 2000), and the cutting edge for this possibility is found among netwar protagonists.

Swarming is a seemingly amorphous, but deliberately structured, coordinated, strategic way to strike from all directions at a particular point or points, by means of a sustainable pulsing of force and/or fire, close-in as well as from stand-off positions. This notion of "force and/or fire" may be literal in the case of military or police operations, but metaphorical in the case of NGO activists, who may, for example, be blocking city intersections or emitting volleys of emails and faxes. Swarming will work best—perhaps it will only work—if it is designed mainly around the deployment of myriad, small, dispersed, networked maneuver units. Swarming occurs when the dispersed units of a network of small (and perhaps some large) forces converge on a target from multiple directions.

The overall aim is *sustainable pulsing*— swarm networks must be able to coalesce rapidly and stealthily on a target, then dissever and redisperse, immediately ready to recombine for a new pulse. The capacity for a "stealthy approach" suggests that, in netwar, attacks are more likely to occur in "swarms" than in more traditional "waves." The Chechen resistance to the Russian army and the Direct Action Network's operations in the anti–World Trade Organisation "Battle of Seattle" both provide excellent examples of swarming behaviour.

Swarming may be most effective, and difficult to defend against, where a set of netwar actors do not "mass" their forces, but rather engage in dispersion and "packetisation" (for want of a better term). This means, for example, that drug smugglers can break large loads into many small packets for simultaneous surreptitious transport across a border, or that NGO activists, as in the case of the Zapatista movement, have enough diversity in their ranks to respond to any discrete issue that arises—human rights, democracy, the environment, rural development, whatever.

In terms of their defensive potential, networks tend to be redundant and diverse, making them robust and resilient in the face of attack. When they have a capacity for interoperability and shun centralised command and control, network designs can be difficult to crack and defeat as a whole. In particular, they may defy counterleadership targeting—a favoured strategy in the drug war as well as in overall efforts to tamp organised crime in the United States. Thus, whoever wants to attack a network is limited—generally, only portions of a network can be found and confronted. Moreover, the deniability built into a network affords the possibility that it may simply absorb a number of attacks on distributed nodes, leading an attacker to believe the network has been harmed and rendered inoperable when, in fact, it remains viable and is seeking new opportunities for tactical surprise. The difficulty of dealing with netwar actors deepens when the lines between offense and defense are blurred, or blended. When *blurring* is the case, it may be difficult to distinguish between attacking and defending actions, particularly where an actor goes on the offense in the name of self-defense. For example, the Zapatista struggle in Mexico demonstrates anew the blurring of offense and defense. The *blending* of offense and defense will often mix the strategic and tactical levels of operations. For example, guerrillas on the defensive strategically may go on the offense tactically, as in the war of the *mujahideen* in Afghanistan during the 1980s, and in both recent Chechen wars with the Russians.

Operating in the Seams

The blurring of offense and defense reflects another feature of netwar (albeit one that is exhibited in many other policy and issue areas): It tends to defy and cut across standard boundaries, jurisdictions, and distinctions between state and society, public and private, war and peace, war and crime, civilian and military, police and military, and legal and illegal. This makes it difficult if not impossible for a government to assign responsibility to any single agency—*e.g.*, military, police, or intelligence—to be in charge of responding.

As Richard Szafranski (1994, 1995) illuminated in his discussions of how information warfare ultimately becomes "neo-cortical warfare," the challenge for governments and societies becomes "epistemological." A netwar actor may aim to confound people's fundamental beliefs about the nature of their culture, society, and government, partly to foment fear but perhaps mainly to disorient people and unhinge their perceptions. This is why a netwar with a strong social content— whether waged by ethnonationalists, terrorists, or social activists— may tend to be about disruption more than destruction. The more epistemological the challenge, the more confounding it may be from an organisational standpoint. Whose responsibility is it to respond? Whose roles and missions are at stake? Is it a military, police, intelligence, or political matter? When the roles and missions of defenders are not easy to define, both deterrence and defense may become problematic.

Thus, the spread of netwar adds to the challenges facing the nation state in the information age. Its sovereignty and authority are usually exercised through bureacracies in which issues and problems can be sliced up and specific offices can be charged with taking care of specific problems.

In netwar, things are rarely so clear. A protagonist is likely to operate in the cracks and gray areas of a society, striking where lines of authority crisscross and the operational paradigms of politicians, officials, soldiers, police officers, and related actors get fuzzy and clash. Moreover, where transnational participation is strong, a netwar's protagonists may expose a local government to challenges to its sovereignty and legitimacy by arousing foreign governments and business corporations to put pressure on the local government to alter its domestic policies and practices.

NETWORKS VERSUS HIERARCHIES: CHALLENGES FOR COUNTERNETWAR

These observations and the case studies presented in this volume lead to four policy-oriented propositions about the information revolution and its implications for netwar and counternetwar (Arquilla and Ronfeldt, 1993, 1996): *Hierarchies have a difficult time fighting networks.* There are examples of this across the conflict spectrum. Some of the best are found in the failings of many governments to defeat transnational criminal cartels engaged in drug smuggling, as in Colombia. The persistence of religious revivalist movements, as in Algeria, in the face of unremitting state opposition, shows both the defensive and offensive robustness of the network form. The Zapatista movement in Mexico, with its legions of supporters and sympathisers among local and transnational NGOs, shows that social netwar can put a democratising autocracy on the defensive and pressure it to continue adopting reforms.

It takes networks to fight networks: Governments that want to defend against netwar may have to adopt organisational designs and strategies like those of their adversaries. This does not mean mirroring the adversary, but rather learning to draw on the same design principles that he has already learned about the rise of network forms in the information age. These principles depend to some extent on technological innovation, but mainly on a willingness to innovate organisationally and doctrinally, perhaps especially by building new mechanisms for interagency and multijurisdictional cooperation.

Whoever masters the network form first and best will gain major advantages: In these early decades of the information age, adversaries who are advanced at networking (be they criminals, terrorists, or peaceful social activists, including ones acting in concert with states) are enjoying an increase in their power relative to state agencies. While networking once allowed them simply to keep from being suppressed, it now allows them to compete on more nearly equal terms with states and other hierarchically oriented actors. The histories of Hamas and of the Cali cartel illustrate this; so do the Zapatista movement in Mexico and the International Campaign to Ban Landmines. Counternetwar may thus require very effective interagency approaches, which by their nature involve networked structures. It is not necessary, desirable, or even possible to replace all hierarchies with networks in governments. Rather, the challenge will be to blend these two forms skillfully, while retaining enough core authority to encourage and enforce adherence to networked processes. By creating effective hybrids, governments may become better prepared to confront the new threats and challenges emerging in the information age, whether generated by ethnonationalists, terrorists, militias, criminals, or other actors.

However, governments tend to be so constrained by hierarchical habits and institutional interests that it may take some sharp reverses before a willingness to experiment more seriously with networking emerges. The costs and risks associated with failing to engage in institutional redesign are likely to be high—and may grow ever higher over time. In the most difficult areas—crime and terrorism—steps to improve intra and international networking are moving in the right direction. But far more remains to be done, as criminal and terrorist networks continuously remake themselves into ever more difficult targets.

RECENT CASES OF NETWAR

Since we first wrote about netwar over seven years ago, there have been at least ten prominent (*i.e.*, front-page) instances of its employment, in conflicts ranging from social activist campaigns to violent ethnic insurgencies. The netwar record has been generally successful. In these ten cases, which feature networked nonstate actors confronting states or groups of states, five netwars have achieved substantial success.

Table: prominent Cases of Netwar, 1994-

Campaign	Dates	Outcome	Type
Protracted Netwars			
EZLN*	984–	Limited success	Autonomist
ICBI	1998–	Limited success	Globalist
Burma	1996–	Failing?	Mixed
Drug Cartels	1994–	Substantial success	Autonomist
Chechnya I	1994–1996	Substantial success	Autonomist
Chechnya II	1999–2000	Failure	Autonomist

Short-Duration Netwars			
Greenpeace	1994	Limited success	Globalist
Battle of Seattle	1999	Substantial success	Globalist
East Timor	1999	Substantial success	Autonomist
Serb Opposition	2000	Substantial success	Mixed

*Zapatista National Liberation Army.

The limits on some successes and the one failure imply a need to take a balanced view of netwar, analysing the conditions under which it is most likely to succeed, fail, or fall somewhere in between. Clearly, there is enough success here to make netwar worth examining more closely. But it is important not to "tout" netwar, as Robert Taber (1970) once did guerrilla war. He was sharply rebutted by Lewis Gann (1970), who pointed out that guerrillas, far from being unstoppable, have often been defeated. Netwar will also have its ups and downs. Our purpose is to uncover and get a deeper understanding of its dynamics.

In Table above the cases are divided into those conflicts that were or have been drawn out, and those focused on specific crises—a useful distinction often made in studies of conflict. Interesting insights emerge. For example, the two most successful protracted campaigns were waged violently by ethnonationalists and criminals who sought freedom from state controls. The short-duration successes also included some use of violence (in two cases), and a global civil society reaction (that threatened a forceful response) to state violence in the other. And, though more muted, most of the other cases have violent aspects. The table distributes netwars by type along a spectrum ranging from those that are globalist in orientation (*e.g.*, the anti-landmine campaign), to those that are autonomist at the opposite end (*e.g.*, the 1994 Chechen effort to secede from Russia). In the middle lie mixed cases where the objective is to gain power locally, but these netwars depend on the protagonists being able to open their societies to democratic, globalist influences.

The two unsuccessful netwar campaigns (in Russia and Burma) have featured networks confronting hierarchical authoritarian governments that have been willing to use substantial force to assert—in the case of Russia, to reassert—their hold on power. These networks' losses to hierarchies, combined with the fact that the principal successes to date have been gained by violent "uncivil society" actors, suggest being cautious about the claims for netwar. That said, the nonviolent International Campaign to Ban Landmines and the Greenpeace effort to curb nuclear testing both achieved reasonable measures of success without engaging in any violence whatsoever. This is a hopeful sign. And, while the civil society campaign to free Burma from authoritarian rule is a partial failure to date, this is a continuing campaign whose ultimate outcome is yet unknown.

Finally, these netwar conflicts feature an uneven split between those about globalist issues—aimed at fostering the rise of a rights- and ethics-based civil society—and the more frequent, somewhat darker "autonomist" variety of netwar, featuring nonstate actors trying to get out from under state controls. Most of the limited successes that have been achieved thus far are globalist in orientation, while most of the substantial successes (save for the Battle of Seattle and Serbia) have been autonomist. It will be interesting, as the instances of netwar increase over time, to see whether this pattern holds. The outcomes of the globalist cases suggest the prevalence of negotiated solutions, while the autonomist conflicts may, in general, have a much more inherently desperate character that drives them to greater violence and less willingness to reach accommodation. All this we will watch in the years to come. For now, these early cases have helped us to develop this taxonomy of netwar, further refining the concept.

Will netwar continue to empower nonstate actors, perhaps reducing the relative power advantage enjoyed by nation states? Civil society networks have already made much use of social netwar as a tool for advancing a globalist, ethics-based agenda focused on broadening and deepening human rights regimes—often in the context of an ongoing effort to foster movement from authoritarian rule to democracy (*e.g.*, Burma). But there is another side of nonstate-actor-oriented netwar, characterised not by globalist impulses, but rather by the desire to avoid state control of a network's criminal, terrorist, or ethnicseparatist agenda (*e.g.*, Hamas and Chechens). While the globalist netwars seem devoted to nonviolent tools of struggle, the autonomists may employ both means of engagement—often with a greater emphasis on violence.

VARIETIES OF NETWAR—DUAL PHENOMENA

Netwar is a deduced concept—it derives from our thinking about the effects and implications of the information revolution. Once coined, the concept helps show that evidence is mounting about the rise of network forms of organisation, and about the importance of "information strategies" and "information operations" across the spectrum of conflict, including among ethnonationalists, terrorists, guerrillas, criminals, and activists. Note that we do not equate ethnonationalists, terrorists, guerrillas, criminals, and activists with each other— each has different dynamics. Nor do we mean to tarnish social activism, which has positive aspects for civil society. We are simply calling for attention to a cross-cutting meta-pattern about network forms of organisation, doctrine, and strategy that we might not have spotted, by induction or deduction, if we had been experts focused solely on any one of those areas.

Netwar can be waged by "good" as well as "bad" actors, and through peaceful as well as violent measures. From its beginnings, netwar has appealed to a broad cross-section of nonstate actors who are striving to confront or cope with their state authorities. Ethnonationalists, criminals, and terrorists—all have found new power in networking. But so too have emerging global civil society actors who have emphasised nonviolent efforts to win the "battle of the story"—a more purely informational dimension of netwar—rather than the violent swarming characteristic of its darker side. Both categories of actors seem to realize, even if only implicitly, that, in the future, conflict will become even more "irregularised," with the set-piece confrontations and battles of earlier eras largely disappearing. While the U.S. military remains focused—in terms of budgetary emphasis, doctrine, and force structure—on the traditional forms of conflict, the rise of netwar should prompt a shift to a nimble "turn of mind," one far less attuned to fighting in the Fulda Gap or the Persian Gulf and more focused on engaging a range of odd new adversaries across a densely interconnected "global grid." The duality of netwar in the real world—dark-side criminals and terrorists on the one hand, but enlightening civil society forces on the other—is mirrored in the virtual world of cyberspace, which is increasingly utilised for crime and terror (still embryonic), along with social activism. At present, social activism is far more robust and established in the cyber realm than is crime or terror. Will this continue to be the case? We think so. Activists will become more adept at integrating the mobilising force of the Internet with the power and appeal of messages aimed at spreading and protecting human rights. Even so, criminal and terrorist organisations will learn how to manipulate the infosphere with increasing skill.

Thus, netwar has two faces, like the Roman god Janus. Janus was the god of doors and gates, and thus of departures and returns, and new beginnings and initiatives. This, in a sense, meant he was the god of communications, too. His double face, one old and looking back, the other younger and peering forward, conveyed that he was an inherently dual god. At the beginning of creation, he partook in the separation of order from chaos. In Roman times, he was identified with the distinction between war and peace, for the gate to his temple at the Forum was kept ceremoniously closed in times of peace and open in times of war—which meant the gates were rarely closed. At the start of the 21st century, the world is again at a new beginning. It is uncertain whether it will be an era of peace or conflict; but how matters turn out will depend to some degree on which face of netwar predominates. This volume explores the two faces of netwar, in three parts. The first part is composed of three chapters that chronicle the increasingly networked nature of major types of "uncivil-society" actors for whom violence is a principal mode of expression.

The analyses by Michele Zanini and Sean Edwards of Arab terrorist groups, by Phil Williams of transnational criminal networks, and by John Sullivan of street-level gangs and hooligans, all speak to the increasingly sophisticated usage of the new information technologies to enhance both these groups' organisational and operational capabilities. The book examines the rise of social netwar, again with three chapters. These chapters examine social netwars waged by networked civil society actors against various types of states. Tiffany Danitz and Warren Strobel show the limitations (but also some successful facets) of social netwar when waged against a resolute dictatorship that maintains a system virtually closed to civil society. The book considers the future of netwar, particularly regarding how technology, organisation, and doctrine interact.

8

THE NETWORKING OF ERROR IN THE INFORMATION AGE

Introduction

The information revolution has fueled the longest economic expansion in history and led to impressive productivity gains in recent years. Along with these benefits, however, has come the dark side of information technology—cyberterrorism. The idea of terrorists surreptitiously hacking into a computer system to introduce a virus, steal sensitive information, deface or swamp a web site, or turn off a crucial public service seriously concerns computer security personnel around the world. High profile attacks—such as the denial-of-service (DOS) attacks against major e-commerce sites Yahoo! and eBay in 1999 or the ongoing "cyber-jihad" against Israeli and American web sites being waged by Pakistani-based hackers in support of the Palestinian "al-Aqsa" Intifadah—continue to raise the specter of cyberterrorism.

The information age is affecting not only the types of targets and weapons terrorists choose, but also the ways in which such groups operate and structure their organisations. Several of the most dangerous terrorist organisations are using information technology (IT)— such as computers, software, telecommunication devices, and the Internet—to better organize and coordinate dispersed activities. Like the large numbers of private corporations that have embraced IT to operate more efficiently and with greater flexibility, terrorists are harnessing the power of IT to enable new operational doctrines and forms of organisation. And just as companies in the private sector are forming alliance networks to provide complex services to customers, so too are terrorist groups "disaggregating" from hierarchical bureaucracies and moving to flatter, more decentralised, and often changing webs of groups united by a common goal.

The rise of networked terrorist groups is part of a broader shift to what Arquilla and Ronfeldt have called "netwar." Netwar refers to an emerging mode of conflict and crime at societal levels, involving measures short of traditional war in which the protagonists are likely to consist of dispersed, small groups who communicate, coordinate, and conduct their campaigns in an internetted manner, without a precise central command. Netwar differs from modes of conflict in which the actors prefer formal, stand-alone, hierarchical organisations, doctrines, and strategies, as in past efforts, for example, to build centralised revolutionary movements along Marxist lines.

This chapter assesses the degree to which—and how—networked terrorist groups are using IT, particularly in the Middle East. The analysis reviews past trends and offers a series of educated guesses about how such trends will evolve in the future. The first section discusses the organisational implications of netwar, especially the degree to which IT is enabling different forms of terrorist structures and command, control, and communications (C3). The second section examines past evidence of terrorist use of IT for offensive netwar, such as destructive and disruptive attacks on information systems and for perception management. The third section contains a speculative look at how future terrorist uses of IT could develop in the near to medium term. The final section concludes with implications for counterterrorism policy.

ORGANISATIONAL NETWORKING AND TECHNOLOGY ACQUISITION

In an archetypal netwar, the protagonists are likely to amount to a set of diverse, dispersed "nodes" who share a set of ideas and interests and who often are arrayed to act in a fully internetted "all-channel" manner. The potential effectiveness of the networked design compared to traditional hierarchical designs attracted the attention of management theorists as early as the 1960s. Today, in the business world, virtual or networked organisations are heralded as effective alternatives to traditional bureaucracies because of their inherent flexibility, adaptiveness, and ability to capitalize on the talents of all of their members.

Networked organisations share three basic sets of features. First, communication and coordination are not formally specified by horizontal and vertical reporting relationships, but rather emerge and change according to the task at hand. Similarly, relationships are often informal and marked by varying degrees of intensity, depending on the needs of the organisation. Second, internal networks are usually complemented by linkages to individuals outside the organisation, often spanning national boundaries. Like internal connections, external relationships are formed and wind down according to the life cycle of particular joint projects. Third, both internal and external ties are enabled not by bureaucratic fiat, but rather by shared norms and values, as well as by reciprocal trust. Internally, the bulk of the work is conducted by self-managing teams, while external linkages compose "a constellation involving a complex network of contributing firms or groups" (Monge and Fulk, 1999, pp. 71–72).

The Emergence of Networked Terrorist Groups in the Greater Middle East

What has been emerging in the business world is now becoming apparent in the organisational structures of the newer and more active terrorist groups, which appear to be adopting decentralised, flexible network structures. The rise of networked arrangements in terrorist organisations is part of a wider move away from formally organised, state-sponsored groups to privately financed, loose networks of individuals and subgroups that may have strategic guidance but that, nonetheless, enjoy tactical independence.

For example, in the Greater Middle East, terrorist organisations have diverse origins, ideologies, and organisational structures but can be categorised roughly into traditional and new-generation groups. Traditional groups date to the late 1960s and early 1970s, and the majority were (and some still are) formally or informally linked to the Palestine Liberation Organisation (PLO). Typically, they are also relatively bureaucratic and maintain a nationalist or Marxist agenda.

These groups have utilised autonomous cells as part of their organisational structure, but the operation of such cells is guided by a hierarchy through clear reporting relationships and virtually little horizontal coordination.

In contrast, the newer and less hierarchical groups (such as Hamas; the Palestinian Islamic Jihad; Hizbollah; Algeria's Armed Islamic Group; the Egyptian Islamic Group; and Osama bin Laden's terrorist network, al-Qaeda) have become the most active organisations (Office of the Coordinator for Counterterrorism, 2000). In these loosely organised groups with religious or ideological motives, operatives are part of a network that relies less on bureaucratic fiat and more on shared values and horizontal coordination mechanisms to accomplish its goals.

The new and more active generation of Middle Eastern groups has operated both inside and outside the region. For instance, in Israel and the occupied territories, Hamas and to a lesser extent the Palestinian Islamic Jihad have demonstrated their strength over the last five years with a series of suicide bombings that have killed more than 100 people. In Egypt, the Islamic Group (also known as al-Gama'a alIslamiya) carried out a 1997 attack at Luxor, killing 58 tourists and four Egyptians. Another string of terrorist attacks (and foiled attempts) has focused attention on a loosely organised group of "Arab Afghans"—radical Islamic fighters from several North African and Middle Eastern countries who have forged ties while resisting the Soviet occupation of Afghanistan. One of the leaders and founders of the Arab Afghan movement is Osama bin Laden, a Saudi entrepreneur based in Afghanistan. To varying degrees, these groups share the principles of the networked organisation—relative flatness, decentralisation and delegation of decisionmaking authority, and loose lateral ties among dispersed groups and individuals. Hamas, for example, is loosely structured with some elements working clandestinely and others working openly through mosques and social service institutions to recruit members, raise money, organize activities, and distribute propaganda (Office of the Coordinator for Counterterrorism, 2000, p. 74).

The pro-Iranian Hizbollah in southern Lebanon acts as an umbrella organisation of radical Shiite groups and in many respects is a hybrid of hierarchical and network arrangements—although the organisational structure is formal, interactions among members are volatile and do not follow rigid lines of control (Ranstorp, 1994, p. 304). Perhaps the most interesting example of a terrorist netwar actor is Osama bin Laden's complex network of relatively autonomous groups that are financed from private sources. Bin Laden uses his wealth and organisational skills to support and direct al-Qaeda (The Base), a multinational alliance of Islamic extremists. Al-Qaeda seeks to counter any perceived threats to Islam—wherever they come from— as indicated by bin Laden's 1996 declaration of a holy war against the United States and the West in general. In the declaration, bin Laden specified that such a holy war was to be waged by irregular, light, highly mobile forces. Although bin Laden finances al-Qaeda (exploiting a fortune of several million dollars, according to U.S. State Department estimates) and directs some operations, he apparently does not play a direct command-and-control role over all operatives. Rather, he is a key figure in the coordination and support of several dispersed nodes.

There are reports that communications between al-Qaeda's members combine elements of a "hub-and-spoke" structure (where nodes of operatives communicate with bin Laden and his close advisers in Afghanistan) and a wheel structure (where nodes in the network communicate with each other without reference to bin Laden) (Simon and Benjamin, 2000, p. 70). Al-Qaeda's command-and-control structure includes a consultation council ("majlis al shura"), which discusses and approves major undertakings, and possibly a military committee. At the heart of al-Qaeda is bin Laden's inner core group, which sometimes conducts missions on its own. Most of the other member organisations remain independent, although the barriers between them are permeable.

According to U.S. District Court testimony in New York, al-Qaeda has forged alliances with Egypt's Islamic Group (leading to an alleged influx of bin Laden operatives into its structure), the National Front in the Sudan, the government of Iran, and Hizbollah. Media reports also indicate that bin Laden has ties with other far-flung Islamic armed groups, such as Abu Sayyaf in the Philippines, as well as with counterparts in Somalia, Chechnya, and Central Asia.

Command, Control, Communications, and the Role of IT

Lateral coordination mechanisms facilitate the operations of networked groups. In turn, such coordination mechanisms are enabled by advances in information technology—including increases in the speed of communication, reductions in the costs of communication, increases in bandwidth, vastly expanded connectivity, and the integration of communication and computing technologies (see Heydebrand, 1989). More specifically, new communication and computing technologies allow the establishment of networks in three critical ways (Monge and Fulk, 1999, p. 84).

First, new technologies have greatly reduced transmission time, enabling dispersed organisational actors to communicate and coordinate their tasks. This phenomenon is not new—in the early 20th century, the introduction of the telephone made it possible for large corporations to decentralize their operations through local branches. Second, new technologies have significantly reduced the cost of communication, allowing information-intensive organisational designs such as networks to become viable. As Thompson (1967) observed, in the past, organisations sought to reduce coordination and communications costs by centralising and colocating those activities that are inherently more coordination-intensive. With the lowering of coordination costs, it is becoming increasingly possible to further disaggregate organisations through decentralisation and autonomy. Third, new technologies have substantially increased the scope and complexity of the information that can be shared, through the integration of computing with communications. Such innovations as tele- and computer conferencing, groupware, Internet chat, and web sites allow participants to have "horizontal" and rich exchanges without requiring them to be located in close proximity.

Thus, information-age technologies are highly advantageous for a netwar group whose constituents are geographically dispersed or carry out distinct but complementary activities. IT can be used to plan, coordinate, and execute operations. Using the Internet for communication can increase speed of mobilisation and allow more dialogue between members, which enhances the organisation's flexibility, since tactics can be adjusted more frequently. Individuals with a common agenda and goals can form subgroups, meet at a target location, conduct terrorist operations, and then readily terminate their relationships and redisperse.

The bin Laden network appears to have adopted information technology to support its networked mode of operations. According to reporters who visited bin Laden's headquarters in a remote mountainous area of Afghanistan, the terrorist financier has modern computer and commu-nications equipment. Bin Laden allegedly uses satellite phone terminals to coordinate the activities of the group's dispersed operatives and has even devised countermeasures to ensure his safety while using such communication systems. Satellite phones reportedly travel in separate convoys from bin Laden's; the Saudi financier also refrains from direct use, often dictating his message to an assistant, who then relays it telephonically from a different location. Bin Laden's operatives have used CD-ROM disks to store and disseminate information on recruiting, bomb making, heavy weapons, and terrorist operations. Egyptian computer experts who fought alongside bin Laden in the Afghan conflict are said to have helped him devise a communications network that relies on the web, email, and electronic bulletin boards so that members can exchange information (FBIS, 1995).

This is a trend found among other terrorist actors in the Middle East. Counterterrorist operations targeting Algerian Armed Islamic Group (GIA) bases in the 1990s uncovered computers and diskettes with instructions for the construction of bombs (FBIS, 1996a). In fact, it has been reported that the GIA makes heavy use of floppy disks and computers to store and process orders and other information for its members, who are dispersed in Algeria and Europe (FBIS, 1996b). The militant Islamic group Hamas also uses the Internet to share and communicate operational information. Hamas activists in the United States use chat rooms to plan operations and activities. Operatives use email to coordinate actions across Gaza, the West Bank, and Lebanon. Hamas has realised that information can be passed relatively securely over the Internet because counterterrorism intelligence cannot accurately monitor the flow and content of all Internet traffic. In fact, Israeli security officials cannot easily trace Hamas messages or decode their content.

In addition, terrorist networks can protect their vital communication flows through readily available commercial technology, such as encryption programs. Examples from outside the Middle East point in this direction—according to one report, Animal Liberation Front (ALF) cells in North America and Europe use the encryption program Pretty Good Privacy (PGP) to send coded email and share intelligence (Iuris, 1997, p. 64). New encryption programs emerging on the commercial market are becoming so sophisticated that coded emails may soon be extremely difficult to break. In fact, strong encryption pro grams are being integrated into commercial applications and network protocols so that soon encryption will be easy and automatic.

Rumors persist that the French police have been unable to decrypt the hard disk on a portable computer belonging to a captured member of the Spanish/Basque organisation ETA (Fatherland and Liberty) (Denning and Baugh, 1997). It has also been suggested that Israeli security forces were unsuccessful in their attempts at cracking the codes used by Hamas to send instructions for terrorist attacks over the Internet (Whine, 1999, p. 128). Terrorists can also use steganography—a method of hiding secret data in other data such as embedding a secret message within a picture file (Denning and Baugh, 1997). Terrorists can also encrypt cell phone transmissions, steal cell phone numbers and program them into a single phone, or use prepaid cell phone cards purchased anonymously to keep their communications secure.

The latest communications technologies are thus enabling terrorists to operate from almost any country in the world, provided they have access to the necessary IT infrastructure; and this affects the ways in which groups rely on different forms of sponsorship. Some analysts have argued that networked terrorists may have a reduced need for state support—indeed, governmental protection may become less necessary if technologies such as encryption allow a terrorist group to operate with a greater degree of stealth and safety (Soo Hoo, Goodman, and Greenberg, 1997, p. 142). Others point to the possibility that groups will increasingly attempt to raise money on the web, as in the case of Pakistan's Lashkar-e-Taiba ("Army of the Pure").

Networked Organisations and IT: Mitigating Factors

To be sure, there are limits to how much reliance terrorist networks will place on information-age technology. For the foreseeable future, electronically mediated coordination will not be able to entirely supplant face-to-face exchanges, because uncertainty and risk will continue to characterize most organisational choices and interactions among individuals. Moreover, informal linkages and the shared values mentioned above—which are critical enablers of networked designs—can only be fostered through personal contact. As Nohria and Eccles argue, electronically mediated exchange can increase the range, amount, and velocity of information flow in a network organisation. But the viability and effectiveness of this electronic network will depend critically on an underlying network of social relationships based on face-to-face interaction (Nohria and Eccles, "Face-to-Face: Making Network Organisations Work," in Nohria and Eccles, 1992, pp. 289–290).

Moreover, while IT-enabled communication flows can greatly help a network coordinate dispersed activities (thus increasing its flexibility and responsiveness), they can also present a security risk. Communication over electronic channels can become a liability, since it leaves digital "traces." For instance, FBI officials have recently acknowledged that they used an Internet wiretap program called "Carnivore" to track terrorist email correspondence at least 25 times. According to *Newsweek,* Carnivore's ability to track Osama bin Laden's email was critical in thwarting several of his strikes.

The case of Ramzi Yousef, the World Trade Center bomber, also provides a revealing example of how information-age technology can represent a double-edged sword for terrorists. Yousef's numerous calls to fellow terrorists during his preparation for the strike were registered in phone companies' computer databases, providing law enforcement officials with a significant set of leads for investigating terrorists in the Middle East and beyond. Prior to his arrest, Yousef unintentionally offered the FBI another source of information when he lost control of his portable computer in the Philippines. In that laptop, U.S. officials found incriminating data, including plans for future attacks, flight schedules, projected detonation times, and chemical formulae (Reeve, 1999, pp. 39 and 97).

There are other examples of how electronic information belonging to terrorist groups has fallen into the hands of law enforcement personnel. In 1995, Hamas's Abd-al-Rahman Zaydan was arrested and his computer seised—the computer contained a database of Hamas contact information that was used to apprehend other suspects (Soo Hoo, Goodman, and Greenberg, 1997, p. 139). In December 1999, 15 terrorists linked to Osama bin Laden were arrested in Jordan; along with bomb-making materials, rifles, and radio-controlled detonators, a number of computer disks were seized. Intelligence analysts were able to extract information about bomb building and terrorist training camps in Afghanistan. In June 2000, the names of 19 suspects were found on computer disks recovered from a Hizbollah-controlled house (see FBIS, 2000). Finally, several encrypted computer records belonging to the millennialist Aum Shinrikyo cult were retrieved by Japanese authorities after an electronic key was recovered (Denning and Baugh, 1997).

Thus, the organisational benefits associated with greater IT must be traded off against the needs for direct human contact and improved security. This makes it likely that terrorist groups will adopt designs that fall short of fully connected, all-channel networks. Hybrids of hierarchies and networks may better reflect the relative costs and benefits of greater IT reliance—as well as further the group's mission. Another important factor determining the adoption of IT by terrorist groups involves the relative attractiveness of high-tech offensive information operations, to which we turn next.

9

TERRORISM AND OFFENSIVE INFORMATION OPERATIONS

In addition to enabling networked forms of organisation, IT can also improve terrorist intelligence collection and analysis, as well as offensive information operations (IO). The acquisition by terrorist groups of an offensive IO capability could represent a significant threat as the world becomes more dependent on information and communications flows. We argue that information-age technology can help terrorists conduct three broad types of offensive IO. First, it can aid them in their perception management and propaganda activities. Next, such technology can be used to attack virtual targets for disruptive purposes. Finally, IT can be used to cause physical destruction.

Perception Management and Propaganda

Given the importance of knowledge and soft power to the conduct of netwar, it is not surprising that networked terrorists have already begun to leverage IT for perception management and propaganda to influence public opinion, recruit new members, and generate funding. Getting a message out and receiving extensive news media exposure are important components of terrorist strategy, which ultimately seeks to undermine the will of an opponent. In addition to such traditional media as television or print, the Internet now offers terrorist groups an alternative way to reach out to the public, often with much more direct control over their message. The news media play an integral part in a terrorist act because they are the conduit for news of the violence to the general population. As Bruce Hoffman has noted, "terrorism ... may be seen as a violent act that is conceived specifically to attract attention and then, through the publicity it generates, to communicate a message" (Hoffman, 1998, p. 131). Terrorists have improved their media management techniques to the point of using "spin doctoring" tactics (Hoffman, 1998, p. 134). In fact, some groups have even acquired their own television and radio stations to take direct control of the reporting of events. Hizbollah, through its television station, has broadcast footage of strikes carried out by its operatives and has a sophisticated media center that regularly—and professionally—briefs foreign journalists. Hizbollah field units have even included specially designated cameramen to record dramatic video footage of Israeli casualties that was then aired in Lebanon and usually rebroadcast by Israeli television. (On these points, see Nacos, 1994.)

The Internet now expands the opportunities for publicity and exposure beyond the traditional limits of television and print media. Before the Internet, a bombing might be accompanied by a phone call or fax to the press by a terrorist claiming responsibility. Now, bombings can be followed—should terrorists so desire—by an immediate press release from their own web sites (at little cost). (For a hypothetical example, see Devost, Houghton, and Pollard, 1997.) The fact that many terrorists now have direct control over the content of their message offers further opportunities for perception management, as well as for image manipulation, special effects, and deception.

An Internet presence could prove advantageous for mobilising "parttime cyberterrorists"—individuals not directly affiliated with a given terrorist group who nonetheless support its agenda and who use malicious software tools and instructions available at a terrorist web site. This scenario would closely resemble the initiatives taken by both the Israeli and Palestinian governments, which have encouraged private citizens to download computer attack tools and become involved in the conflict surrounding the al-Aqsa Intifadah. Web sites can also be used to refine or customize recruiting techniques. Recording which types of propaganda receive the most browser hits could help tailor a message for a particular audience. Using some of the same marketing techniques employed by commercial enterprises, terrorist servers could capture information about the users who browse their web sites, and then later contact those who seem most interested. Recruiters may also use more interactive Internet technology to roam online chat rooms and cyber cafes looking for receptive members of the public, particularly young people. Electronic bulletin boards and user nets can also serve as vehicles for reaching out to potential recruits. Interested computer users around the world can be engaged in long-term "cyber relationships" that could lead to friendship and eventual membership.

Disruptive Attacks

Netwar-oriented terrorists can also use IT to launch disruptive attacks—that is, electronic strikes that temporarily disable, but do not destroy, physical and/or virtual infrastructure. If the ultimate goal of a terrorist is to influence his opponent's will to fight, IO offer additional means to exert influence beyond using simple physical attacks to cause terror. Disruptive attacks include "choking" computer systems through such tools as e-bombs, fax spamming, and hacking techniques to deface web sites. These strikes are usually nonlethal in nature, although they can wreak havoc and cause significant economic damage.

To date, disruptive strikes by terrorists have been relatively few and fairly unsophisticated—but they do seem to be increasing in frequency. For example, in 1996, the Liberation Tigers of Tamil Eelam (LTTE) launched an email bomb attack against Sri Lankan diplomatic missions. Using automated tools, the guerilla organisation flooded Sri Lankan embassies with thousands of messages, thus establishing a "virtual blockade."

Japanese groups have allegedly attacked the computerised control systems for commuter trains, paralysing major cities for hours (Devost, Houghton, and Pollard, 1997, p. 67). In 2000, a group of Pakistani hackers who call themselves the Muslim Online Syndicate (MOS) defaced more than 500 web sites in India to protest the conflict in Kashmir (Hopper, 2000). Finally, Pakistan's Lashkare-Taiba claimed to have attacked Indian military web sites in early 2000.

Disruptive rather than destructive actions take place for several reasons. For example, terrorists who rely on the Internet for perception management and communication purposes may prefer not to take "the Net" down, but rather to slow it down selectively. In addition, groups may want to rely on nonlethal cyber strikes to pressure governments without alienating their own constituent audiences. Terrorist groups may also follow the lead of criminal hackers and use the threat of disruptive attacks to blackmail and extort funds from private-sector entities (*e.g.*, the ongoing "cyber jihad" against Israel may come to target commercial enterprises that do business with the Israelis). For instance, in the early 1990s, hackers and criminals blackmailed brokerage houses and banks for several million British pounds. Money can also be stolen from individual users who visit terrorist web sites.

Destructive Attacks

As mentioned earlier, IT-driven information operations can lead to the actual destruction of physical or virtual systems. Malicious viruses and worms can be used to permanently destroy (erase) or corrupt (spoof) data and cause economic damage. In the worst case, these same software tools can be used to cause destructive failure in a critical infrastructure like air traffic control, power, or water systems, which can lead to casualties. Indeed, it is likely that information operations that result in the loss of life may offer the same level of drama as physical attacks with bombs. Also, striking targets through electronic means does not carry the risks associated with using conventional weapons—such as handling explosives or being in close proximity to the target.

Offensive IO: Mitigating Factors

The extreme case where the use of IT results in significant human losses has yet to occur. The lack of destructive information attacks is arguably influenced by the relative difficulty of electronically destroying (rather than disrupting) critical infrastructure components—the level of protection of existing infrastructure may be too high for terrorists to overcome with their current IT skill set. In fact, a terrorist organisation would first have to overcome significant technical hurdles to develop an electronic attack capability.

Concentrating the necessary technical expertise and equipment to damage or destroy targeted information systems is no easy task, given the computer security risks involved. In developing and increasing their reliance on electronic attacks, terrorist organisations may be assuming risks and costs associated with the relative novelty of the technology. Terrorists wishing to expand the scope of their offensive IO activities would have to continue upgrading and researching new technologies to keep up with the countermeasures available to computer security experts and systems administrators. This technology "treadmill" would demand constant attention and the diversion of scarce organisational resources.

Another important determinant in netwar terrorists choosing lowlevel IT is that such conventional weapons as bombs remain more cost-effective. In fact, most terrorism experts believe that existing groups see their current tactics as sufficient and are not interested in branching into computer network attacks. Since current tactics are simple and successful, there is no built-in demand to innovate: bombing still works. As long as current tactics enable these groups to accomplish their short-term goals and move toward their longterm goals, there will be no strong incentives to change behavior. In addition, the fragility of computer hardware may make a physical attack on these targets more attractive because such an attack is significantly less challenging from a technical standpoint than attempting a virtual attack (Soo Hoo, Goodman, and Greenberg, 1997, p. 146).

Disruptive attacks may be easier to carry out, but because of their very nature they do not produce the same kind of visceral and emotional reaction that the loss of human life does. Indeed, some terrorism analysts argue that it is unlikely that terrorist groups will turn to disruptive attacks as the primary tactic. Brian Jenkins points out that IT-enabled disruptive strikes do not produce the immediate, visible effects. There is no drama. No lives hang in the balance .... Terrorist intentions regarding cyberterrorism are even more problematic. Linking the objectives of actual terrorist groups to scenarios of electronic sabotage that would serve those objectives is conjecture. In addition, many computer security experts believe that even disruptive attacks remain technologically challenging for most terrorist groups and too undervalued by the media to make them attractive for terrorists (Soo Hoo, Goodman, and Greenberg, 1997, pp. 145–146).

EVALUATING PAST, PRESENT, AND FUTURE TRENDS

Given that information technology brings drawbacks as well as benefits, the terrorist groups examined here have not chosen to rely exclusively on IT to coordinate their operations and execute attacks. The available evidence suggests that netwar terrorists have embraced IT for organisational purposes, especially to facilitate C3, but they have been either unable or unwilling to attempt more ambitious offensive IO. However, the benefits clearly outweigh the risks when it comes to utilising IT for perception management and propaganda.

Future Developments in Information-Age Terrorism

Were the trends described above to persist, one could speculate that future netwar actors will continue to consolidate their IT use primarily for organisational purposes, with some emphasis on perception management on the offensive 10 side. Under these conditions, networked terrorists would still rely on such traditional weapons as conventional bombs to cause physical violence. But they will also transmit information on how to build such weapons via CD-ROMs or email, use chat rooms to coordinate their activities, and use web sites to publicize and justify their strikes to a global audience.

The al-Aqsa Intifadah in the West Bank and Gaza highlights how protracted IO campaigns could be waged in conjunction with a campaign of conventional violence. Mirroring the real-world violence that has resulted in hundreds of casualties, a conflict has also been waged in cyberspace over economic and propaganda stakes. Palestinian hackers who support the al-Aqsa Intifadah have been waging a cyberjihad against Israeli government and commercial targets, defacing web sites and conducting DOS attacks. More than 40 Israeli sites have been hit, including the Tel Aviv Stock Exchange and the Bank of Israel. Israeli hackers have counterattacked, hitting more than 15 different Palestinian targets, including Hizbollah,

Hamas, and the Palestinian National Authority. As the disruptive attacks have escalated, individuals and groups have joined both sides, from professional hackers to "script-kiddies" (relative amateurs who rely on off-the-shelf and easy to use tools). (See Lemos, 2000.)

That said, the swift and unpredictable changes associated with technology suggest that other outcomes are possible. The question is, will terrorists have the desire and opportunity to significantly increase their reliance on IT—primarily for offensive purposes—in the future? Several factors could influence such a shift, including the degree to which new technology will serve their main strategic goals in a safe and effective manner. For instance, the introduction of easy-to-use, "unbreakable" encryption programs to support email and file exchange will encourage netwar terrorists to adopt such techniques. Moreover, terrorist access to technologies that can be readily employed without extensive internal development efforts —by group members and part-time "volunteers" or through "hackers for hire" — will be a critical facilitating factor. Equally important, the relative vulnerability of the information infrastructure plays a role in this calculus. These possible developments would likely prompt the evolution of current netwar terrorist groups toward greater reliance on IT for offensive purposes and could also encourage the emergence of new and completely virtual groups that exclusively operate in cyberspace.

The Evolution of Current Groups

As Brian Jackson notes, the introduction of new technologies in an organisation follows a complex and often lengthy process. Not only do innovative systems have to be developed or acquired, but organisational actors have to become familiar with new systems and be able to use them effectively (Jackson, unpublished). Given the challenge, terrorist groups are likely to channel their scarce organisational resources to acquire those IT skills that have the greatest leverage for the least amount of cost and effort.

This line of reasoning can help explain terrorists' recent emphasis on using communications technology for organisational purposes: Having access to the Internet and cellular telephones is not overly complicated, and it plays a significant role in enabling dispersed operations, a key goal of netwar groups. This reasoning also suggests that over time terrorist groups might begin to experiment more aggressively with information-age technologies for offensive information operations, as they become more familiar with such innovations. Indeed, some may follow a "migration" pattern. The knowledge of IT issues gained by relying on technology to facilitate interactions among group members, or to gain a web presence, might eventually be expanded and harnessed for increasingly offensive uses.

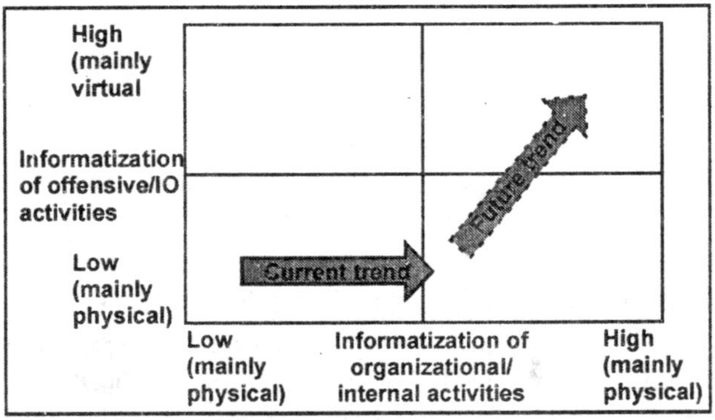

Fig.: Possible Shifts in the Use of Technology

The pace with which current groups move through such a path is also dependent on the degree of cooperation and information exchange among netwar terrorists. Such cooperation has often occurred in the past—for instance, Islamic radicals have organised "terror conferences"(Kushner, 1998, p. 41), while European terrorist groups such as the Irish Republican Army entered into joint ventures with counterparts across the globe to learn from one another and disseminate knowledge (such as designs of booby traps and radio-controlled bombs). (See Wilkinson, 1986, p. 40.) Given the loose and reciprocal nature of ties between actors in networks such as al-Qaeda, it is entirely possible that those with IT skills would be leveraged globally and placed at the disposal of the organisation's various members. Lastly, as leading-edge groups begin to move toward the upper-right quadrant of Figure above, other groups may be tempted to follow suit: Terrorists that hitherto had decided to adopt a low-technology profile for their offensive operations could be emboldened by successful instances of IT attacks by others (Jackson, unpublished).

The Emergence of New Groups

An alternative hypothesis to the notion that existing terrorist groups should be watched for signs of movement toward cyberterror is that qualitative improvements in the informatisation of networked terrorists will only be witnessed with the emergence of newer, and more technologically savvy, groups. Just as Hamas and al-Qaeda have overshadowed the PFLP and other Marxist groups formed in the 1960s, new-generation groups may further advance the trend toward networked and IT-reliant organisations. New groups could even be led by individuals who are technically skilled, suggesting the rise of a hybrid breed of "terrorists cum hackers." Like hackers, they would undertake most of their attacks in cyberspace. Like terrorists, they would seek to strike targets by both disruptive and destructive means to further a political or religious agenda.

The possibility that innovation will take place only with the advent of new groups finds support in previous work by such terrorism experts as Hoffman, who describes most groups today as operationally conservative (Hoffman, "Terrorism Trends and Prospects" in Lesser et al., 1999, p. 36). Aside from organisational inertia, current groups may also be hesitant to further rely on IT for offensive purpose because of large, "sunk costs" in traditional tactics, training, and weapon stockpiles. Existing groups wishing to "amortize" such capital cost may be unwilling to direct scarce resources toward the development of new and radically different offensive techniques.

POLICY IMPLICATIONS

The acquisition and use of information-age technology by terrorist groups are far from certain. Indeed, the scenarios painted above are not mutually exclusive. It is conceivable that current groups will acquire new IT skills over time and adopt more-offensive IT strategies. New hacker/terrorist groups may also emerge to compound this problem. Some terrorist networks may even become sophisticated enough to sustain and coordinate offensive campaigns in both the virtual and physical realms. What is certain, however, is that counterterrorism policy will be able to counter the dangers associated with terrorist IT use only if it becomes attuned to the information age.

Counterterrorist policies and tactics could even alter the speed with which terrorists become informatised—groups facing a robust counterterrorism campaign may have less time and resources to acquire new technologies. For such reasons, it seems advisable that counterterrorism policymakers and strategists bear in mind the following recommendations.

First, monitor changes in the use of IT by terrorist groups, differentiating between organisational and offensive capabilities: Counterterrorism policies will have to take into account the type of IT capabilities developed by each group, targeting their specific technological vulnerabilities. Evaluating how IT shapes a group's orga-nisational processes and offensive activities will remain a critical component of the threat assessment. Monitoring the shift in capabilities for each type of IT use and then examining trends in the aggregate can also help forecast future terrorist behavior. Among the most significant trends to be carefully examined is the possible emergence of a new, and potentially dangerous, breed of terrorists—groups that are highly informatised along both the organisational and offensive axes. In this regard, a number of "signposts" should be identified and tracked. These would include significant increases in the level of technical expertise of known leaders and their subordinates, increases in the frequency of disruptive attacks, increases in the seizures of IT equipment owned by terrorists, the presence—and successful recruiting—of "hackers for hire," and the availability of effective and relatively secure off-the-shelf information technologies (including those that facilitate hacking).

Second, target information flows: Since network designs are inherently information intensive, counterterrorism efforts should target the information flows of netwar groups. Intercepting and monitoring terrorist information exchanges should remain a top priority, and the implementation of "Project Trailblaser" by the National Security Agency—to develop a system that can crack new encryption software, fiber-optic cables, and cellular phone transmissions—represents a useful addition to America's signals intelligence capability (Kitfield, 2000). Equally important, policymakers should consider going beyond the passive monitoring of information flows and toward the active disruption of such communications. To the degree that erroneous or otherwise misleading information is planted into a network's information flows by what are seemingly credible sources, over time the integrity and relevance of the network itself will be compromised. This in turn could breed distrust and further cripple a group's ability to operate in a dispersed and decentralised fashion—essentially eliminating a netwar group's key competitive advantage.

Increased emphasis on targeting information flows should not exclude nonelectronic efforts to gather intelligence and undermine the network. Indeed, human intelligence will remain an important tool for intercepting (and injecting) information not transmitted through electronic means of communication. This is an especially pressing concern, given that several intelligence observers have pointed to a lack of U.S. capability in this area.

Third, deter IT-based offensive IO through better infrastructure protection: Changes in the vulnerability of critical infrastructures can significantly alter a terrorist's IT calculus. If such infrastructures, such as those that manage air traffic control, were to become relatively more vulnerable, they might become more attractive as targets: Terrorists could strike at a distance, generating as much—if not more—destruction as would have been caused by the use of traditional weapons. U.S. policy should identify specific vulnerabilities to expected threats and develop security techniques that mitigate each. An analysis of these issues is beyond the scope of the current chapter, but there are numerous studies that explore this process, including RAND's *Securing the U.S. Defense Information Infrastructure: A Proposed Approach* (Anderson et al., 1999). The FBI's National Infrastructure Protection Center and other newly created organisations represent useful steps in this direction. Counterterrorist agencies may also want to consider the option of employing a large number of hackers and leveraging their knowledge for defensive and possibly even retaliatory purposes.

Fourth, beat networked terrorists at their own game: "It takes networks to fight networks. " Governments wishing to counter netwar terrorism will need to adopt organisational designs and strategies like those of their adversaries. This does not mean mirroring the opponent, but rather learning to draw on the same design principles of network forms. These principles depend to some extent upon technological innovation, but mainly on a willingness to innovate organisationally and doctrinally and by building new mechanisms for interagency and multijurisdictional cooperation. The Technical Support Working Group (TSWG) is a good example of a nontraditional government interagency group with more than 100 member organisations from at least 13 federal agencies and a growing number of local and state agencies. Its principal aim is to help develop and deploy technologies to combat terrorism. Another example is the Counter-Intelligence 21 (CI-21) plan, a set of reforms that seek to increase the level of cooperation between counteri-ntelligence personnel at the CIA, FBI, and the Pentagon (Kitfield, 2000). If counterterrorism agencies become ready and willing to rely on networks of outside "ethical hackers" in times of crisis, the need to coordinate beyond the boundaries of government will increase.

Supporters of these initiatives rightly recognize that the information age and the consequent advent of netwar have blurred the boundary between domestic and international threats, as well as between civilian and military threats. This in turn demands greater interagency coordination within the counterterrorism community. As terrorist groups evolve toward loose, ad-hoc networks that form and dissipate unpredictably, so must counterterrorism forces adopt a more flexible approach that crosses bureaucratic boundaries to accomplish the mission at hand. While militaries and governments will never be able to do away with their hierarchies entirely, there is nevertheless much room for them to develop more-robust organisational networks than they currently have—a change that may offset some, if not all, of the advantage now accruing mostly to networked terrorist groups.

10

CRIMINAL NETWORKS AND MILITARY DISRUPTIONS

In a recent analysis of global trends, the U.S. National Intelligence Council included a short section on criminal organisations and networks. It noted that criminal organisations and networks based in North America, Western Europe, China, Colombia, Israel, Japan, Mexico, Nigeria, and Russia will expand the scale and scope of their activities. They will form loose alliances with one another, with smaller criminal entrepreneurs, and with insurgent movements for specific operations. They will corrupt leaders of unstable, economically fragile, or failing states, insinuate themselves into troubled banks and businesses, and cooperate with insurgent political movements to control substantial geographic areas.

In other words, there is a growing recognition that organised crime is increasingly operating through fluid network structures rather than more-formal hierarchies. However, the traditional paradigm for studying organised crime emphasised identifying the hierarchical or pyramidal structures of criminal organisations. Finding its fullest expression in the 1967 report on organised crime by the President's Commission on Law Enforcement and Administration of Justice and in Donald Cressey's famous analysis in *Theft of the Nation,* this interpretation of organised crime was based on the example provided by La Cosa Nostra in the United States. It emphasised the existence of a "nationwide illicit cartel and confederation," the governing role of a national commission, hierarchical structure, and the clear division of labor between local branches.

Cressey's analysis, though, provoked several pioneering studies that challenged the mainstream interpretation of organised crime as having a rational corporate structure, arguing not only that organised crime was much more fluid than portrayed by the conventional wisdom, but also that patron-client relations and network structures played a pivotal role. Francis Ianni looked at the role of African American and Puerto Rican criminal networks in New York, while Joseph Albini contended that even Italian organised crime in the United States could best be understood through patron-client relations rather than formal hierarchies. In an important historical study of organised crime in New York, Alan Block discovered that it was not only more fragmented and chaotic than believed, but also that it involved "webs of influence" that linked criminals with those in positions of power in the political and economic world. These patterns of affiliation and influence were far more important than any formal structure and allowed criminals to maximize opportunities.

More recently, Gary Potter has suggested that organised crime in the United States can best be understood in network terms, while Finckenauer and Waring, in a study on Russian émigré criminals in the United States, concluded that they operate largely through network structures. Of particular importance is the work of Malcolm Sparrow, who not only applies concepts from social network analysis to the operation of criminal networks, but also offers innovative insights into ways in which the vulnerabilities of these networks might be identified and exploited. My own work has also moved in this direction.

This emphasis on criminal networks reflects a growing acknowledgment, among researchers into crime, that there is no single, dominant organisational structure with universal applicability, and the realisation by law enforcement agencies that they are seeing patterns of organised crime that do not fit the traditional hierarchical structure. The German BKA (the equivalent of the American FBI), for example, has observed that most of the criminal organisations it investigates are "loose, temporary networks" and that "lastingly established, hierarchical structures" are rather in the minority. In the BKA's view, the evidence in Germany suggests that even hierarchical organisations such as the Italian Mafia families allow their local branches considerable discretion.

Perhaps even more significant, a major study of organised crime in Holland noted great variations in collaborative forms and concluded that the frameworks need not necessarily exhibit the hierarchic structure or meticulous division of labor often attributed to mafia syndicates. Intersections of social networks with a rudimentary division of labor have also been included as groups in the sub-report on the role of Dutch criminal groups, where they are referred to as cliques. As is demonstrated ... there can be sizeable differences in the cooperation patterns within these cliques and between the cliques and larger networks of people they work with on an incidental basis.

In other words, there is a growing recognition that organised crime often operates through fluid networks rather than through more formal hierarchies. Important as they are, none of these studies systematically explores the advantages of network structures as an organisational form for criminal activities. This chapter identifies both the characteristics of networks that make them an ideal form for organising criminal activities and the specific characteristics of criminal networks themselves. This conceptual analysis of criminal networks also draws insights from social network and business theories and moves beyond theory to draw implications for policymakers concerned with developing strategies to combat criminal networks.

BACKGROUND ON NETWORK ANALYSIS

Networks are one of the most common forms of social organisation. They are simultaneously pervasive and intangible, ubiquitous and invisible, everywhere and nowhere. Networks are not an exclusive organisational form and often exist within more traditional hierarchical structures, cutting through divisions based on specialisation or rank. It is also possible to have networks in which hierarchical organisations are key participants. Networks are also an important complement to markets, making them more efficient, reducing transaction costs, and providing increased opportunities for both buyers and sellers.

These characteristics—their pervasiveness, their capacity to coexist both within and outside hierarchies, their ability to make markets more efficient by facilitating directed flows of information and commodities—give networks an elusive quality. In some respects, they appear little more than plastic organisations that can be molded in many different ways. Networks vary in size, shape, membership, cohesion, and purpose.

Networks can be large or small, local or global, domestic or transna-tional, cohesive or diffuse, centrally directed or highly decentralised, purposeful or directionless. A specific network can be narrowly and tightly focused on one goal or broadly oriented toward many goals, and it can be either exclusive or encompassing in its membership. Networks facilitate flows of information, knowledge, and communication as well as more-tangible commodities. As communications have become cheaper and easier, networks have expanded enormously. Indeed, technological networks facilitate the operation of larger and more-dispersed social networks and can even act as a critical force multiplier for certain kinds of social networks. Against this background, the analysis here seeks to:

- Delineate very briefly the underlying concepts and ideas that encourage and facilitate analysis of criminal organisations in terms of network structures. These include social network analysis, a growing literature on network business organisations (a concept developed most fully in the idea of the virtual corporation), and previous studies of organised crime that have emphasised the importance of networks rather than the more traditional hierarchical structures.
- Identify the characteristics of networks that make them attractive to criminals and to elucidate further the major characteristics of criminal networks.
- Specify critical roles in criminal networks, bearing in mind that there are network roles that relate to the functioning of the network and substantive roles related specifically to the nature of the criminal enterprise. In some cases, these two roles might overlap; in others, however, they will be quite distinct.
- Highlight and assess the operations of criminal networks. In effect, the analysis will examine a case study of a criminal network that penetrated a legal institution—the Bank of New York.

- Outline ways in which governments and law enforcement agencies can attack networks more effectively. This requires an analysis of network vulnerabilities and how these can be exploited.

Some Underlying Analytic Concepts

The Network: A network can be understood very simply as a series of nodes that are connected. The nodes can be individuals, organisations, firms, or computers, so long as they are connected in significant ways. The focus here, of course, is on networks that originate and operate in order to obtain financial rewards through and from illicit activities. As such, this analysis draws on three separate strands of research: social network analysis, discussions of network business organisations, and previous work on criminal organisations (work that departs significantly from the emphasis on formal hierarchies that was long part of the dominant paradigm in the study of organised crime).

Social Network Analysis: Social network analysis originated in several fields, including anthropology, sociology, and social psychology. Perhaps the most important of the early pioneers was J. L. Moreno, who, in the 1930s, developed the notion of a "sociogram." This was a picture in which people (or more generally any social units) are represented as points in two-dimensional space, and relationships among pairs of people are represented by lines linking the corresponding points.

The essence of this type of approach is its focus on "the relationships or ties between the nodes or units in the network." These ties can be based on a variety of underpinning factors, such as "kinship, material transactions, flow of resources or support, behavioral interaction, group co-memberships, or the affective evaluation of one person by another." In many cases there will be some kind of exchange between the nodes, whether of commodities or services (broadly defined to include information and favours). Whatever the basis for the relationship, however, the network concept emphasises the linkages among actors.

Accordingly, social network analysis examines such issues as the importance or prominence of particular individuals in the network;

the concept of centrality, *i.e.*, the individual in the network with the most—or most important—ties to other actors; the notions of closeness and distance based on communication paths among the actors in the network; the notion of cohesive subgroups, that is, subsets of actors among whom there are relatively strong, direct, intense, frequent, or positive ties; the extent to which the relationships and transactions within it are regulated by explicit or tacit rules; and the number and diversity of actors within the network. Whatever the focus, however, there is a recognition of the flexibility and dynamism of social networks, qualities that stem from the ways in which ties are constantly formed and strengthened or weakened and broken.

Partly because of this dynamism, some sociologists conclude that network-based organisations are capable of superior performance than are more traditionally structured hierarchical organisations, especially in terms of adaptability to changes in their environment. This conclusion is reinforced by a growing literature on business networks—literature that has particular relevance to the discussion here since organised crime is perhaps best understood in quasi Clausewitzian terms as the continuation of business by criminal means.

Business Networks: The focus on networks in business has emerged in response to the limitations, rigidities, and inefficiencies associated with strict hierarchical structures, the need to exploit globalisation through partnerships and strategic alliances, and a desire to emulate the Japanese success with the *keiretsu* (regularised networks of suppliers that enhance the efficiency of the production process). It has also emerged out of a recognition that understanding the opportunities provided by "structural holes" (see below) can be critically important for the success of a business in a competitive environment.

The notion of business networks has been developed most explicitly, however, in the concept of the virtual corporation and its dependence on what are sometimes termed "agile networks." Such notions place considerable emphasis on flexible internal communication networks; connections to other organisations; shared interests in obtaining certain outcomes; the need to respond rapidly to external opportunities and challenges; the capacity for environmental scanning, rapid information-processing, and quick decisionmaking; and the capacity of the organisation to learn and adapt.

It is clear even from this abbreviated discussion of network organisations in business that a rich and varied research agenda has resulted in many important insights, some of which are as relevant to the functioning of criminal networks as they are to any other kind of enterprise network. Indeed, another important strand of research underlying the present analysis is the studies of networks that have been undertaken by analysts focusing directly on organised crime.

Dimensions of Criminal Networks

Although networks are an important, and somewhat neglected, form of criminal organisation, they are not the sole or exclusive form. The traditional hierarchical model long associated with Mafia families in the United States, for example, does not need to be jettisoned: After all, it is possible to have networks of hierarchies, hybrid organisational forms with some hierarchical components and a significant network dimension, and even a network of networks. If networks come in a great variety of shapes, however, they vary along several critical dimensions.

First, a network can be created and directed by a core of organisers who want to use it for specific purposes (a "directed network") or it can emerge spontaneously as a mechanism to add efficiency to the functioning of a market (a "transaction network"). The Colombian cocaine trade in the 1980s and early 1990s was very much a directed network—at least at the core—which came into existence to transport cocaine to the United States. The heroin trade from Southeast Asia, in contrast, is far more of a transaction network, in which brokers play a critical role at almost every stage of the process.

Producers supply heroin to independent distributors, and it is then passed along a chain of brokers until it reaches the retail market. In practice, of course, a directed network can be part of a larger transaction network, and it appears that with the demise of the large, vertically integrated networks operating out of Medellín and Cali, the Colombian cocaine trade has increasingly taken on this hybrid quality.

Second, networks can range from small, very limited associations at the local level to transnational supplier networks that move a variety of goods, either licit or illicit—or even both—across national borders. Membership can be determined by a particular characteristic, such as ethnicity, or can be relatively open. Supplier networks are likely to be multiethnic when instrumental considerations outweigh the desire or need to maintain a high degree of exclusiveness.

Among the larger criminal networks, it is possible to identify both key individuals and key companies or firms through which they operate. One of the best examples of an extensive transnational criminal network is that revolving around Semeon Mogilevich. Based in Hungary, Mogilevich is reputed to have close links with the Solntsevo criminal organisation in Moscow, with prostitution activities in Frankfurt, with the Genovese family in New York, and with Russian criminals in Israel.

For several years, Mogilevich operated in part through a company called Magnex YBM operating in the United States and Canada (where it was engaged in money laundering—the process of turning criminal proceeds into clean money by hiding origin and ownership—and stock fraud) and also had a network of companies in the Bahamas, the British Channel Islands, and the Caymans. Significantly, as a key figure in this transnational network, Mogilevich is far less vulnerable than a traditional Mafia don or family head, and, despite continued allegations about his role, he has never been convicted of any crime.

Third, networks can be highly structured and enduring in nature or they can be loose, fluid, or amorphous in character, with members coming and going according to particular needs, opportunities, and demands. Some individuals or even small organisations will drift in and out of networks when it is convenient for them to do so. Other networks will have a more enduring membership. In yet other cases, there will be some members who provide continuity (and direction) to the network, while others will play an occasional or ephemeral part. There will be both "embedded ties" and enduring relations based on high levels of trust, mutual respect, and mutual concern; but also more fleeting relations based on nothing more than a shortterm coincidence of interests. A similar dynamism is evident in the way in which criminals develop and use front companies, creating them wherever opportunities exist and abandoning or closing them whenever they become the targets of law enforcement investigations.

Last, networks can be focused very narrowly on a single purpose or on the supply of a single product, or they can supply a broader range of illegal products or engage in more diverse criminal activities. Colombian and Mexican drug trafficking organisations, for example, engage in a very narrow range of activities.

Although there has been a tendency to traffic in more than one kind of drug, essentially they are in the drug trafficking business and little else. Russian and Chinese criminal organisations, in contrast, have a very diverse portfolio of criminal activities, trafficking in drugs, stolen cars, arms, prostitution, antiquities, and endangered species, yet also engaging in various forms of extortion and financial fraud.Whatever their precise characteristics, networks provide criminals with diversity, flexibility, low visibility, durability, and the like. Indeed, their attractions are very considerable:

- Networks can often operate clandestinely. The more visible a criminal enterprise the more likely it is to be attacked by law enforcement. One of the most significant points about networks, however, is that they are not immediately and obviously visible. Criminal networks can hide behind various licit activities, can operate with a lower degree of formality than other types of organisation, and can maintain a profile that does not bring them to the attention of law enforcement. In some cases, of course, the network will be exposed. Significantly, though, when the FBI began to investigate the Mogilevich criminal network, there was considerable surprise at its extensiveness.
- Even when they are targeted by law enforcement, many criminal networks are inherently dispersed, with the result that they do not provide obvious centers of gravity or loci for law enforcement attacks. Lacking a physical infrastructure or a large investment of sunk costs that would add significantly to their vulnerability, networks can also migrate easily from areas where risks from law enforcement are high to areas where the risks are much lower.

- Criminal networks, especially when they are transnational in character, can exploit differences in national laws and regulations (Israel, for example, only criminalised money laundering in 2000) by engaging in what might be termed jurisdictional arbitrage. Throughout the 1990s, for example, criminals from the former Soviet Union flooded into Israel, exploiting both the law of return and the lack of anti–money laundering measures. In some cases, money from Russia was used in Israel to buy up virtually bankrupt businesses that would then start to make "profits" that flowed back to Russia. In some instances transnational criminal organisations also create jurisdictional confusion, making it difficult for any single nation's law enforcement agencies to act effectively against them. Laundering money through a series of firms and banks in multiple jurisdictions, for example, makes it arduous and costly for law enforcement to follow the money trail.

Networks also offer opportunities for both redundancy and resilience. In network structures, it is easier to create redundancies than it is in more formal and rigid organi-sations—so that even if part of the network is destroyed it can still operate. Furthermore, degradation of a network does not necessarily lead to its demise: Networks are very resilient and can easily be rebuilt.

In view of these advantages, it is not surprising that network structures have become particularly prevalent in contemporary organised crime, whether in the United States, Europe, or states in transition such as Russia, Ukraine, other newly independent states of the former Soviet Union, South Africa, and Cambodia, or even China and Cuba. Accordingly, the analysis now looks at the main characteristics of criminal networks, characteristics that help make them extremely difficult to combat.

11

Criminal Network Operation

Network Cores

Networks of any substantial size will generally have both a core and a periphery, reflecting asymmetries of power, influence, and status within the network. The core is characterised by dense connections among individuals who, in the case of a directed network, provide the steering mechanism for the network as a whole. Usually the originators of the criminal enterprise, the core members initiate specific criminal activities, arbitrate disputes, and provide direction. Their relationship is often underpinned by bonding mechanisms that help to create high degrees of trust and cohesion.

In many cases, bonding will be directly related to family or kinship: Many Italian Mafia groups are still organised along family lines, while Turkish drug trafficking and criminal organisations are often clan based. Other bonding mechanisms include ethnicity and common experience in which the participants develop a strong sense of trust and mutual reliance. Membership in youth gangs or time spent together in prison can also provide critical bonding mechanisms. In the United States, the Mexican Mafia (which is not actually Mexican) started as a prison gang in Southern California but has developed much more extensively. Yet, it is the common experience that continues to give the core of the network a capacity to operate with confidence that disloyalty or defection are unlikely.

If network cores exhibit strong collective identities, cohesion does not necessarily enhance—and can actually reduce—the capacity to obtain information and "mobilize resources from the environment."

Indeed, recent trends in network analysis posit an inverse relationship, in general, between the density/intensity of the coupling of network ties on the one hand and their openness to the outside environment on the other. This explains the attraction of a two-tier structure in which the weaknesses of the core in carrying out the functions of information acquisition are more than offset by the periphery.

Network Peripheries

This zone features less dense patterns of interaction and looser relationships than the core. Yet, these characteristics play a critical role in networks, exhibiting and exploiting "the strength of weak ties." In effect, the periphery allows the network to operate at a far greater distance—both geographically and socially—than would otherwise be the case, facilitating more-extensive operations, more-diverse activities, and the capacity to carry out effective intelligence collection. The Cali cartel, for example, was generally thought of as a highly centralised and structured organisation. In fact, it was a networked structure with a set of key figures at the core and a periphery that included not only those directly involved in the processing and transportation of cocaine, but also taxi drivers and street vendors who were an invaluable source of information at the grass-roots level.

For criminal networks, this capacity is critical, because it allows them to anticipate and thereby to neutralize many law enforcement initiatives. Indeed, sensitivity to both threats and opportunities is vital to the continued functioning of criminal networks, making them highly adaptable. In this sense, criminal networks resemble agile corporations: The ability to obtain advance warning is complemented by a capacity for rapid reconfiguration of internal structures and operational activities. Because they have limited fixed assets, networks not only have limited exposure to risks but also adapt in ways that further reduce this exposure and exploit the paths of least resistance.

Criminal Networks As Defensive Structures

If criminal networks usually have early warning mechanisms that provide the first line of defense against law enforcement, there are also additional defensive mechanisms that can be integrated very effectively into their network structures. As I have noted elsewhere:

Two-tiered networks ... with both core and periphery have formidable internal defense mechanisms. While it is possible for law enforcement to infiltrate the periphery of the network, getting in to the core is much more difficult partly because entry is dependent on a high level of trust that is based on bonding mechanisms rather than functional utility.

Moreover, there will usually be several nodes in the network which act as built-in insulators between core and periphery, distance the core leaders from operations, and make it very difficult for law enforcement to strike at the center of gravity as opposed to nibbling around the edges. The concomitant of this, of course, is that the periphery is where the risks from law enforcement are greatest. Ultimately, however, this is not too serious a problem ... if parts of the periphery are seriously infiltrated or compromised, they can simply be discarded and new members recruited for the outer reaches of the network.

Compartmented networks are good at protecting not only the core membership but also information (while also having effective information flows from periphery to core) that could compromise criminal operations or the integrity of the network. Criminal networks compartmentalize knowledge and information, making it difficult for law enforcement to have more than localised effects on their operations. This is not to deny that, on occasion, there will be defectors or informants whose testimony enables law enforcement to inflict considerable damage, as happened to the Sicilian Mafia in the 1980s.

For the most part, however, networks are very good at self-protection. This is even true when they operate outside the home state—where ethnicity and language become additional defensive mechanisms. U.S. law enforcement agencies, for example, find it difficult to infiltrate Nigerian and Chinese networks in the way they did La Cosa Nostra. Electronic surveillance is also highly problematic since many of the networks use unfamiliar languages or dialects. An additional problem is that criminal networks based on ethnicity are generally located in ethnic communities that offer cover, concealment, and a constant supply of recruits. This is an important factor, for example, in explaining the success of Turkish drug trafficking organisations, and more recently Albanian criminal networks in Western Europe.

Criminal Networks As Facilitators of Cooperation

Even distinctively ethnic networks are not exclusive in their collaboration. Part of the reason for this is that although such networks do not lack organisational identities, they are not overly preoccupied with organisational form. Criminal networks come together with one another when it is convenient or beneficial for them to do so without this being a threat to their identity or *raison d'etre.* Connections among different criminal networks became a major feature of the organised crime world during the 1990s. Colombian Sicilian networks brought together Colombian cocaine suppliers with Sicilian groups possessing local knowledge, well-established heroin distribution networks, extensive bribery and corruption networks, and a full-fledged capability for money laundering. Italian and Russian criminal networks have also forged cooperative relationships, while Colombian and Russian criminals have been meeting in various Caribbean islands to engage in guns-for-drugs deals. The importance of these network connections has been evident in increased seizures of cocaine imported to, or transshipped through, Russia.

There have also been reports of Colombian money laundering activities taking place in Russia and Ukraine, something that would not be possible without some kind of network collaboration. The result of such collaboration, of course, is the creation of a network of networks. These super-networks or pan-networks come into existence for various reasons and operate at a variety of levels, varying in scope, duration, and intensity. As Clawson and Lee put it: At the lowest level are simple buyer-seller deals involving relatively small investments, little advance planning, and relatively little interaction between the parties. At the highest level is what might be called strategic cooperation, which encompasses the principles of long-term agreements, large volume shipments of both drugs and money, and the creation of specialised infrastructure to facilitate these flows.

The latter can appropriately be characterised as strategic alliances. Some criminal networks develop steady supplier relationships with one another along the model of the Japanese *keiretsu,* while others develop contract relationships for the provision of certain kinds of services, such as transportation, security, contract killing, and money laundering. Turkish drug traffickers in Belgium, for example, can buy services from Georgian car thieves to meet their transportation needs. Even some of the more traditional criminal organisations, such as the Sicilians, are also reliant on networks of cooperation to ply their criminal trade. Indeed, Turkish drug traffickers in Italy have links with the Sicilian Mafia, the Sacra Corona Unita, and the Calabrian 'Ndrangheta.' In 1993, a narcotics trafficking network in Turin involved Calabrians, Turks, Pakistanis, and members of the Cali drug trafficking organisation, forming what was clearly a highly cosmopolitan criminal network. In short, the internal flexibility of network organisations is mirrored in the capacity of criminals to form and operate flexible alliances and other cooperative ventures. Indeed, network structures facilitate cooperation among criminal enterprises in the same way they facilitate cooperation in the licit business world.

Criminal networks are also able to draw on a whole set of support structures, whether through acts of paternalism in the community or through more strictly financial considerations. Among the support structures are groups that provide false documentation, front companies, transportation, and a financial infrastructure that can be used to move the proceeds of crime. The creation of false documents facilitates the movement of various kinds of contraband and people and offers an extra layer of protection for those involved in criminal activities. A hint of the scale of the support structure was revealed in May 1998 when agents from the Los Angeles branch of the Immigration and Naturalisation Service (INS) disrupted a counterfeit document operation and seised more than 24,000 counterfeit documents, sophisticated printing equipment, and 50,000 blank social security cards.

Criminal Networks as Boundary Spanners

Another closely related advantage of criminal networks is their capacity to flow around physical barriers and across legal or geographical boundaries. Networks transcend borders and are well-suited for business operations in a world where responding to the opportunities and challenges posed by globalisation has become an imperative. It is no exaggeration to suggest a natural congruence between transnational Another closely related advantage of criminal networks is their capacity to flow around physical barriers and across legal or geographical boundaries. Networks transcend borders and are well-suited for business operations in a world where responding to the opportunities and challenges posed by globalisation has become an imperative. It is no exaggeration to suggest a natural congruence between transnational or cross-border activities and network structures, irrespective of whether the networks operate exclusively in the legitimate sector or in supplying illicit (prohibited or stolen) goods and services.

The capacity to cross national borders creates several advantages for criminal networks. It enables them to supply markets where the profit margins are largest, operate from and in countries where risks are the least, complicate the tasks of law enforcement agencies that are trying to combat them, commit crimes that cross jurisdictions and therefore increase complexity, and adapt their behavior to counter or neutralize law enforcement initiatives. One important boundary crossing, of course, is that between the criminal world and the "upperworld." Criminal networks extend across this boundary in ways that are sufficiently important to require discussion in a separate category, which follows below.

Criminal Networks as Creators and Exploiters of Corruption

In a series of widely cited studies, Ronald Burt has provided considerable insight into the effective functioning of networks by means of his concept of structural holes. Defining structural holes as the separation between nonredundant contacts, Burt contends that the information benefits provided by large diverse networks are greater than those provided by small homogenous networks since size and diversity provide more nonredundant contacts. Consequently, extending networks to cover structural holes provides important competitive advantages. Closely related to this, he argues, relationships can be understood as social capital that can be exploited to benefit the enterprise. Networks provide access to people with specific resources, which create mutually advantageous information benefits and exchange relationships. This is as relevant to organised crime as to business and helps to explain why criminal organisations extend their networks into the licit world. Further, extending a network into government provides access to both information and power.

For criminal networks, spanning structural holes is particularly beneficial when it also involves crossing from one domain into another. By crossing from the underworld into the worlds of government, business, and finance, criminal networks not only identify and exploit new criminal opportunities, but also enhance their capacity to protect existing activities and opportunities. The specific connections that facilitate criminal entry into the licit world can be understood as gateways or portals, while the relationships at the boundaries of the criminal network and the world of government and/or licit business can prove vital to a whole series of criminal operations and activities. For criminal organisations involved simply in theft, for example, the critical node is the person who can fence the goods, who in effect transfers them from the criminal network back into the world of legitimate business and commerce.

At a more sophisticated level are found the lawyers, accountants, bankers, and other financial professionals who help criminals both to conceal and to invest their profits. This facilitates the flow of criminal proceeds back into the legitimate financial system, where it rapidly becomes indistinguishable from money that has been obtained by legal means. In New South Wales, for example, lawyers, accountants, and financial managers have been categorised as "gatekeepers" for organised crime and targeted accordingly.

Perhaps most important of all, however, are the members of law enforcement agencies and government officials whose link to criminal networks involves exchange of information or protection for money. In the case of politicians, the exchange can be about personal gain but might also be about assistance in mobilising the vote, support for electoral campaigns, criminal assistance in providing information about political opponents, or even in intimidating and, in extreme cases, eliminating political enemies.

In the case of law enforcement personnel or members of the judiciary, the aim of the criminals is to minimize risks by undermining enforcement efforts, suborning the judicial process, and neutralising the criminal justice system. In short, criminal organisations extend their reach by coopting individuals and organisations in ways that facilitate, enhance, or protect their activities. The corruption networks they create are dynamic rather than static, increasing in significance as corrupted officials become more senior. In these circumstances, the exchange relationship between them becomes much more substantial in terms both of the favours done by the official and the payoffs provided by the criminal. While the official is not part of a criminal enterprise, he has become a vital node in a criminal network, providing important services including timely intelligence about law enforcement initiatives. In countries such as Turkey, Mexico, Colombia, Nigeria, and Russia, criminal networks have extended their reach into the domains of both commerce and government, thereby increasing their capacity to accrue large profits while simultaneously reducing the risks they have to confront.

Criminal Networks as Robust and Resilient Organisations

Networks are highly resilient, partly because of what might be termed loose coupling. Charles Perrow distinguishes between tightly coupled and loosely coupled systems. He contends that tightly coupled systems are the least stable because disturbances involve a chain reaction or, at the very least, serious knock-on effects. In contrast, "loose coupling gives time, resources, and alternative paths to cope with the disturbance and limits its impact." Criminal networks—apart from the core—are based largely on loose coupling. Even if some parts of the network are destroyed, the effects are limited since other parts are left intact. In a loosely coupled network, knock-on or cascading effects are limited and damage to one part of the network does not undermine the network as a whole. Loose coupling also preserves more diversity, in response offering considerable latitude in the decision of which parts of the network should respond, in what manner and in what location.

Resilience, however, stems not only from the capacity to limit the damage that is inflicted but also from the ability to mitigate consequences. Criminal networks often develop certain forms of redundancy that facilitate recovery if part of the network is degraded or damaged. In legitimate business, redundant contacts in networks and indeed redundancy in general—are generally seen as wasteful and inefficient. For criminal networks, such costs are greatly outweighed by the benefits of redundancy in the face of attack and degradation by law enforcement.

The more redundancy in the network, the more options there are to compensate for law enforcement successes whether in finding new ways of moving illicit commodities to the market or alternative routes and methods of repatriating profits. In effect, redundancy enables members of the network to take over tasks and responsibilities from those who have been arrested, incarcerated, or killed by law enforcement. The diversity of different connections allows the network to function even if some connections are broken—not least because the nodes and connections that remain intact can be redirected. In effect, network redundancy makes it possible to maintain organisational integrity even in an extremely inhospitable environment.

Criminal Networks As Synergistic Organisations

Although social networks exist independently of technological networks, there are major synergies among the two distinct network forms. The ability of transnational criminal networks to exploit the information and communication networks that developed during the 1990s provides major multiplier benefits. While exploitation of information technologies is certainly not the sole prerogative of networkbased organisations, networks are extremely well placed to exploit new technological opportunities. Indeed, many criminal organisations have been using technology as a force multiplier to carry out their entrepreneurial activities with greater efficiency at lower cost.

There is one set of technologies in particular that could give them an enormous advantage in their continued competition with law enforcement—strong forms of encryption. One of the most potent weapons of law enforcement in its struggle with organised crime has been the capacity to monitor communications among criminals—in effect, to identify and listen in on network connections. Encryption provides opportunities to neutralize this capacity and offers criminal networks a form of strategic superiority—the equivalent of an effective strategic defense initiative, at very low cost and based on off-theshelf technologies.

In sum, criminal networks provide moving and elusive targets that operate across enemy lines, infiltrating law enforcement agencies and governments, avoiding confrontation in favour of cooption and corruption. They are resistant—although not impervious—to damage and have qualities that facilitate recuperation and regeneration. Before looking more fully at criminal networks in action, however, it is necessary to identify some of the critical roles that their members must play if the network is to maximize its potential.

12

MEASURES TO CONFRONT

It is clear from the foregoing examples of criminal networks in action that they are formidable. This does not mean that they are invulnerable, however. Indeed, there are several ways in which governments and law enforcement agencies can respond more effectively to the challenges posed by criminal networks. Although criminal networks are resistant to disruption and have high levels of redundancy and resilience, they are not impervious to attack by law enforcement. The nature of these networks, however, suggests that the attacks need to be carefully orchestrated, finely calibrated, and implemented in a comprehensive and systematic fashion. Indeed, there are several important prerequisites for initiating effective attacks on networks, especially clear delineation of objectives and enhanced intelligence assessments.

In attacking networks, it is vitally important to determine the major objectives: Are they to destroy the network, simply to degrade its capacity to carry out criminal actions, or to detach the network from its support apparatus in the licit world? The objectives can range from making operations more difficult for the network through creating instability in the environment to more direct attacks on the network itself that are aimed at disruption of its activities, dislocation or degradation of its capabilities, or even its compete destruction. While all are legitimate objectives, it is essential that there is clarity about precisely which of them is being chosen.

Even clear articulation of objectives is no guarantee that they will be achieved. One of the major problems in dealing with criminal networks is the absence of adequate models about precisely how these networks function. This is paralleled in the business world by a lack of understanding of why business networks succeed or fail. In neither domain has there been sufficient comparative work identifying patterns of success or failure. Specifically in relation to criminal networks, there has been little sustained empirical research on how these networks respond to different law enforcement initiatives. It is clear that networks react quickly and effectively to measures such as interdiction efforts and, for example, move their operations or find new modes of concealment and deception.

What is less clear, however, is the exact nature of their response when damage is inflicted upon them. If part of the network is compromised, for example, is it simply jettisoned or amputated and other components given increased responsibilities in an attempt to compensate, or are efforts made to regenerate the damaged portion of the network? Similarly, it is not always clear where the network starts and ends and whether an apparently successful attack has actually fulfilled its objective of significantly degrading or destroying the network. Damage assessment is always difficult; when it involves networks, it is even more problematic than usual.

To overcome these problems it is essential to develop more effective intelligence about criminal networks. In this connection, various software companies, working closely with the law enforcement community, have developed some important tools to assist with the intelligence analysis task. The three major packages are Orion Leads produced by Orion Scientific Systems, and Watson Powercase (formerly owned by Harlequin) available from Xanalys. Although these packages differ slightly in both power and usability (with some trade-offs between these two characteristics), they all have capabilities that assist in the identification of criminal networks. All of them, for example, have a component that facilitates telephone toll analysis of patterns of interaction among key individuals. The results of this analysis can be fed into what is generally referred to as association, network, or link analysis.

Such an approach helps to identify and assess the relationships or connections among people and organisations involved in crime, in effect helping to understand and visualize the network. Although it is often used for tactical purposes and for specific cases, link analysis could also be a valuable tool for strategic purposes. It could help, for example, in identifying some of the more important nodes in the network, in identifying key individuals who carry out the various network functions identified in the previous section, and in locating the portals or gateways through which the criminal network successfully crosses into the licit world. It could also be used strategically as an aid to damage assessment. In effect, the analytic intelligence process facilitates both identification and mapping of criminal networks.

Understanding network structures and operations makes it easier to identify vulnerabilities against which concentrated attacks should be directed. Particularly important in this connection is the identification of critical nodes. A critical node in a network is one that generally has a high level of importance and a low level of redundancy. The importance can reflect the existence of certain specialised skills (which can be substantive in terms of the specifics of the criminal enterprise or related to the operation of the criminal network as a network) or the position of the node within the network. The low level of redundancy stems from the lack of adequate substitutes for those with these skills.

In terms of network functions, a critical node might be a person who is well connected and the focus for dense connections. If this person is removed and there are no readily available communication links, then the network could be severely degraded. On the other hand, even a few alternative communication links can provide the basis for reestablishing enough connectivity for the network to continue to function. In addition to those nodes that are obviously critical, there are those that can become critical because of more general damage inflicted on the network. These nodes—the ones that are important but highly redundant—can become critical if they are attacked simultaneously or in close succession to one another. While this requires effective coordination, it is certainly an option that needs to be considered.

In attacking networks, it is also critical to target the boundaries, either from one network to another or from the criminal world to the upperworld. Particularly important in this connection are network extenders and crossover figures (defectors from the licit world), individuals who, in effect, straddle the boundary between the licit and illicit sectors and provide an important gateway for the criminals into licit financial, political, administrative, or business institutions.

Indeed, it is essential to disentangle the crime-corruption networks (and the nature of the exchanges between criminals and their clandestine supporters in the licit world) and thereby provide opportunities to detach the network from its various support structures. In part, the struggle between law enforcement and organised crime networks can be understood in terms of a competition in crossovers—informants and defectors from criminal networks on the one side and corrupted politicians, bureaucrats, law enforcement personnel, and members of the judiciary on the other.

Closely related to their ties to the upperworld, criminal networks can become deeply embedded in certain social, political, and economic structures that need to be attacked as a system. Perhaps the best example is the world of offshore financial centers and bank secrecy havens, which can be understood as a set of interlocking services provided to criminal networks that enables these networks to move, hide, and protect the proceeds of their criminal activities. Ironically, the providers of these services enjoy the protection of sovereignty. In effect, this puts the network crossovers out of reach and makes it necessary to attack the support system and not simply the network itself.

The other obvious target for attack is the network core. If the network is functioning effectively, however, and the insulation processes are working as intended, then this will prove extremely difficult. If the core figures are identified and removed, one of two results is possible. The first is that the network is so well-established—with the steering mechanisms so deeply embedded in operational procedures that operations have become more or less independent of the core group— that it can continue to function. A variation on this is that some of the figures who have been close to the core, but not necessarily part of it, can substitute for those removed from the steering group. The second possibility is that attacking the core group will significantly degrade the network and along with other measures, such as an attack on the gateways, will either force it to cease operating or, at the very least, significantly degrade its capacity and reach.

In effect, the options being discussed so far are all part of an external attack on the network. It is also possible to initiate internal attacks on criminal networks, however, where the objective is to create dysfunctional relations that seriously degrade the capacity of the network to function effectively. One option, for example, might be to destroy trust through misinformation and actions designed to create suspicion and acrimony. One way of doing this would be to identify some of the network crossovers and, rather than remove them, use them to feed misinformation into the network. Not only could this have a corrosive internal effect, but also it could encourage the criminals to move in directions that make them increasingly vulnerable to external attack.

One other important component of the response to defeating criminal networks is that governments and law enforcement agencies, in effect, need to mimic network structures. One of the advantages criminal networks enjoy is that they are smart, future-oriented organisations locked in combat with governments that, by contrast, are often hobbled by a variety of constraints. Governments still operate along hierarchical lines and are further hindered by bureaucratic rivalry and competition, interagency antipathies, and a reluctance to share information and coordinate operations. Working from John Arquilla's and David Ronfeldt's proposition that it takes a network to defeat a network, the most successful attacks on criminal networks are likely to be those carried out by innovative law enforcement structures that transcend the normal bureaucratic way of doing business. Joint task forces, in which there are a pooling of resources and information and a concerted attack on a particular criminal network, provide an important value-added approach to attacking criminal networks. They can be particularly useful where they involve transnational cooperation in response to a transnational criminal network.

Joint undercover operations have been particularly successful in this respect, largely because they provide access to crucial parts of the criminal network. Operation Green Ice in the early 1990s, for example, involved law enforcement agencies from eight countries and resulted in around 200 arrests in the United States, Spain, Italy, and Britain. In some cases, cooperation of this kind is even being institutionalised. One of the most forward looking agencies in responding to transnational criminal networks through the creation of its own networks has been the Financial Crimes Enforcement Network at the U.S. Treasury (FINCEN). Although FINCEN has its problems—and has been criticised, among other things, for its lack of performance indicators—its importance reflects the way in which the U.S. government has decided to attack not only criminal kingpins and criminal networks, but also the proceeds of crime.

A key part of this has been an effort to combat money laundering by making it more difficult to introduce dirty money into the financial system without triggering either cash transaction reports (CTRs) or suspicious activity reports (SARs). In addition, the United States has developed laws for asset seizure and asset forfeiture that allow the confiscation of criminal profits. FINCEN has played a key role in this strategy and has acted as liaison with the financial community, encouraging banks to take on responsibilities such as "know your customer" requirements and the exercise of due diligence in all transactions. It is also the repository for the information provided by the banks through the CTRs and SARs.

Fincen is one model of what has become known as a financial intelligence unit (FIU). Many other countries have developed their own variants of these units. Australia, for example, has its Transaction Reports and Analysis Center, known as AUSTRAC, while in Bermuda there is a Financial Investigation Unit. Generally FIUs have reporting and analytic functions; in some countries FIUs also have investigative responsibilities. The challenge, however, is that dirty money has become highly mobile, moving rapidly through multiple jurisdictions before being hidden in safe havens that place a high premium on financial anonymity and bank secrecy. The response to this has been to create a network of FIUs known as the Egmont Group. Established in 1997, the Egmont Group FIUs meet regularly for plenary sessions, while also exchanging information through a secure web site.

As of May 2000, the Egmont Group had 53 operating units in as many countries. Although the national FIUs vary considerably in terms of skills, resources, and available technology, the network facilitates a multinational effort to combat money laundering. Given the speed, ease, and anony-mity with which money can be moved around the global financial system, the Egmont Group, by itself, does not level the playing field, but it does make it less uneven.

Such developments are important, particularly when combined with what is a growing trend toward intelligence-led law enforcement. Yet there is still a gap between the prevalence and sophistication of criminal networks on the one side, and law enforcement networks on the other. Closing this gap and developing more-effective strategies to attack criminal networks has to be one of the priorities in government efforts to combat transnational organised crime in the 21st century. This requires changes in attitudes and ways of thinking, in organisational structures, and in the relationship between intelligence and action. Without these changes, criminal networks will continue to retain important advantages over those who are trying to combat them.

13

POTENTIAL ATTACK

Contemporary society is undergoing significant changes that promise to alter—and in fact are altering—the nature of conflict and crime. Two significant factors are technological and organisational changes that enhance the power of relatively small groups. The information revolution allows small groups to exercise power and extend their influence in seconds, across vast distances. Accompanying this access and ability to move information via the Internet, cell phone, fax, and emerging digital technologies is a shift from hierarchies to network forms of organisation.

These two factors are ushering in an era of asymmetric threats, where nonstate actors can extend their influence and challenge states and their institutions to gain social, political, or economic influence. This chapter examines the potential for certain small groups—in particular, urban criminal gangs—to embrace network forms of organisation and doctrine, and to utilize advanced information technology to wage netwar. This potential lies on the blurry border between crime and warfare and threatens to change the faces of gangsterism and terrorism. It challenges state institutions such as the police, the military, courts, and political leadership to develop responses that protect the public and preserve civil order. The mutation of traditional urban gangs into a new generation that is organised and operates in the manner of many highly networked triads, cartels, and terrorists is highlighted. The chapter shows that politicisation, internationalisation, and sophistication are three factors that influence gang organisation and help explain how a net-based threat can mature. Finally, the example of Black Bloc anarchists, who utilize sophisticated networked tactics and violence to stimulate political action, is reviewed to illustrate the difficulties police encounter when facing networked adversaries.

THREE GENERATIONS OF URBAN GANGS

The information revolution is changing the nature of conflict and crime. Organisational changes benefit from these new technologies. As described by RAND analysts John Arquilla and David Ronfeldt, networks can prevail over hierarchies in this postmodern battlespace: "Power is migrating to small, nonstate actors who can organize into sprawling networks more readily than can traditionally hierarchical nation-state actors." This conforms to the prediction made by eminent military historian Martin van Creveld, In the future war, war will not be waged by armies but by groups whom today we call terrorists, guerrillas, bandits and robbers, but who will undoubtedly hit on more formal titles to describe themselves.

Thus, netwar may result, in some cases, in a distinct and perhaps refined form of what we generally refer to as terrorism. In netwar, alliances between and among state and nonstate actors can fuel conflict. Combinations of "internetted" transnational criminal organisations (TCOs), triads, cartels, cults, terrorists, gangs, and other entities replace their more state-oriented predecessors. Again, Arquilla and Ronfeldt are instructive with their view that "netwar" [is] an emerging mode of conflict (and crime) at societal levels, involving measures short of war, in which the protagonists use—indeed, depend upon using—network forms of organisation, doctrine, strategy and communication.

In the past, loosely organised violent criminal entities like gangs were discounted as serious terrorist threats and excluded from discussions of classic terrorism. But recognition of new technological and organisational factors shows that such entities are especially well-suited to exploit new forms of conflict. Arquilla and Ronfeldt observe that netwar is about Hamas more than the PLO, Mexico's Zapatistas more than Cuba's Fidelistas, the Christian Identity Movement more than the Ku Klux Klan, the Asian Triads more than the Sicilian Mafia, and Chicago's Gangsta Disciples more than the Al Capone Gang. With a focus on gangs that especially concern urban police agencies, this chapter explores the convergence of some of these groups on the road to netwar. Gangs operating in urban areas have gone through three generational changes—from traditional turf gangs, to marketoriented drug gangs, to a new generation that may mix political and mercenary elements. Particularly important for this evolution are trends in the degree of politicisation, internationalisation, and sophistication of a gang.

Politicisation refers to the scope of political activity embraced by the gang. For example, most gangs are largely criminal enterprises, but some have begun to adopt varying degrees of political activity. At the low end, this activity may include dominating neighborhood life and creating virtual "lawless zones," application of street taxes, or taxes on other criminal actors. Gangs with more sophisticated political attributes typically co-opt police and government officials to limit interference with their activities. At the high end, some gangs have active political agendas, using the political process to further their ends and destabilize governments.

Internationalisation refers to the spatial or geographic reach of the gang. Most gangs are extremely local in nature, generally spanning several blocks of turf. Other gangs operate as confederacies of smaller "cliques," working across entire metropolitan regions and nationally across state boundaries. At the high end, some gangs are crossborder, transnational, or even international in scope with outposts in foreign cities.

Sophistication addresses the nature of gang tactics and strategies, the use of weapons and technology, and organisational complexity of the gang. Gangs can demonstrate their sophistication in one or more of these areas. For example, a gang could use sophisticated infantry tactics to conduct ambushes, utilize networked organisational forms, or utilize information technology. The simplest indicator of sophistication is the ability to seek and forge alliances or networks of smaller gangs. This potential is often underestimated, since networks (such as the umbrella "Crip," "Blood," "Folk," and "People" groupings) do not generally adopt the hierarchical forms of traditional organised criminal entities familiar to police. It is important to recognize that networks are not less sophisticated than hierarchies, just different. To a large extent, the diffusion of information technologies and/or networked organisational forms among urban gangs remains largely unstudied.

Each generation, as described below, has different characteristics, which affect the potential for what gangs may do on their own, when drawing inspiration from major criminal and terrorist organisations, or even when linking up with these organisations. The characteristics of these three gang generations. The attributes of gangs, hooligans, and anarchists in terms of the indicators of politicisation, internationalisation and sophistication.are discussed more clearly.

The First Generation—From Traditional Street Gang to Soccer Hooligans

Traditional street gangs operate at the low end of extreme societal violence. Primarily turf-oriented, they are characterised by loose leadership with a focus on loyalty and turf protection in their immediate neighborhoods. Members of such gangs engage in opportunistic criminal activity, including rivalry for drug sales as lone individuals and as a gang competing with other gangs. These *first-generation* (turf) gangs are limited in political scope, are localised (often by city blocks), and are not highly sophisticated.

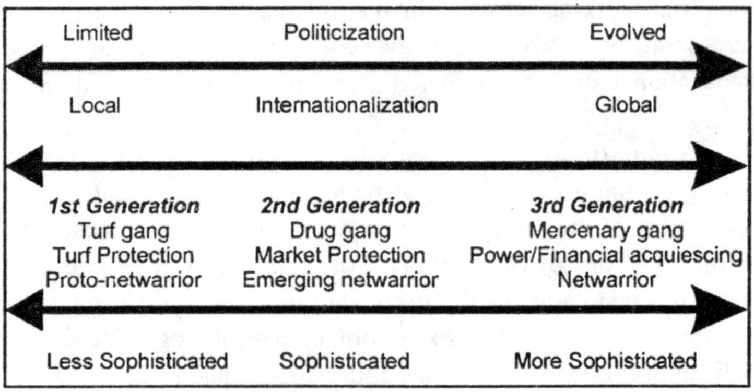

Fig: Characteristics of Street Gang Generations

While traditional street gang activity does not constitute terrorism in the classic sense, it acts as a conflict generator that may provide the necessary foundation for some groups to evolve into complex internetted criminal entities, or even netwarriors. Examples of traditional gangs include the Chicago-based "Folk" and "People" Nations and Los Angeles–based "Crips," "Bloods," and their ubiquitous Hispanic counterparts including the notorious "18th Street" gang. Such street gangs, while violent, have been viewed as outside of the realm of true terrorism because of their lack of formal organisation.

In fact, one noted Los Angeles gang investigator, Wesley McBride, describes traditional gang activity as "disorganised crime in action." Yet informal, network-like organisation is one of the factors that may make netwar more difficult to combat than classic terrorism.

Analyst Robert J. Bunker sees this as one of the factors that may contribute to the rise of nonstate "soldiers." Other factors contributing to this emergence include failed communities with disintegrating social structure and increased sophistication. In Bunker's view, terrorism is an insidious form of warfare based on social rather than political considerations. He sees "armed nonstate actors intent on legitimising forms of behavior that current societies consider to be criminal or morally corrupt" as a major security threat, with networked threats potentially organising into "new warmaking entities, the smallest of which will be subnational groups, such as armed bands, private armies, and local crime organisations." In that context, a web of dispersed, interconnected "nodes" gains relative advantage, since doctrine or common purpose is more important than hierarchical leadership. This view is similar to the observations of Arquilla and Ronfeldt regarding the emergence of netwar where societal-level conflicts are waged through internetted modes of communication, leading to the enhanced standing of nonstate actors.

While street gangs may be in a position to exploit changes in social organisation, the majority of street gangs remain firmly in the first (turf focus) or second (nascent organised crime groups with a drug focus) generation. Gangs that span the first and second generations include some Crip and Blood sets, as well as a few Hispanic gangs such as 18th Street. These gangs tactically employ limited quasi-terrorism to support their activities. Like other organised crime groups, such street gangs use criminal terror, targeting each other, or interfering agencies, to sustain spatial or economic spheres of influence—"turf" or "markets." Finally, some gangs are becoming increasingly mobile, gaining in sophistication, developing links with organised crime entities, and maintaining caches of weapons financed by the large sums of money obtained from multistate or cross-border narcotics distribution networks.

An interesting variation on the traditional turf gang is the rise of soccer hooligans in Europe; for them, the important turf is not a neighborhood per se, but more a "virtual turf," as represented by their favourite local or national soccer team. Football hooligans are largely a European gang form, and soccer or football violence is a major social ill throughout Great Britain and the rest of Europe. Roving bands of thugs looking for street battles mar football games throughout the continent, injuring participants, police, and bystanders alike. These bands, known as "firms," differ from normal football supporters, since violence for violence's sake takes precedence over team success. Firms travel from stadium to stadium via ferry and train to engage their adversaries. They act like ethnonationalist marauders. British firms include the infamous "super-hooligan" armies, such as the Inter City Firm from West Ham and the Service Crew from Leeds. Other notable firms include Chelsea's Headhunters and Milwall's Bushwhackers. These firms generally have about 20 hardcore members, with total membership into the hundreds. British police divide football supporters into three categories. Category A involves typical fans; Category B consists of hooligans who occasionally embrace violence; and Category C is reserved for hardcore violent hooligans. All can engage in violence under certain circumstances.

British police estimate that there are approximately 600 hardcore (or Category C) hooligans in Great Britain. Up to 250–300 associates who participate in violence when under the influence of alcohol (Category B) supplement the violence orchestrated by the hardcore Category C nucleus. Category A members, the more typical football supporters, provide the outer fringe of the phenomena. Continental firms include Ultra Sur, which supports Real Madrid; Milan's Tiger Commandos and the Red and Black Brigade; as well as Barce-lona's Boixos Nois (Crazy Boys).

What appears to have originated as spontaneous violence is now carefully coordinated and orchestrated. Hooligans are integrating network and hierarchical command and control to enhance their combat effectiveness with technology. Firms of opposing hooligans now use wireless technology and the Internet (email, *etc.*) for both marshalling their own combatants and challenging their opponents. For example, Milwall's Bushwackers are believed to have used Internet tools (an interactive web site and real-time messaging) to organize and coordinate the violent activities of hooligans traveling to a match in Cardiff, where 14 people were hurt and 6 arrested.

Messages had been posted both during and throughout the week prior to the game, demonstrating the dangers of organised gangs of hooligans using the Internet. Police and the National Criminal Intelligence Service (NCIS) in the U.K. believe the Cardiff melee confirms their fears that organised soccer firms are turning to modern technology, including computers and mobile phones, to avoid police intervention. Wireless technology allows the firms to coordinate their battle plans and issue tactical operations to precision-guide both pulsing and swarming attacks across Europe's borders.

Second-Generation Street Gangs—The Influence of Organised Crime

Entrepreneurial, drug-centered street gangs occupy the *second generation.* Interested in market protection, these gangs view drugs as a business. They use violence to control their competition and assume a market rather than a turf orientation. With a broader, marketfocused political agenda, these gangs operate across a greater geographic (sometimes multistate) area, tend to have centralised leadership, and conduct more-sophisticated operations, particularly for market protection. Second-generation gangs, like the first, are firmly established criminal threats. But while first-generation gangs operate much like clans, these second-generation types operate more like professional businesses. Drug selling becomes a necessity rather than an optional individual activity.

Second-generation street gangs utilize violence in a manner similar to that of drug cartels, narcoterrorists, and other organised crime groups. These gangs' activities—partly because of their focus on market protection—fall into the center of the range of politicisation, internationalisation, and sophistication. Market protection may necessitate a step toward the use of violence as a political means, and these groups can be expected to exploit both violence and new forms of technology to extend their place in the criminal marketplace.

Crime and violence often blur when criminal enterprises seek to incapacitate enforcement efforts by the state, its police, and security forces. The use of violence as political interference has traditionally been a phenomenon of failed states, but a similar phenomenon occurs when street gangs exploit "failed communities" and dominate community life. As this exploitation occurs in the United States (particularly in neglected inner cities), it reflects what has already occurred in other countries where organised crime has taken hold in embattled "lawless zones." Particularly worrisome is narcoterrorism, which emerged as a result of collaboration between terrorist or guerrilla insurgents and drug cartels, and which involves the use of terror in support of cartel business. While the Andean cocaine trade and Colombian cartels are notorious for the use of narcoterrorism, recent instances of such terror are also evident in Mexico.

The extensive terror and disruption practiced by narcotics producing and trafficking cartels can incapacitate government enforcement efforts, paralyze the judiciary, fuel corruption, and destabilize local communities and nation states alike. Colombian experiences include bombings of public facilities, banks, commercial facilities, and aircraft and assassinations of supreme court justices, cabinet-level officials, magistrates, police officers, and journalists. Mexican cartels have targeted police officials in both Mexico and U.S. border states as well as journalists. Needless to say, cartels in both nations also target rival cartels.

Colombia's Medellín and Cali cartels and, more recently, the ArellanoFélix and other cartels in Mexico have employed extreme violence to further economic—and de facto emerging political—goals. Colombian *narcotraficantes* have recruited members from guerrilla insurgencies, such as FARC (Fuerzas Armadas Revolucionarias de Colombia), ELN (Ejército de Liberación Nacional) and M-19 (April 19th Movement); utilised guerrillas to conduct mercenary operations when their terrorist capability eroded; and solicited terrorist specialists, perhaps including the ETA (Basque Fatherland and Liberty), for technical assistance. Colombian cartels also on occasion target insurgent groups, such as M-19 and FARC themselves, while Peru's

Sendero Luminoso (Shining Path) has used the drug trade to support its insurgency. Such examples illustrate the complex intertwining of politics, crime, and terrorism.

The interaction between cartels and terrorists poses a significant threat to legitimate governments. In this mix, drugs finance terrorists, while terrorists protect drug operations. Building upon relationships initially forged as marriages of convenience, the armed militias supporting contemporary cartels are equipped with modern weapons and seek to disrupt and preempt rather than merely react to government enforcement efforts. For example, FARC and ELN, with an estimated combined strength of 25,000 members, routinely disrupt oil pipelines and carry out wide-ranging acts of urban terrorism to undermine public support for the government. The links between terrorist and organised crime (including drug traffickers) extends beyond the Andean drug states to form an integral node in the global network of organised criminal entities.

Drug cartels are not the only organised crime groups to engage in terrorist-like violence (or quasi-terrorism) to support their goals. Other nonstate actors—including millennialist cults and such transnational criminal organisations as the Asian Triads and other criminal enterprises—are also players. The Sicilian Mafia, the Russian mafiyas, and recently the Chinese 14K Triad have embraced bombings and high-order violence to influence government activity and achieve their goals. The Sicilian Mafia has links with Colombian cartels, La Cosa Nostra (the American Mafia), and many Asian organised crime groups. Its tactics have included assassination, bombings, and kidnapping. Targets have included the police (including senior officers of the Carabinieri), magistrates, justices, and their families. Public buildings, such as police stations, railway stations, restaurants, courts, and department stores, have also been attacked.

The Sicilian Mafia provides many useful insights into networking and politicisation. The Sicilian Mafia (like the Colombian and Mexican cartels and at times the Russian mafiyas) is highly politicised, at times even capturing state institutions. As described by the Italian Parliamentary Anti-Mafia Commission, the Sicilian Mafia is a genuine criminal counter-power, capable of imposing its will on legitimate states. Of undermining institutions and forces of law and order, of upsetting delicate economic and financial equilibrium and destroying democratic life. Indeed, Manuel Castells sees the Sicilian Mafia as part of a "global, diversified network, that permeates boundaries and links up ventures of all sorts." This network, which allows traditional criminal entities to escape the controls of a given state at a given time, includes the American Mafia, the constellation of Russian *mafiyas,* Colombian and Mexican cartels, Nigerian criminal networks, Chinese triads, and the Japanese *Yakuza* (itself a network of constituent entities including the *Yamagachi-gumi,* with 26,000 members in 944 networked gangs; the *Inagawa-kai;* and the *Sumiyoshi-kai*).

Castells observes that the Sicilian Mafia, by linking with this diffuse global network, remains one of the most powerful criminal networks in the world. Drawing from its deep penetration of the Italian State, particularly its political influence over the Christian Democratic Party, the Mafia was able to exert its presence throughout Italy's political, business, and financial infrastructure. When the state sought to reassert its autonomy, the Mafia reacted with unprecedented violence and brutality. When the state prevailed in its efforts to limit the Mafia's control of government institutions, the Mafia strengthened its international linkages and enhanced its networking, providing flexibility and versatility to the organisation. As a result, the Sicilian Mafia and its allied organisations embrace networking both internally in their own organisations and externally with other criminal organisations as a way to counter state interference. Thus flexible networking among local turfs and strategic alliances with other traditional criminal enterprises allow the Sicilian Mafia, like its partners, to achieve global reach.

Russian organised crime groups, loosely known as the mafiyas, have utilised similar approaches, adding trafficking in weapons of mass destruction and local political dominance in parts of the former Soviet Union to their repertoire. Russian mafiyas operate in 60–65 countries and include about 6,000 separate groups, 200 of which operate in the United States. Within this series of loose, dynamic networks of semiautonomous entrepreneurs are a collection of gangs, crews, and individuals operating in a dozen major networks in up to 20 American cities. With a flexible and diffuse structure, these mafiya nodes are responsive to new threats and opportunities and are virtually impossible to decapitate. These groups are flexible and often seek alliances with a variety of entities, including former KGB operatives and other criminal enterprises, including partnerships or service provision to relatively low-level gangs. A good example of a contemporary TCO, these mafiyas are often better organised and financed than the police. Their activities cross so many borders that intergovernmental coordination is awkward. In brief, they are less constrained by bureaucracy, have more money, and have access to the best technology.

Triads are also players in the quasi-terrorist game. The Hong Kong– based 14K Triad has conducted an extended terror campaign in Macao. Utilising petrol bombs, attacks on police and journalists with secondary devices, and attacks against infrastructure and public places, this campaign illustrates the use of terror as a political tool by a criminal enterprise. The 14K campaign exists within the vacuum of power resulting from the transition from Portuguese to Chinese rule. This transition has yielded an intertriad war, where organised crime groups including Hong Kong triads, mainland Chinese gangs from Guangdong Province, and corrupt security officials interact in an ever shifting web of alliances, business deals, and violence. Within this framework, the 14K campaign seeks to influence the police, government agencies, casino watchdogs, and other criminal groups.

These trends in transnational crime—and criminal netwar—abroad have, to some extent, worked their way into the United States. Further penetration must be guarded against, especially to prevent their linking up with American gangs. A danger is that gangs like the Bloods, Crips, or Gangster Disciples will be drawn increasingly into serving as wholesale trafficking and distribution networks for foreign cartels.

Third-Generation Gangs: Social, Political, and Mercenary Objectives

The overwhelming majority of street gangs are first or second generation. However, a small number of gangs in the United States and South Africa are also moving into the next generation. A *third-generation* gang is a mercenary-type entity focused on power and financial acquisition. These criminal netwar actors have significant political aims, aspire to operate at the global end of the spectrum, and are more sophisticated than first- and second-generation gangs. Currently, no gang is fully within the third generation, but some are moving swiftly along the spectra of politicisation, internationalisation, and sophistication. These gangs can be expected to utilize terrorism (including for hire) to advance their influence and can be expected to challenge the institu-tions of the nation state.

For the most part, these gangs are mercenary in orientation; however, in some cases they share some political and social objectives. Examples of third-generation evolution among gangs in Chicago, San Diego, Los Angeles, and Cape Town, South Africa are provided in the following discussion. The potential for third-generation street gangs first emerged in Chicago. It is home to approximately 125 gangs, including some of the most complex, well-disciplined gangs in the nation. A few demonstrate the sophistication and political savvy of third-generation evolution. These gangs not only create and sustain alliances, but act as paramilitary groups embracing terrorism or terrorism for hire.

The "El Rukn" gang (currently known as the "Black P Stone Nation"), which sought to carry out terrorism for hire on behalf of Libya is an early example. Members of the gang once traveled to Libya, trained for terrorist operations in abandoned buildings, and sought to arm themselves with rocket-propelled grenades. Under the leadership of Jeff Fort, the gang diverted economic development funds into criminal activity and later endeavoured to conduct terrorist operations for hire. If successful, the gang might have blown up airplanes and buildings on behalf of Moammar Qaddafi, and obtained payments in the millions of dollars. Fort is currently in prison for a 1986 mercenary conspiracy.

An example of high-level violence among Chicago gangs is demonstrated by the Four Corner Hustlers faction of the Vice Lords, who plotted to blow up the Chicago Police Department Area 4 headquarters using an M72A2 light antiarmor weapon system rocket. Politicisation, which signals a shift from a second- to a third-generation gang, is also found among Chicago gangs. Gang "empowerment" and political evolution are illustrated in the example of the 30,000member Gangster Disciples (GDs) and their political arm 21st Century VOTE. The GDs conduct drug trafficking activities in 35 states, in some cases controlling entire housing projects, schools, and streets. The gang has evolved from a turf-based street gang utilising murder and drive-by shootings to settle disputes into a complex organisation that conducts overt political activity.

Police intelligence gathering can be hampered as gangs evolve into third-generation types with political agendas—in Chicago, a 1982 injunction barred surveillance, infiltration, and dossier compilation on groups, including gangs, that played political roles. Such wellintentioned but naive restraint can have particularly alarming consequences. In addition to maintaining a political action committee funded through a "street tax" on gang members, GD members infiltrate police and private security agencies, sponsor political candidates, register voters, and sponsor protest marches. A rival gang, the Unknown Conservative Vice Lords, has embraced similar activities, including establishing a nonprofit political association known as the United Concerned Voters' League. This political dimension signals a shift from a second- to a third-generation gang, where power acquisition rather than simple market protection is a motivating concern.

Internationalisation is another indicator of gang evolution. Gangs in Los Angeles and San Diego are notable in this respect. Los Angeles gangs currently have outposts in Tijuana, Mexico; Managua, Nicaragua; San Salvador, El Salvador; and Belize. Police in these jurisdictions are concerned about the evolution of these gangs into drug mafias. In El Salvador, home to an estimated 10,000 L.A.-style gangs, some elements are merging with local *maras,* yielding the potential for lethal criminal coalitions. Traditional L.A. rivals Mara Salvatrucha (MS) and Eighteenth Street (18th Street) have outpost affiliates that have clashed in San Salvador, utilising AK-47s and hand grenades. In Tijuana, 18th Street has expanded its scope to include trafficking in stolen vehicles from the United States and moving illicit small arms into the United States.

San Diego's Calle Treinta (30th Street, Barrio Logan, or Logan Heights) gang has ventured into the third generation in conjunction with the Arellano-Félix (Tijuana) cartel. Members of Calle Treinta have been recruited in true mercenary fashion, with as many as 30 members abandoning their turf orientation and turning to acting as proxies for the Arellano organisation. This is not the only recent example of gangs acting as mercenaries for drug mafias. Brazilian street gangs active in Rio de Janeiro's *favelas* provide an interesting parallel to the Logan Street gang experience, selling their services to drug traffickers and embracing combat training to strengthen their hold on their *favelas* and to ward off competition from others.

During their heyday, Calle Treinta's international gang combat left a trail of over 200 bodies from San Francisco to Tijuana to Venezuela. Notorious activities include a 1993 San Diego shootout killing 26 and the 1993 slaying of Cardinal Juan Jesús Posadas Ocampo in Guadalajara. Calle Treinta members have been linked to assassinations, driveby shootings, and torture slayings on both sides of the border. In November 1997, a Mexican judge issued an arrest warrant for seven "Logan 30s" members, believed to be in San Diego, for the Tijuana assassination attempt of J. Jesús Blancornelas, publisher of the Tijuana paper *Zeta.* Blancornelas observes that the cross-fertilisation of street gangs and drug traffickers results in "a binational army of killers working in both Mexico and America." Barrio Logan provided the cartel with imported *pistoleros,* who had the advantage of being able to float between nations, thus complicating apprehension and prosecution.

An emergence of third-generation street gangs has also occurred in South Africa, where both street gangs and countergang vigilante groups are politically active and conduct quasi-terrorist or terrorist campaigns. Pagad (People Against Gangsterism and Drugs) is notable in this regard. Primarily Muslim in orientation, Pagad is a vigilante group battling gangs in Cape Town and the Western Cape. Its activities have resulted in a near war, reaching the level of civil conflict with terrorist attacks (bombings and armed assault). Pagad maintains a paramilitary, G-Force, organised into small cells at the neighborhood level. These cells have the capacity to operate undetected and independent from central control. Some members are believed to be veterans of Islamist campaigns in Bosnia, Lebanon, and Afghanistan. Pagad also has links, including shared leadership, with the Islamistoriented Qibla Mass Movement. Pagad currently is believed to be nurturing an alliance with the Pan Africanist Congress (PAC), an outgrowth of the relationship between PAC's former military wing Apla and Qibla, forged during the armed struggle against apartheid.

Cape area gangs, with an estimated 400,000 members, have evolved a political dimension as well. The Hard Livings gang is in conflict with Pagad for both political and criminal transgressions. Hard Livings developed links with the African National Congress during Hard Livings' opposition to South Africa's apartheid regime. These links were formed when Umkhonto weSizewe guerrillas relied upon gang safe houses and trafficking routes. Now, both Pagad and the Hard Livings gang participate in conventional politics—and South African police observe that these gangs have better organisational networks in Cape Flats and other Western Cape towns than do traditional political actors. For example, Pagad spent considerable effort arranging political alliances for the 1999 elections; and Hard Livings sponsors the Die Suid-Afrikaan party and Community Outreach Forum (CORE). Hard Livings member Rashied Staggie, an influential CORE member and frequent spokesman for its political positions, including support of the South African Olympic Committee's bid to host the Olympics, publicly voiced an interest in standing for office in that election. Staggie is the twin brother of Rashaad Staggie, who was assassinated in a Pagad attack in 1996.

VIOLENT NETWAR—THE ADVERSARIES AFTER NEXT

Few criminal gangs, even in the third generation, have become fullfledged terrorist organisations as well. But there is some crossfertilisation occurring in terms of organisational designs, strategies, and tactics. Thus, it behooves an analyst concerned about the future evolution of gangs to be cognizant of trends in the world of terrorism that could lead to imitation by criminal gangs or, worse yet, to links and alliances with criminal gangs, either as proxies or partners.

Trends Linking Terrorists and Criminal Gangs

Today's terrorists, characterised by religious and social motivations, stand at the threshold of netwar. The lighting rods of postmodern conflict, these terrorists eschew terrorism's classic political motivations and instead seek broader religious or social change. This resurgence of religious terrorism involves Shi'a and Sunni Islamists seeking to replace the secular state, such Christian fundamentalists as the Army of God in the United States, the racist Christian Identity movement, and some fundamentalist Jews in Israel. Millenarian cults have also sprung up, perhaps best exemplified by the Aum Shinrikyo's international conspiracy to wield weapons of mass destruction, which culminated in a campaign of chemical and biological assaults, including the sarin attack on the Tokyo subway. Aum continues to exist and is once again building membership under the name Aleph.

These postmodern religious zealots rely in large measure on common philosophy rather than rigid individual command and control to reach their ends. Exemplified by the Aryan Nation's ambassador-atlarge Louis Beam's "Leaderless Resistance," calls to action through "fictional" manifestos, web pages, Usenet news groups, and radio shows allow like-minded extremists, in a decentralised way, to select their own course of action under a common philosophical umbrella. The Army of God, for example, provides a call to action in "Rescue Platoon." This "fictional" web site account gives operational and tactical advice and recommends targets (both venues and thinly veiled individuals)—thereby, in actuality, laying the blueprint for a terrorist antiabortion campaign.

An internetted coordinating structure allows what Bruce Hoffman has termed the "amateurisation of terrorism," where an ad hoc amalgamation of like-minded individuals can come together for a specific, perhaps one-time operation with or without coordination from a nonstate network actor. A good recent example of such a nonstate network is found in the interaction between Osama bin Laden's *alQaeda* (The Base) and the International Islamic Front Against Jews and Crusaders.

Bin Laden not only provided philosophical guidance to his own network (al-Qaeda), but was able to bring together an amalgam of separate but like-minded groups, including Gama's al-Islamiya (Egypt), the Ulema Society and Harkat-ul-Ansar (Pakistan), and the Jihad Movement (Bangladesh), into a networked alliance. This alliance, sharing the goals of the Islamic Army for the Liberation of the Holy Places, was able to come together to conduct specific operations in the near-simultaneous bombing of the U.S. embassies in Kenya and Tanzania. A similar "one-time" coalition, guided by Bin Laden, is thought to be responsible for the 1993 bombing of New York's World Trade Center. Such groups are not susceptible to preemption through pressure on a state sponsor, since they are not guided by a single "opposing state." Rather, they occupy an amorphous space, cloaked in anonymity and deniability.

The groups discussed in this chapter all share a common evolution toward becoming violent, pernicious network-based threats to domestic and international security. Those at the lower stages (turf gangs and soccer hooligans) are similar to the more advanced groups (cartels and terrorist networks), in that all exhibit the adoption of networked organisational designs and strategies and an ability to integrate new technological tools to enhance their virulence and lethality. All types are difficult to counter precisely because of their multicephalic, networked nature. For example, the killing of Pablo Escobar weakened the Medellín cartel but did little to permanently inhibit the Colombian cartels, and the imprisonment of Larry "King" Hoover and other key GD leadership has had little effect on the gang's continued success. While all use violence to varying degrees to pursue their ends, some of these groups are particularly dangerous because of their ability to learn to exploit the benefits of the network form. Like some militant net-activists, violent networked groups benefit from the obscurity and near simultaneous transmission of information inherent in new network-enhancing technology.

It appears that contact with other sophisticated networked groups may help to "revolutionize" groups at the lower stages of progress, enabling them to become full-fledged criminal and terrorist netwar actors. Such cross-fertilisation—whether it occurs in prison, where lesssophisticated gangs learn from more-seasoned organised crime groups, or when groups come together to conduct criminal activity— has clearly sped movement toward enhanced sophistication. As these groups become more sophisticated and obtain more skills and technology through the vast amount of illicit funds at their disposal, it may only be a matter of time until they learn to attack cyber as well as physical infrastructures, and to use information warfare to their advantage.

Groups with a natural network structure are able to quickly learn to exploit new technologies and organisational ideas to make the group more successful. Such was the case when insurgent guerrillas conducted joint operations with Colombian cartels; when ANC guerrillas converged with South African gangs, and Islamist guerrillas came in contact with Pagad; when Mexican cartels recruited San Diego gangs; and when Los Angeles street gangs merged with local *maras* in El Salvador. Such cross-fertilisation has particularly ominous overtones as these networked gangs come into continuing contact. Such contact allows these criminal partners to exploit existing smuggling and distribution channels, obtain funds for purchasing weapons and technology, co-opt local police and government officials, and learn from each other's experience. When more-evolved TCOs, terrorists, and gangs converge, the potential for truly more terrible netwar actors arises.

To combat groups evolving along this path requires that police, security agencies, and other government offices quickly recognize the threats that can be posed by internetted adversaries, and thus craft networks of their own. Police, military, and security forces must learn to integrate network forms into their hierarchical structures to enable rapid, robust, and flexible response across organisational and political boundaries. Otherwise, networked adversaries may exploit the gaps and seams between governmental organisations. These must be filled through innovative, multilateral, interagency collaboration. An important strategic intelligence task for police and law enforcement agencies combating these groups is identification of evidence of the diffusion of information technologies and/or networked forms among urban gangs, hooligans, and violent anarchist cells.

Lessons from Observing Social Activists and Anarchists

The disturbances associated with the World Trade Organisation (WTO) meeting in Seattle, Washington, between November 29 and December 3, 1999, are illustrative for police and law enforcement officials seeking to cope with networked adversaries. The WTO meeting brought 8,000 delegates from 135 nations, as well as a number of nongovernmental organisations for the WTO ministerial meeting. A number of dignitaries, including the U.S. president and the secretary of state, were present in Seattle for the sessions. Prior to the meeting, the Federal Bureau of Investigation warned Seattle authorities of the potential for disturbances, cyber activity, and demonstrations from a wide variety of social activist organisations.

When the WTO meeting sought to initiate its sessions, a confluence of loosely organised social activists converged on the sessions in both physical and cyber space. What ultimately transpired involved a unique combination of social netwar and violent demonstrations as anarchists, legitimate demonstrators, and opportunist criminals converged and met a police force unprepared for postmodern net conflict. The Seattle police encountered a diverse, yet cohesive coalition of demonstrators with the objective of shutting down the WTO. This loosely organised coalition used and exploited intelligence, the principles of mass and maneuver, good real-time communications, and well-practiced techniques to meet its objectives. Ultimately, the police were overrun by this unique combination, demonstrating their failure to discern between lawful demonstrators, anarchists, opportunists, and bystanders. As a result, the WTO sessions and ceremonies were disrupted, and police credibility was challenged, particularly as the demonstrations were seen on global television and simultaneous demonstrations spilled over in cities across the globe.

What occurred in the Battle of Seattle, which resulted in 601 arrests and $3 million in property damage, was more than a tactical and intelligence failure of a single police force. Rather it became an example of the challenges that hierarchical organisations face when confronting networked adversaries with faster reaction cycles. The opposing force (demonstrators and anarchists) in Seattle were systematic, wellorganised, and well-funded. Using extremely good modern communications, including live Internet feeds, they were able to execute simultaneous actions by means of pulsing and swarming tactics coordinated by networked and leaderless "affinity groups." The social netactivists were able to combine simultaneous physical protests and cyber activity (including virtual sit-ins and denial-of-service attacks) to communicate their antiglobalist, anti-WTO message.

While over 160 social activist groups (including the Direct Action Network, Rainforest Action Network, The Ruckus Society, Free Mumia supporters, Earth First!, Green Peace, and others, including the Zapatista National Liberation Army, which was among the first groups to embrace "social netwar") physically converged on Seattle, a group of approximately 180 black-clad anarchists fomented violent action, while other unknown actors in Seattle and elsewhere struck in cyberspace.

Hackers probed the Seattle Host Organisation's web site nearly 700 times looking for weaknesses and tried to hack into the web site 54 times in a continuing attempt to bring down the site. While the email attacks (directed denial-of-service attacks) were repelled, the WTO home page at www.wto.org was brought down briefly. The WTO also faced simultaneous infrastructure attacks as saboteurs claiming to be the Green Rennet Brigade cut power to the WTO's Geneva headquarters. The legitimate social activists are not the concern in this discussion. While the vast majority of the protestors were non-violent, there was a small band of people dressed in all black, with masks covering their faces, who caused destruction and tried to incite the crowd to violence.

These black-clad actors were the Black Bloc, a "loosely organised cluster of affinity groups and individuals" who roamed downtown Seattle, remaining constantly in motion, pulsing and swarming to avoid engagement with the police as they targeted corporate organisations. The Black Bloc was most active on November 30 (N30), causing property damage to sites owned by Occidental Petroleum, Bank of America, US Bancorp, Washington Mutual, Old Navy, Banana Republic, the GAP, NikeTown, Levi's, McDonald's, Starbucks, Warner Bros., and Planet Hollywood. Slingshots, sledgehammers, paint balls, and eggs filled with glass etching solution were employed.

According to a communiqué by the N30 Black Bloc, anarchists planned to physically strike out against capital, technology, and civilisation, exploiting the inability of police forces to shift from their planned method of addressing illegal demonstrations through crowd dispersal. The Black Bloc refers more to a tactic employed by loosely organised, fluid, and dynamic groups that come together in shortterm affinity groupings, than to any defined, regular group. This loosely organised coalition, embracing network organisation and tactics, frustrated police efforts to gain the situational awareness needed to combat the seemingly chaotic Seattle disturbances. The groups facing the Seattle police were not "disorganised." They were organised as a network, something hierarchies have difficulty addressing.

BUILDING A RESPONSE TO NETWORKED THREATS

Responding to networked crime groups will require new and innovative responses from states and their law enforcement agencies. Such traditional responses as "counterleadership targeting" (*e.g.*, the takedown of Pablo Escobar or attempts to capture Osama bin Laden) have dominated strategy to date, with little long-term effect. Networked groups are resilient. Their organisational flexibility allows them to absorb such shocks and rechannel their efforts to remain intact. This organisational ambiguity frustrates hierarchical organisations, since their efforts to contain the opposing criminal forces are frequently too rigid or too slow to stop these adversaries.

Networked threats require a response from either a network or a hybrid (that is, a blend of a hierarchy and a network). The capabilities to address these types of threats may be contained in another agency or another discipline altogether. The traditional organisational "stovepipes" of law enforcement and state agencies give networked adversaries the ability to exploit the seams and gaps of traditional responses. Recent interagency coordination among federal entities to build flexible, tailored response capabilities shows that some progress is being made at the national level. A concluding point of this chapter is that much more progress must be made at the local and metropolitan levels, particularly to coordinate activities among a range of local, state, and federal offices, in areas that may range from intelligence gathering to emergency response.

An example of such an effort is found in the Los Angeles County Operational Area's Terrorism Early Warning Group (TEW). TEW was designed to address emerging threats and to deny networked adversaries the ability to maneuver in the gaps between traditional response organisations. TEW is a hybrid organisation that blends networked organisational features with traditional government structures. Bringing together law enforcement, fire service, and health authorities at all levels of government, TEW serves as a mechanism for monitoring terrorist trends and potentials, assessing threats, sharing information, and rapidly disseminating alerts and warnings. TEW is organised as a plenary open forum with three subcommittees: a Playbook Committee for developing response information (target) folders and playbooks to guide response, an Emerging Threat Committee to address upcoming threats in the five–ten year range, and a Net Assessment Group for providing decision support in actual incidents (threats or attacks).

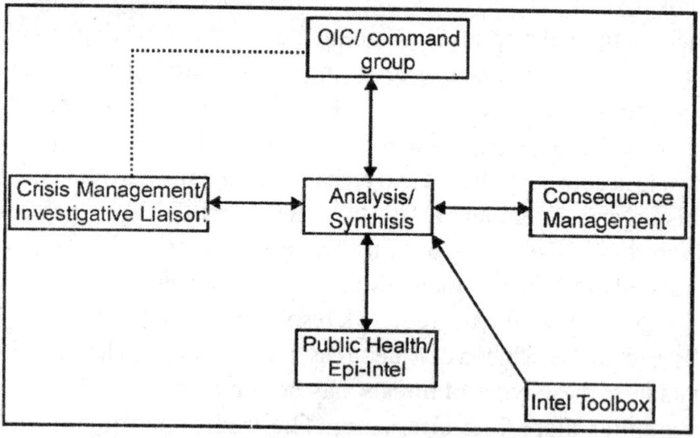

Fig: Terrorism Early Warning Group/Net Assessment Organisation

Prior to an incident or specific threat, TEW serves as an indications and warning apparatus. When a specific threat warrants a potential response, the Net Assessment Group is convened from the multidisciplinary, interagency response community to assess the effects of the event, monitor situation status, and provide the Unified Command with potential courses of action to mitigate or respond to the situation. The Net Assessment Group has a networked architecture and is designed to plug into existing response structures and command pathways. This organisation includes an officer in charge (OIC) or command group, and an analysis/synthesis element for coordinating the group's tasking and decision support products. The consequence management element assesses the effects of an incident and the necessary elements of response. The crisis management/investigative liaison (law-intel) element provides investigative support and obtains information about the threat derived from investigative sources.

The public health/epidemiological (epi-intel) element links disease surveillance (human, veterinary, and food surety) with incident response. Finally, TEW utilises an "intelligence toolbox" consisting of virtual reachback to technical specialists or advanced technology tools (forensic intelligence support such as plume modeling, field analytical and laboratory capabilities, decision models, and gaming) to help project incident consequences and the event horizon.

Since its inception, TEW has employed open source intelligence (OSINT), including links to networked Internet-based OSINT tools and relationships with external academic specialists to scan the horizon for emerging threats and to act as a forum for monitoring specific threats, building response capabilities, and supporting decisionmaking efforts.

As such, TEW forms a network to speed an integrated and effective response to a range of threats—networked and otherwise. Recognition of these threats and use of the benefits that may stem from networked forms of organisation are essential to limiting the growing, evolving specters of big-city gangs, transnational organised criminal enterprises, and terrorism, as well as the possible blending of these adversaries into compound netwarriors.

14

Organised Cyber Crime

The merger of transnational crime, terrorism and corruption is profound. The idea that these ideas can be discussed separately is problematic. Such compartmentalisation limits our ability to analyze and address the diverse forms of transnational criminal activity. Highly corrupt societies give little opportunity for legitimate social mobility and their high level corruption is a deterrent to economic growth and investment. Under these circumstances, the employment opportunities of transnational crime groups provide a desirable economic alternative to youth without legitimate opportunities. Terrorist groups flourish in environments where youths have limited chance for advancement within their societies.

The phenomena of transnational crime, terrorism and corruption are all too often viewed as separate phenomena. These phenomena have grown in tandem because the economic and political conditions that give rise to these phenomena are quite similar. The evolution of the transnational crime-ideologically based or economically based depends on specific environmental factors that have proliferated in many developing and transitional countries that have not successfully integrated into the global Economy.

Terrorists and transnational criminals use many of the same strategies to promote their operations, chief among these being the use of information technology to plan and realize the activities. The rise of greater international mobility and the proliferation of information technology throughout the world have facilitated the growth of both transnational crime and terrorism. The ease of communications in the contemporary era makes the location of groups and actors less significant than it was previously. The ability to exploit security holes in the system makes crime groups and terrorists operate out of unexpected locales rather than their home territories.

Most transnational crime and terrorist groups are based in transitional and developing countries. The illicit businesses are now the largest and most profitable to be located in the developing world. For example, the drug trade now represents about 7% of world trade according to late 1990s estimates of the United Nations. Their vast profits and enormous assets make them powerful actors in their home countries and in their regions. Because they are so large relative to the legitimate businesses based in their region or in the countries through which they operate, they have a large influence on politics and business.

The vast profits of illegal businesses allow them to hire the best specialists domestically and internationally. Facilitating this trade, is an ever greater reliance on information technology to promote their activities secretly. For example, international drug traffickers are among the most widespread users of encrypted messages, coded messages by cell and satellite phones and use anonymiser features on computers. They also are able to hire technical specialists capable of using steganography and other means to make messages hard or impossible to decipher. This access to high level specialists allows illicit businesses and terrorist organisations to transcend borders and operate internationally without detection. Often the crime and terrorist groups do not need to go outside their region to hire such technical specialists. Some of the leading specialists in the technical area are located in regions that house major transnational crime groups and terrorist organisations.

The presence of many highly trained technical specialists in the countries of the former Soviet Union and in the Indian subcontinent means that transnational crime groups means that a vast array of specialists are available for hire. While some specialists will not work for criminal or terrorist organisations willingly, some will do it unaware of their employers whereas others will agree to provide assistance because well-paid legitimate employment is scarce in their region. The widespread problem of corruption in many developing countries allows the proliferation of transnational organised crime and terrorism. The official corruption facilitating this activity may assume many different forms and is not just based on bribery. Top government officials provide falsified documents to smuggled criminals and terrorists, restrain law enforcement from acting against suspicious groups and provide them a safe space to operate.

Because of this, criminals can use the high level technology available in the former Soviet Union and the Punjab region to facilitate not only their own crime and terrorist groups but those of other regions of the world which find save haven on their territory. In this way criminals exploit information technology to carry on their operations in a safe and secure manner. The connections between transnational crime and terrorism are not unique to developed and developing countries. As investigations in the advent of September, 11th have shown, terrorists in developed countries use criminal activity to survive. Arrests in Spain revealed that terrorists were selling counterfeit airline tickets to survive and such groups in the United States were surviving by means of money laundering and other criminal offenses.

Organised Crime, Terrorism and Use of Information Technology

Technology links developed and developing regions by facilitating financing, rapid planning, and all forms of information sharing. Legitimate corporations have exploited the technological revolution to full advantage by use information technology to coordinate their international operations in developed and developing countries. This has helped them overcome problems of inefficient postal services, time differences among different regions and problems of international communication in a multi-lingual environment. The linking of the developed and developing world in the technology area has provided financially beneficial to multinational corporations. They have been able to outsource work so that data processing and other information technology functions can be performed in regions with technical capacity but low labour costs.

Transnational criminal organisations, criminal and terrorist, also take advantage of the possibility of uniting the developed and developing country by information technology. Drug traffickers use encrypted messages to direct their operations. Terrorists use the anonymiser feature of computers to coordinate their activities across countries. Websites facilitating all forms of transnational crime, for example dissemination of child pornography or recruitment sites for terrorist organisations, are often posted in developing countries without the law enforcement capacity to bring down these sites. Furthermore, law enforcement in these developed countries cannot hire or retain the personnel needed to combat the criminal activity of transnational crime groups.

The low salaries and the corruption of law enforcement means that individuals with highly developed technical skills cannot find desirable employment in the state sector. Computer experts in developing countries choose not to work for low law enforcement salaries, instead they work for the private sector and others will work consciously or unknowingly for criminal and terrorist groups.

In some countries, even if the state paid adequate wages, the state law enforcement sector may not be a legitimate alternative to the criminal sector. The institutionalised corruption of much of law enforcement and its close links with the criminal sector in some regions of the world means that the criminals can pay for specialists within and outside the government.

In the developed countries, there is a shortage of personnel with adequate IT skills. Many of those who work in the high technology sector in Europe and the United States are immigrants from less developed countries and are not able to serve law enforcement in the countries in which they reside. Moreover, law enforcement has not been able to compete with the private sector in terms of the pay it offers or the promotional options which it provides to make it an employer of choice to talented IT specialists. Criminals have been very successful in exploiting the international inconsistencies in the system and the failure to regulate technology across jurisdictions.

As the love virus from the Philippines illustrates, there are limits on sanctioning offenders whose crimes are extremely costly to society because individual countries have not enacted legislation. While the perpetrator of the love virus did not intentionally cause the harm to computer systems around the world, individuals who intend to cause serious harm exploit the environments in which there is little regulation of computers and little law enforcement capacity to act against this crime. One website containing child pornography was posted on a website indicating that it was located in a Central Asian country. Over four million individuals downloaded images from the site before it was brought down. The reason being is that there were an absence of computer specialists in that country to take down the website. The lack of coordinated legislation has been exploited not only by criminals but by terrorists as well. The hijackers of the September, 11th planes were aware that their phones and cell phones might be tapped. Before post-September, 11th legislative changes, separate warrants were needed to tap each phones in the three jurisdictions of the Washington area — Virginia, Maryland and the District of Columbia. The terrorists exploited this knowledge of the limits of law enforcement and used different phones in these different jurisdictions to prevent monitoring of their conversations. Just as the future terrorists exploited jurisdictional differences in the Washington metropolitan area to reduce risk, they also did the same internationally.

Much of the plotting for the September, 11th attack was carried out in Germany that has the greatest limits on undercover activity. With its protections on the right to privacy and its limitations on police powers, a legacy of the abuses of the Nazi era, terrorists could use the advance telecommunications networks to their advantage without detection. Intelligence and analysis by the terrorist cells helped ensure the ultimate security of operations with access to the most sophisticated information technology. The merger of transnational organised crime with terrorism is seen on a regular basis. Terrorists use criminal activity to support their operations. The growth of information technology facilitates terrorists' attempts to gain significant profits with relatively low risk. Terrorists can finance their operations without resorting to violent assaults or bank robberies that would raise the risk of detection.

Criminal activity committed internationally via the Internet supports terrorist activity as they can tap into credit card bases and commit various forms of lucrative fraud. Ukrainian specialists at a TraCCC conference in 2000 reported that their country is the source of many financial crimes committed by computer and the Internet. But while Ukraine may be the source country for much of this criminality, it is not now clear that only Ukrainians are committing this crime. There are many foreigners using the computer resources of Ukraine and they may be also contributing to this economic crime because they have identified this country as one with limited capacity to act against this crime. By means of corruption, they are able to obtain the right to reside and operate within the country.

Countries with high capacity in information technology and low capacity to act against crime committed using computers and telecommunications become havens for transnational crime and terrorism. The concept of a safe haven acquires a different concept when the weapon is not a conventional one but a piece of information technology which allows plotting, financing and possibly even executing a serious crime.

Information Technology is Central to Commission of Organised Crime and Terrorism. Before the advent of widespread information technology, the pace of international communications and transactions was slower. Secure measures of communications required trusted carriers, funds could be moved only slowly and planning across borders was slow and laborious. In the age of information technology, messages can be transmitted instantly without leaving a trace, massive wire fund transfers can occur across multiple jurisdictions in an hour and international plotting can occur within chat rooms and protected communications within a computer system. There has been a movement of money to areas where regulation is less. Even traditional systems of underground banking such as *hawala* or Chinese underground banking have been revolutionalised by the ability to provide almost instantaneous instructions on the delivery of funds.

The criminal and terrorist exploitation of information technology has proceeded in tandem with its growth by the legitimate multinational community. In fact there is evidence that those who seek to promote illicit ends have been as fast if not faster to introduce this technology into their operations. The possibilities of introducing technology rapidly into transnational crime groups and terrorist organisations exists because the most modern organised crime groups and terrorist cells are organised as networks. Unlike the traditional mafia structure or the traditional top down corporation that react slowly to innovation, these new transnational criminal actors enjoy enormous flexibility. They have high level technical specialists within their organisations or employ the top specialists.

Both terrorists and transnational criminal organisations such as Colombian drug traffickers or Russian-speaking organised crime have used the full variety of information technology to achieve their desired results. This includes cell phones, satellite phones, computers, and virtual private networks. The latter are particularly valuable for undetected international operations. Anonymity increases the difficulty of decoding encrypted messages.

Both encryption and anonymisers are increasingly used by transnational crime groups. Once encrypted messages represented a very small share of the communications of transnational crime groups. But the use and the sophistication of the encryption have been increasingly exponentially. Therefore, increasingly messages are staying outside the capacity of law enforcement and the intelligence community to decipher. With the enhanced information gathering in the contemporary era, which law enforcement and intelligence cannot digest, those messages which are encrypted have even less chance of being incorporated into the analysis needed to address these groups.

Private safe, secure and rapid communications are key to the spread of organised and ideologically motivated transnational crime. The anonymity offered by computers in internet cafes and computer services allows criminal groups in many parts of the world to interact. Investigators found that terrorists in the United States used computers as Kinko's, a computer and copy store, to conduct their businesses. In other countries, millions have access to Internet through anonymous computers that sell their services by the hour. Without knowing the identity of those who use the computers and using constantly changing on-line addresses, messages are not traceable. Instant messenger provide the possibility of on-going interactive communication without leaving a trace that investigators can follow Information technology facilitates many aspects of the operation's of transnational crime groups and terrorists from their financing, to the documents that they need for their operations.

The transnational illicit actors are able to produce fraudulent documents on the computer to provide them new identities, covers and to provide a paper trail, which covers their operations. Human smugglers produce high-quality false identity papers for those who need new identities. These computer-produced documents may be of such high quality that their fraudulent nature is not discernable to even sophisticated law enforcement. Computer systems help finance criminal and terrorist operations. The revolution in information technology has facilitated covert banking, more efficient underground banking, electronic fund transfers, and the use of debit and credit cards. Piracy and counterfeiting of goods, facilitated by information technology, is an important financial source for criminal groups. This is particularly true in the software area and other areas involving intellectual property. Criminals and terrorists can commit fraud on the Internet, can solicit banking information from gullible citizens, tap into insufficiently protected banks of credit card information or even tap into the online orders of some mail-order businesses. These are not hypotheticals but examples of the kind of financial activity used by these groups already detected by international law enforcers. The logistics of transnational crime groups and terrorists are aided by information technology. The Internet aids the transport, tracking, monitoring and diversion of shipments. Part of the reason that drug traffickers can respond quickly to law enforcement crackdowns is that they monitor their shipments through elaborate computer systems. Identifying points of vulnerability, they are able to rapidly reroute their shipments to reduce the risk of intervention.

Combing analysis with sophisticated computer programs, Colombian drug traffickers ensure that over sixty to seventy percent of drugs shipped enter the United States successfully. Less covert means can be used by terrorist organisations that use the worldwide web to recruit and fund raise. Sites can be posted and taken down as needed. Therefore, they can reach a broad audience in many regions of the world. Those who are the most likely recruits for terrorist organisations are youthful males who are also the individuals in their countries most likely to have access to computers and the Internet. Therefore, investment in information technology provides a very valuable marketing tool to reach the most receptive audience.

Problems of Cooperation– Domestic and International

Many of the problems that impede transnational crime and terrorist investigations have already been cited. But examining them together reveals the fundamental challenges which exist in this age in which there are such discrepancies available to investigators and intelligence in the developed and developing and transitional worlds. Furthermore, the fact that the ransnational groups have been among those to take most advantage of the globalised information system, highlights the very serious problems that exist in a world where laws are state-based and criminals and terrorists operate across many states simultaneously to carry out their activities.

The presence of so much of the information technology system in private hands and the presence of control over this system lying in state hands provides very serious impediments to regulation and control. The concept of public-private partnerships which exists in the United States is not an internationally recognised concept. It works haltingly in the United States and often proceeds only as an alternative to state intervention in the operations of Internet service providers (ISPs). Cooperation with law enforcement in pursuing purveyors of child pornography on the Internet is a preferential alternative for many ISPs rather than search warrants being issued to have access to their data bank. Much tracking of crime committed over the Internet can be done by American law enforcement because so much Internet traffic is routed through the United States.

But in traffic that does not pass through the U.S., the situation is more difficult. Different legal codes and procedures impede cooperation on the international levels. Many countries lack needed laws to address computer crime and crimes committed by means of information technology. Compounding the problem is that the global information infrastructure is outside the jurisdiction of anyone country. Criminals and terrorists, as previously mentioned, exploit the weaknesses in laws and law enforcement capacity to execute their crimes. These are not casual decisions on how top operate effectively by computers but are instead based on calculations and careful training and analysis.

Future Trends

Over the past years there has been a rise in the use of existing forms of carrying out covert operations by means of information technology. These include ever greater use of encryption, money transfer facilitated by computer system and increasing fraud over the internet. With the retention by top information technology specialists by transnational crime groups and terrorists, we can expect to see new and innovative uses of information technology by these groups. Of greatest concern to many governments and international financial systems is the possibility of serious intrusions into critical systems. These intrusions could include the introduction of viruses that would destroy critical data, the posting of harmful websites that cannot be brought down and even the full scale incapacitation of critical computer systems.

The disruption of international financial markets remains a serious concern. The present interdependence of the world's economic system means that a disruption in one region of the world will have ripple effects in other regions. The constant monitoring of stock, bond and commodity markets by financial analysts world wide means that an intrusion and/or disruption of these systems would not go unnoticed. It would send shock waves outside of the market which is the source of the problem.

Money laundering is increasing with the amount of money outside regulated markets growing. This is a result of the growth of the illicit global economy that is supported by the profusion of offshore havens. The proliferation of information technology increases the possibility of moving money covertly outside of any system of regulated banking. Therefore, the recent crackdowns on the banking sector and The Patriot Act, which has ripple effects in international financial markets, means that illicit and terrorist money may increasingly be pushed outside the regulatory system. Movement of money through tangible commodities, businesses and *hawala* like currency transfers may be ever more possible because of the monitoring and facilitation of computer systems.

One distinct concern is that there will be more successful mergers and/or cooperation between organised criminal and terrorists in the information technology area. Cooperation between organised criminals and terrorists exists in Latin America, Europe, Asia and other regions of the world. Information technology expertise may be commissioned by one type of transnational criminal group and then subsequently exploited by another either for mutual advantage or as a business proposition. Already there is enhanced exploitation of areas with sophisticated information technology and corrupt officials and corrupted and incapable law enforcement.

This means, for example, that members of terrorist organisations can pay corrupt officials to obtain residence permits in a region where there is a high level of IT capacity. Then they can use the Internet resources or even finance their IT outlets and market them as public facilities. Incompetent law enforcement will not think to look at public Internet outlets as havens for terrorists. If they were to detect such a phenomena, they could be bribed to look the other way. In this way terrorists have secured a safe physical space but also a safe space in which to run their operations. Enhanced mobilisation and recruitment for terrorism by the Internet is an existing concern. This mobilisation can be of funds and people. By using steganography, disclosing secret messages within other messages or pictures, communications can be made secretly to a large number of people. Without the linguistic capacity or the intelligence capacity to intervene in these groups, technology can be used to ever greater advantage.

Legitimate civil liberties concerns in many countries may curtail or limit monitoring of information technology. Because most information technology is controlled by the private sector, it is their primary concern to protect their customers rather than to counter transnational crime or terrorism. As cooperative as information technology companies may be, once a risk is defined, their initial interests are to make a profit rather than to prevent a crime or a terrorist act. The constitutional protections existing in countries which now enjoy information technology dominance place a premium on the privacy and rights of citizens. Therefore, the possibilities for information gathering are limited.

Tools to Respond

A strong dichotomy exists between the way states and multinational organisations respond to transnational crime and terrorism generally, and the particular threat posed by cybercrime committed by these groups. Because information technology is primarily in the private sector, public private partnerships are needed to locate abuse of the Internet by transnational criminals. This may include network monitoring by private corporations to detect suspicious websites or usage patterns. The development of international teams of computer specialists incorporating information technology specialists from developing countries with advanced computer skills to work in cooperative ways to monitor transnational crime and terrorism. International cooperation in a mutual process of information sharing is a key response to the problem. There is a need to develop and support international security research teams with specialists from both developed and developing countries. There are a need or partnership relationships in which both parts of the team believe that it is in their interests to respond to any manifestations of transnational crime and terrorism that are evident through investigations of cybercrime. This may include a system of rewards that provide multinational incentives rather than those which are based on the country in which the investigation may occur. The rewards may be too low for the investigators and the chance of corruption may be too great.

There is a need for citizen assistance in identifying problematic and suspicious websites. Citizen support has been particularly valuable in identifying child pornography websites in the United States and in sites that are lures by human traffickers in Russia. In both of these countries, citizen groups have warned of abuses in order that Internet service providers can bring down these websites. This may not be possible in many situations where the citizens have sympathy with the goals and objectives of the terrorists but it can be most effectively done in cases of sexual exploitation, financial fraud on the Internet and potentially in relation to money laundering schemes on the Internet. Penalties should be established for computer specialists who assist in international organised crime and terrorism. Just as the legal system has moved against lawyers and accountants and money launderers who serve criminals and terrorists, there needs to be the ability to readily prosecute the computer facilitators. There needs to be the harmonisation of laws that individuals cannot operate out of safe havens which allow individuals to commit computer crimes without any risk of arrest and prosecution.

Investigations of the information technology component of the crime and the terrorist act must be an integral part of the overall investigation and not exclusively the domain of computer specialists. Coordination among citizens, private corporations, states and multinational organisations is central to addressing cybercrime that facilitates organised crime and terrorism.

Transnational criminals and terrorists have been major beneficiaries of globalisation because they benefit from more open borders, greater international mobility and faster and more secure communications. Although the information technology revolution has provided the opportunities for greater access to information and democratisation of societies, this development has benefited not only legitimate users but those which seek to harm others on the personal and political level. International drug traffickers have exploited information technology to full advantage. They are not alone. Child pornographers and terrorists have exploited to this technology to their enormous advantage. The expansion of international communications in the coming years will require much thinking on the appropriate balance between the protection of national security, the most effective means to protect the integrity of financial markets and of individuals from fraudulent schemes or potential sexual exploitation. The ease and security with which transnational criminals and potential terrorists can transmit information, will provide a challenge in many areas that are not even foreseen at the present time.

Even in countries that do not place a premium on privacy over national interest, like China, they cannot monitor the content of the messages which are communicating over their ever proliferating computer systems within their country. Therefore, the potential for abuse is even higher in societies that place a premium on free exchange of information. The challenges to regulation are formidable. Telecommunications systems are often in private hands. Therefore, their control is outside of state authority. The concept of public-private partnerships is a concept alien to many states where the government is authoritarian, corrupt or infiltrated by organised crime. Compounding the problems is the lack of harmonisation of laws dealing with the regulation of information technology. Even in the presence of laws, many countries do not have the law enforcement capacity or the even the computer equipment to adequately investigate the crime or detect threats to the system. In contrast, in the United

States, there is such formidable data collection from computer systems that analysts are unable to digest the information they possess. Therefore, there is a curious imbalance between the most technologically powerful country in the world that is overwhelmed with information and developing and transitional countries, which cannot seek the information they need. This dichotomy between the most affluent and least affluent countries seen in many other areas of the contemporary world has startling consequences for the all the world. The imbalance between too much information and too little, increases international political, financial and personal security. The full consequences of this will be seen in the coming years.

Putting Cyberterrorism into Context

With the growth of the Internet in both its size and functionality from the 1970s through to the present, we have seen a massive change in both the nature of the threats and the level of malicious attack activity directed against Internet-connected systems. During the last decade, broad sections of government and industry have embraced the Internet as a generally reliable and cost-effective platform for business critical communication and services. During the same period, with increased exposure to and dependence on Internet connectivity and dependent services, government, media and the public have also increasingly given more attention to the potential threat of cyberterrorism to these Internet-connected systems, particularly for the critical information infrastructures of nation states. In this regard, Australia is no different from most affluent and technology dependent nations.

For sometime now (even dating back to the Gulf War in 1991) there has been a heightened level of interest in the potential threat of cyberterrorism coupled with an unhelpful amount of hype and misinformation surrounding the use of the term.

Part of the problem is one of definition - there are broadly different definitions as to what actually constitutes 'cyberterrorism'. There are a number of well-accepted definitions which share common similarities and are outlined below. But increasingly, there are a number of loose definitions which are promulgated to encourage the purchase of particular computer security products or services or to generate interest in a story by the media. If these definitions are not clearly articulated, an uninformed reader/viewer may rely on their own, possibly misinformed, understanding of the nature of the threat of cyberterrorism. As long as the term 'cyberte-rrorism' continues to be used loosely and inconsistently, misinformation and hype associated with the threat will remain.

Before defining 'cyberterrorism' it is necessary to define and understand what we mean by 'terrorism' — afterall there should be similarities between the usage of the terms. The United States' State Department defines terrorism as politically motivated acts of violence against non-combatants. In Australia, the recently enacted Security Legislation Amendment (Terrorism) Act 2002 defines a terrorist act to mean: an action or threat of action where:

(a) the action falls within subsection (2) and does not fall within subsection (2A); and

(b) the action is done or the threat is made with the intention of advancing a political, religious or ideological cause; and

(c) the action is done or the threat is made with the intention of:

  (i) coercing, or influencing by intimidation, the government of the Commonwealth or a State, Territory or foreign country, or of part of a State, Territory or foreign country; or

  (ii) intimidating the public or a section of the public.

(1) Action falls within this subsection if it:

  (a) causes serious harm that is physical harm to a person; or

  (b) causes serious damage to property; or

  (c) causes a person's death; or

  (d) endangers a person's life, other than the life of the person taking the action; or

  (e) creates a serious risk to the health or safety of the public or a section of the public; or

  (f) seriously interferes with, seriously disrupts, or destroys, an electronic system including, but not limited to:

  (i) an information system; or

(ii) a telecommunications system; or

(iii) a financial system; or

(iv) a system used for the delivery of essential government services; or

(v) a system used for, or by, an essential public utility; or

(vi) a system used for, or by, a transport system.

(1A) Action falls within this subsection if it:

(a) is advocacy, protest, dissent or industrial action; and

(b) is not intended:

(i) to cause serious harm that is physical harm to a person; or

(ii) to cause a person's death; or

(iii) to endanger the life of a person, other than the person taking the action; or

(iv) to create a serious risk to the health or safety of the public or a section of the public.

In a study of 109 academic and official definitions of terrorism, three common elements were identified:

- the use of violence
- political objectives
- the purpose of sowing fear within a target population

For cyberterrorism to apply, these same elements should also exist as they do in the following definitions:

1. According to the US Federal Bureau of Investigation:

   Cyberterrorism is any premeditated, politically motivated attack against information, computer systems, computer programs, and data which results in violence against non-combatant targets by sub-national groups or clandestine agents.

2. A definition of cyberterrorism proposed by the US National Infrastructure Protection Center is a criminal act perpetrated by the use of computers and telecommunications capabilities, resulting in violence, destruction and/or disruption of services to create fear by causing confusion and uncertainty within a

given population, with the goal of influencing a government or population to conform to a particular political, social, or ideological agenda.

3. Dorothy Denning defines cyberterrorism as unlawful attacks and threats of attack against computers, networks, and the information stored therein when done to intimidate or coerce a government or its people in furtherance of political or social objectives. Further, to qualify as cyberterrorism, an attack should result in violence against persons or property, or at least cause enough harm to generate fear.
4. James A. Lewis, Centre for Strategic and International Studies (2002) defined cyberterrorism as the use of computer network tools to shut down critical national infrastructures (such as energy, transportation, government operations) or to coerce or intimidate a government or civilian population.

Interestingly, two of the definitions (2 and 4) specify that computer systems or telecommunication cababilities are used to conduct cyberterrorist attacks. The other two definitions (1 and 3) only specify that computer and information systems are the targets of cyberterrorist attacks. Arguably both elements should apply. While an information system can be attacked in any number of ways (eg, conventional methods involving bombing, arson, *etc*), for an act to be classed as *cyber*terrorism, the attacker must use information systems or other electronic means to launch the attack (as applies to the term 'bioterrorism', where the method of attack is a toxic biological agent). Cyberterrorism is but one form of cyber attack. Too often the terms cyberterrorism and cyber attack are used interchangeably and may result in a misunderstanding of the cyber threat in general and the threat of cyberterrorism in particular. These definitions demonstrate that for cyberterrorism to be perpetrated there are at least three elements which must be satisfied in order to distingish a cyberterrorist attack from an ordinary cyber attack. Denning notes that politically motivated cyber attacks that lead to death or bodily injury, explosions, or severe economic loss would be examples of cyberterrorism. Serious attacks against critical infrastructures could be acts of cyberterrorism, depending on their impact. Attacks that disrupt non-essential services or that are mainly a costly nuisance would not. Most cyber attacks in Australia, even 'serious' ones, will be offences under the Commonwealth *Cybercrime Act 2001* or similar State legislation rather than offences under the *Security Legislation Amendment (Terrorism) Act 2002*. To date, there is no known publicly reported incident of cyberterrorism in the world that meets the first three definitions outlined above.

The fourth definition, has been met, but only in so far as there have been several serious cyber attacks against critical information infrastructures but these are not assessed to be politically motivated.

What Cyberterrorism is not

In contrast to the above definitions, cyberterrorism has been used improperly to refer to the use of:

- Encryption technologies for secure electronic storage of data and communication by and between supporters/members of known terrorist groups;
- Various forms of electronic communications (web sites, email *etc*) for the purposes of recruiting supporters, organising and communicating the messages (propaganda) of known terrorist groups;
- The occasional use by known terrorist groups of cyber attack techniques which are incapable of causing bodily harm, fear or serious economic damage; and
- The occurrence of port scans from countries considered to sponsor terrorism or which harbour known terrorist groups.

What is the Threat of Cyberterrorism?

Assessments of the threat of cyberterrorism require an assessment of the intent and capability of attackers to cause fear and/or physical harm through cyber attack techniques. Except perhaps for national security agencies which are tasked with collecting and analysing intelligence about terrorist threats, there are few who are able to comment authoritatively on the intent or capability of known terrorist groups to conduct acts of cyberterrorism. Notwithstanding this, there are however, some factors which are relevant to an assessment of the threat.

Terrorists by and Large are not Innovators

Despite a relatively long history of terrorism, to date terrorists' modus operandi mostly has involved the threat of physical harm; actual maiming or killing of people; and damage to property. In the vast majority of cases, terrorists have used conventional methods which involve the use of affordable, accessible and volatile substances, eg improvised explosive devices or weaponry. Less often non-conventional methods have been used such as the Aum Shinrikyo sarin gas attack on the Tokyo subway in 1995. But through the use of a chemical weapon, Aum Shinrikyo still sought to cause physical harm to a large group of people - necessary for instilling fear within a target population.

Terrorist Attacks on Critical Infrastructures have Used Conventional Methods of Attack

Terrorists have frequently targeted critical infrastructure and sometimes this has been to cause disruption only. For example, during the 1990s, some of the operations planned and conducted by the Provisional Irish Republican Army were assessed to have the primary goal of causing damage and disruption to critical infrastructures while minimising harm to people.

Two examples include the October 1992 week-end bombing of the Square Mile financial district of London. and the planned bombing of six substations of the London power grid in 1997. At other times terrorists have targed critical infrastructures, including critical information infrastructures to maximise disruption in addition to generating fear through deliberate attacks on human life (as occurred with the World Trade Center attacks).

Cyber Attack as a Tool for Terrorism has Limitations and would not be Regarded as the Tool of Choice by most Terrorists

- Uncertainty of attack impact

  A computer network attack on a critical information system such as a Supervisory Control and Data Acquisition (SCADA) system that controls devices which provide essential services such as power or gas, may potentially cause a harmful and unwanted incident that could seriously damage property or endanger lives. This is the essential concern associated with a cyberterrorist attack. While this is a possibility, unless the attacker has an intimate knowledge of the system being targeted then the best an attacker can expect is that the impact will be unknown or unreliable.

Add to this the ability of network operators to manually over ride critical systems in the event of a malfunction or fail safe mechanisms to be triggered, then it is more difficult for an attacker to be certain his actions will achieve the desired result. By contrast, the impact of a conventional attack, on a critical information system or other target, is immediate and unequivocal and would require significantly less knowledge of the inner workings of the system itself.

- Recovery from a cyber attack is likely to be quicker and easier

  A computer network or electronic attack on critical computer control systems, such as SCADA systems, requires the attacker to manipulate data within that system to affect the way the systems being controlled by the attacked system, function. Once a computer network attack has been detected and diagnosed, corrections can usually be made to prevent further damage and compromise to the system itself and to the systems it controls. Recovery from a computer network attack on a critical information system can occur more quickly than a conventional attack - perhaps requiring a reinstall of operating system or other critical applications, back-up files, or additonal network hardening *etc*. By contrast, a conventional attack will usually involve serious physical damage and require the rebuilding of complex pieces of equipment and facilities which is likely to take considerably more time and resources than would be to recover from the system changes due to a cyber attack. If recovery is able to occur quickly then from a terrorist perspective, the attack may be less effective as a means of instilling fear or causing serious damage.

- Plausible deniability

"Plausible deniability" in the context of cyber attacks generally refers to the ability of an attacker to conceal the true source of the attack, ie plausibly deny they did it. But 'plausible deniability' may also extend to the attacked site. In the event a critical service disruption or malfunction occurs due to a cyber attack, without evidence of clear physical damage, operators may plausibly deny the cause of the disruption or malfunction was due to a cyber attack. The detection and correct diagnosis of a cyber attack relies on the examination and analysis of largely hidden computer forensic evidence (assuming it is collected and retained for examination). By contrast, conventional attacks exhibit clear observable physical evidence that an attack took place. Denying it would be more difficult, if not infeasible. Regardless of how successful a cyber attack may prove to be in causing serious disruption to critical services or serious economic damage, without the targeted population being aware that the disruption was the result of a terrorist operation, then the incident loses its ability to generate fear and be an effective tool of terror, and becomes indistinguishable from other prolonged disruptions to essential services that have occurred in Australia and elsewhere.

Vulnerability of Critical Information Aystems to Cyber Attack

Finally, an assessment of the threat of cyberterrorism depends on the extent to which critical information systems are vulnerable to cyber attack. The greater their perceived and actual vulnerability, the more likely a terrorist may consider or experiment with cyber attack and the easier an attack will be. In theory, if the systems are recognised as being critical then the owners and operators of these systems should seek to mitigate the risk by protecting against cyber attacks to these systems - not only from cyber terrorists, but from others who may hold greater intent and capability to conduct attacks, including disgruntled employees or contractors, competitors, or ordinary hackers (attackers), or possibly nation states with identified information warfare programs during times of war.

If critical information infrastructures are being protected to the extent required of a critical system, ie commensurate with the risk, then the opportunities for targeting these systems by terrorists or others *should* theoretically be low. (Admittedly, *"should be"* and *"will be"* are not the same and this assumption may not apply to all critical systems. There have been an increasing number of reports claiming that some SCADA and other critical information systems are vulnerable to cyber attack, but while relevant, is beyond the scope of this current paper).

What is the Threat of other forms of Politically-Motivated Cyber Attacks?

During recent international conflicts or events and particularly since the emergence of the world wide web in the early 90s, politically motivated cyber attack activity or 'hacktivism' has been used as a form of protest around the world. But in comparison to other cyber attacks, it occurs less often. Politically motivated cyber attacks were launched during the Balkans conflict, during globalisation talks and in response to the Bali bombings, to name just a few examples.

Politically motivated cyber attacks, as a form of protest, usually involve web site defacements (with a political message) or some types of denial of service (DoS) attack and are usually conducted by loosely organised hacker groups or individuals, with hacker skills, sympathetic to a particular cause or who align themselves with a particular side in a conflict. For example, the downing of a US spy plane in Chinese airspace, resulted in an increase in attacks from both Chinese and US hackers (mostly web site defacements) who were apparently displeased with 'the other side'.

Another example occurred, in 1997 when a group aligned with the Liberation Tigers of Tamil Elam (LTTE) reportedly swamped Sri Lankan embassies with 800 e-mails a day over a two-week period. The messages read "We are the Internet Black Tigers and we're doing this to disrupt your communications." While the cyber attack was politically motivated, from the outset the attack was incapable of harming people or property or instilling fear into the target population. Its impact was primarily designed to cause disruption to the Sri Lankan embassies' email operations but with alternative forms of electronic communications available to the embassies, in all likelihood, the attack did not have a serious impact on critical lines of communication.

While DoS attacks have been used as form of political protest, they are most effective when the attacker publicly advertises the reason for the attack, eg through virtual-sit-ins which invite participation from ordinary Internet users as a form of political protest. Such attacks are usually symbolic expressions of protest and while they may be illegal are not intended to, or are incapable of causing damage or disruption sufficient to endanger life or cause serious economic damage. Such attacks are likely to continue on an opportunistic basis in response to international and global conflict.

What is the Threat of Common forms of Cyber Attack?

Any organisation with an Internet connection faces a significant threat of cyber attack. The rate of malicious scanning that occurs against networks, the rate of new information about serious computer vulnerabilities and the frequency of reports of serious computer attacks crime demonstrate that the opportunities for attack are numerous as are the number of attackers willing to launch such attacks. The motives for other forms of cyber attack also vary and may range from illicit financial gain, personal use of resources, competitor advantage or malicious damage. Additionally, many attacks are indiscriminate, as attackers are less concerned with who they are attacking rather than launching the attack itself.

Conclusion

The threat of cyber attack for organisations with Internet connections is high. For the most part this threat has little to do with the occurrence of conventional terrorist attacks, increased international tensions or nation state conflicts. Certainly, these events may increase the threat of politically motivated web site defacements or other forms of politically motivated low impact cyber attack, but only slightly. These forms of attack still occur relatively infrequently, despite tumultous events over the last few years, and requires a system to be vulnerable in order for a compromise to succeed. Cyberterrorism, while possible, is assessed to be very unlikely - and indeed, as far as we and others are aware - there have been no reported cases of it which match the above definitions. At present, terrorists seem to prefer the mileage to be gained from conventional methods of attack.

Misuse of the term or a pre-occupation with cyberterrorism as the seeming greatest source of threat may divert attention from addressing other forms of cyber attack which are capable of causing serious harm to organisations and infrastructures and which have occurred far more often and will continue to do so. Our focus should be on preventing serious and harmful cyber attack regardless of who conducts them or what their motives may be. If organisations are taking steps to protect themselves from ordinary cyber attacks of the type that are reported in the media and the *2003 Australian Computer Crime and Security Survey*, then they will be well placed to protecting against all forms of cyber attack.

As a final footnote, the Canberra bushfires earlier this year illustrated how a natural disaster, assessed to be a one in a hundred year event, was able to disrupt and damage critical telecommunications, power, gas, water and sewerage infrastructures, for an extended period of time and affected individuals, businesses, government and organisations that depended on these services. Organisations and businesses should therefore ensure they focus on managing all threats - deliberate, accidental or natural - logical or physical - and implement appropriate security measures to manage that risk. This includes having in place sound disaster recovery or business continuity plans and computer incident response plans.

Cyber Terrorism: Mass Destruction or Mass Disruption?

Just days after the September 11 terrorist attacks the U.S. Federal Bureau of Investigation began warning the public that the potential for future attacks exist, and among the threats was that of cyber terrorism. The concept is not a new one, such attacks have been taking place between Palestinian and Israeli groups, and between U.S. and Chinese sources, in response to political conflicts. And now, in light of new terrorism and cyber exclusions in insurance policies, commercial insurance buyers are wondering how to protect themselves from the potential threat of today's "hacktivists" becoming tomorrow's cyber terrorists, and weapons of mass disruption turning into weapons of mass destruction. Al-Qaida, (the notorious terrorist group formed by Osama bin Laden, has not engaged in computer-based attacks in the past. However, in the wake of the World Trade Center (WTC) attacks, bin Laden has suggested that Al-Qaida has the expertise to use computer technology as a weapon, reports Canada's Office of Critical Infrastructure Protection and Emergency Preparedness (OCIPEP).

In response to reports from the FBI about the potential threat of cyber attacks in the wake of September 11, OCIPEP began issuing such advisories, and notes that "retaliatory cyber attacks" against coalition countries, primarily in the form of website defacements had already begun. In late November, the Canadian government helped draft the Council of Europe's Convention on Cybercrime, an international effort to deal with issues of terrorist financing, money laundering and cyber terrorism. The September 11 terrorist attacks changed perceptions of the world's security infrastructure, and the insurance industry's understanding of risk. What had once been inconceivable was now reality and so began the process of imagining the unimaginable in terms of catastrophic risks. Cyber terrorism, a heretofore unconsidered threat, was suddenly put on the world stage amongst a host of new potential threats.

Digital Pearl Harbour

When the U.S. government's new cyber terrorism expert, Richard Clarke, suggested the possibility of a "digital Pearl Harbor", he was greeted with skepticism. The concept of one, large-scale attack on the Internet seems far-reaching, despite the claims of Al Qaida and other Muslim extremist groups who claim to, or are known to, use the Internet as a tool.

Tensions between the U.S. and China following the accidental bombing of the Chinese Embassy in Belgrade led to a cyber conflict. In the U.S., key government sites, including the Energy Department, the Interior Department and even the White House were targeted. The Chinese domain, ".cn", and that of Taiwan, ".tw", became the two most defaced domains behind ".com" last year. India (.in) and Pakistan (.pk) saw similar increases in the number of web site defacements due to political tensions. Following NATO air attacks on Serbia in 1999, hackers began to tap into U.S. defense computers and those of other defense related businesses. And, since September 11, several high profile U.S. government sites have been defaced, some bearing the Saudi flag and threatening messages aimed at the U.S. The groups involved, sometimes called "cyber mujihadeens", have hit sites including the U.S. Army Waterways Experiment Station and the National Institute of Health's Human Genome Project.

Striking at.ca

Canada is not immune to the cyber threat, experts say. Matai points out that the ".ca" domain experienced a similar increase in defacements last year, with 215 hits, up from 59 in 2000 and 52 in 1999. He notes that many Canadian sites bear the ".com" domain, as well as ".org" and ".net", also popular targets. Hits are similarly not aimed solely at government sites, he adds. "Admittedly there is some bias of attacks towards high profile sites such as whitehouse.gov or fbi.gov, however more and more attacks are on commercial web sites."

"The 11 September attack had an even deeper ripple effect: the temporary disruption of the entire U.S. financial and transportation infrastructure," notes the OCIPEP report. "If the terrorists did not fully anticipate these aftershocks, they can see them clearly now. This raises the possibility that those responsible may shift their sights away from primarily symbolic targets, such as heavily populated buildings or sports stadiums, toward critical infrastructures."

There are about 10,000 "serious grade crackers" using original code attack systems, as opposed to what Matai calls "script-kiddies", or hackers who rely on ready-made tools. "In terms of defacement attacks on large corporations, attackers penetrate the systems as multi-level attacks using subterfuge and social engineering," he explains. Criticisms of lax electronic security are still being heard, despite the growing awareness created by large-scale attacks such as the "I Love You" and "Melissa" viruses, and worms like "Nimda" and "Code Red". Criticisms of lax electronic security are still being heard, despite the growing awareness created by large-scale attacks such as the "I Love You" and "Melissa" viruses, and worms like "Nimda" and "Code Red". "My own opinion is that the potential is there (for cyber terrorists to attack), everyone's networks are so poorly protected, but no one has taken advantage of it," says Chuck Wilmink, director of the Canadian Center for Information Technology Security (CCITS). A study by the U.S.-based Computer Security Institute reports that 85% of companies admit to having their networks breached in 2000, and 64% acknowledge significant financial losses due to those breaches. A recent report by the U.S. Congress gave two-thirds of American's federal agencies failing grades in cyber security, including the departments of Defense, Justice, Energy and Treasury.

Similarly, in Canada, a 1999 Senate report pointed to the potential for a major cyber attack in Canada, and admitted that the FBI has characterised Canada as a "hacker haven". Perhaps fortunately, Canada is more often a base for hackers to attack other countries, rather than a target itself. "Canadian hackers have traditionally tended to attack outside of Canada as opposed to within," says Matai. He notes that Canada's quieter political demeanor means that it is less often viewed as a target. ".ca Canadian sites are less vulnerable than.com or .uk because Canada is not seen to be so aggressive on the world stage." "I really don't think we've ever considered Canada to be at the same threat level (as the U.S.)," says Max London, manager of public affairs for OCIPEP. However, OCIPEP has issued the FBI warnings post-September 11, giving companies advance warning in the event of a cyber attack. Ultimately, London explains, corporations are responsible for their own security systems.

He notes that OCIPEP is aware of "hacktivist" activity in Canada, specifically "around some of the larger meetings", such as the G-8 Summit or World Trade Organisation meetings. However, these are a far cry from the threat by a foreign government or terrorist organisation that might harm Canada's critical infrastructure, including systems that support communications, transportation and services such as health care and finance. With the "increasing dependence and increasing interconnectivity" of such systems comes ă greater risk, however. In the past, OCIPEP has been involved in public awareness campaigns around threats including the "Code Red" worm, which was viewed as "a very real threat to the Internet", and has worked with the U.S. National Infrastructure Protection Center (NIPC), an FBI operation, to disseminate infornation. The NPIC issued warnings in mid-October of a potential cyber threat aimed at the U.S. power grid, and yet another aimed at online financial sites.

Insurer Reaction

Canada's insurers have been jumping into the terrorism risk fray since September 11, trying to understand what exposures they might face in the future. Just as no one predicted the events that represent the largest insurance loss in history, there is fear of what other unforeseen risks may lie ahead. As insurers met through the Insurance Bureau of Canada's (IBC) terrorism task force to discuss the new risk horizon, cyber threats were one possibility on the table, says Anne MacKenzie, assistant vice president, claims technical, at the Dominion of Canada General Insurance Company and a member of the task force. She adds, however, that they did not top the list of concerns for several reasons, including the notion that terrorists generally tend towards visible, high profile acts. "It's usually physical acts of terrorism," she says. "Terrorists like to put the population at fear." OCIPEP also notes that terrorists have traditionally relied on "bombs over bytes" as the weapon of choice.

Cyber terrorism has not dominated discussion of electronic risks, adds Jennifer Soper, assistant vice president, technology, at St. Paul Canada. Most of the talk seems centered around the major viruses that have plagued companies. This is partly because many companies do not see themselves as targets for such acts. "When you're not in the Fortune 500 or brand name companies, you can get an 'it can't happen to me', almost false sense of security." She adds that companies often do not discuss the nature of attacks, and still have a "keep it in the closet" attitude about cyber security breaches. The benefit is that this policy of silence denies attackers the desired result of publicity. However, terrorists may soon find that cyber attacks will gain them the same kind of notoriety as physical attacks, MacKenzie adds. "Nothing would scare people more than to learn that terrorists had hacked into government sites".

Exclusions

Commercial insurance buyers are no doubt facing a tough market in the post-September 11 era, although the situation was already beginning to grow bleak prior to the terrorist attacks. Reinsurers had already stated their intention to introduce cyber exclusions into their treaties, leaving insurers to follow suit.

However, insurers assert that cyber or "data" coverage was never really part of commercial general liability (CGL) policies. In light of the potential for differing interpretations (such as the U.S. case of Ingram v. Micro, where it was found that business interruption due to computer failure should be included in CGL policies), more specific wording was added to most policies. "The data exclusion was just a clarification to make sure consumers knew what they were buying, there never was coverage for data," explains MacKenzie. This clarification is apparent in most policies as of yearend 2001, adds Dominion president George Cooke. "Our view is that the wordings don't do anything the old wordings didn't do, they're just clearer."

However, the wordings have left many companies scrambling for coverage, Soper says. "What is available is not widely available." Companies will either have to negotiate coverage as a limited buy-back option in existing policies, or hunt it down as a separate policy from another carrier. "In terms of coverage, if there is anything going on it is on a customer-by-customer level. It has to be." Given the difficulty in quantifying cyber risks, there is no "one size fits all" policy. Cooke says he is concerned with the lack of cyber coverage available, but acknowledges that insurers simply are not in a position to offer it. "It's a situation that troubles me. But we can't buy coverage [in the reinsurance market], so it's impossible for us to offer it."

September 11 did not help the situation either. He predicts that notwithstanding the terrorist attacks, cyber coverage would have been a top issue for insurers, but given the shift in priorities, insurers were unable to come up with private market capital solutions in advance of yearend commercial policy renewals. "September 11 kind of eclipsed concerns over whether we should be developing new products to deal with cyber risks," says MacKenzie. However, she adds, "we will want to revisit it" in the future.

Overriding Concern

Regardless of new cyber covers, with the current terrorism exclusions being written, any act deemed as "cyber terrorism" would not be covered, as the terrorism exclusion would be overriding. In the wake of September 11, with reinsurers refusing to cover terrorism in their treaties, insurers were forced to either introduce similar exclusions in their policies or to negotiate a deal with the government, which would act as excess of loss reinsurer through a "terrorism pool" arrangement. By yearend, no such pool had been devised, despite lengthy discussions between IBC representatives and the government. "The nature of the discussions evolved as the market evolved," says Cooke, who is also chair of the IBC. "The decision was taken to wait. It was probably a smart decision."

The U.S. government's inability to come to a solution prior to breaking at the end of the year was among the contributing factors. Cooke recognises that it was "politically difficult" for the Canadian government to come forward with a solution before the U.S., given the fact that the situation was not of the same scale here. This situation may change as the U.S. House reconvenes in late January. "People have said that the government wasn't prepared to act, but I don't buy that," he adds. "Minister Peterson and the staff in Finance were seriously engaged in discussions and are prepared to act if the need arises." The need for a solution may not be quite as pressing as originally thought, with renewals moving along despite the lack of a solution, and the fact that many commercial policies on target risks have not yet reached renewal.

However, Cooke still feels a solution is needed. The government has consulted with other associations, most notably the Canadian Bankers Association (CBA), who claim that there is no need for the coverage. "I think they're wrong," Cooke says, but their resistance makes it difficult for insurers to press for a solution. He is most displeased with the view that insurers are looking for a "bail out". "We are not doing an 'Air Canada' here. We're more than prepared to take our pains for our past sins." But without reinsurance coverage in place, it is not economically feasible for insurers to offer the coverage. The terrorism task force was "driven by the sudden recognition that there was now infinite risk and infinite exposure and that wasn't economically sustainable," says MacKenzie. "It [terrorism coverage] isn't anything we could write even if we wanted to." With no cap on the exposure, insurers would be leaving themselves open to unquantifiable risks, a situation that extends into the domain of cyber terrorism. "Putting a box around the exposure" or quantifying the risk is especially difficult with cyber risks, says Soper.. "The 'net is worldwide. It is difficult to know where it (an attack) is going to come from, and how it's going to come."

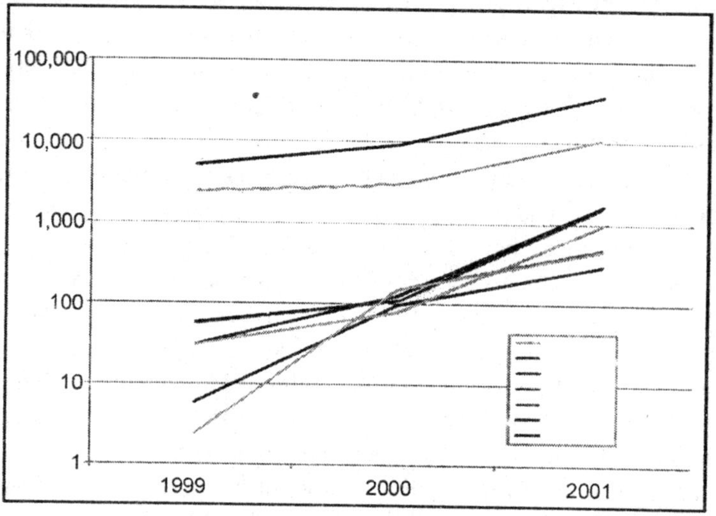

Fig: Global Hot Spots – Defacements by Domain (1999-2001)

She adds, "It's hard when you're an industry that likes to put dollars and cents to things. There's just no history. You can't go into the archives and pluck out something and say 'this is going to work for me today'." September 11 was a "humbling" experience for the industry, says MacKenzie, and as the industry learns more about that event, "we realize we don't know about all the risks".

Table: Web Site Defacements, 2001 (increase over 2000)

Location Incidents	Domain	Number	Percentage Increase
Canada	.ca	215	265
China	.cn	1298	1326
Taiwan	.tw	1355	1178
Israel	.il	413	220
India	.in	250	205
pakistan	.pk	72	300

UK government	.gov.uk	43	378
UK organisations	.org.uk	25	400
UK companies	.co.uk	385	181
US government	.gov.com	248	37
US military	.mil.com	n/a	128

Prior to September 11 "there was a sense that we could talk about 100-year events and worst case scenarios...everyone's trying to come up with scenarios, however, the end of the conversation always comes to the same conclusion, we just can't imagine."

15

Internet Warfare

The inclusion of Terrorism and Internet Warfare within the subject of Internet Crime is testimony to a problem with enormous scope. Furthermore, to look beyond the traditional criminology community for ideas on how to view this issue is also recognition that Internet Crime could be a problem quite different from crimes not manifest in Internetworking. Traditionally the topic of warfare has suggested involvement of military forces and military action. In the consideration of Internet Warfare, the intent of this paper is to be able to apply some military insight into the problem. However, criminology itself is not an area of military business. Where crime and warfare merge is on the aspect of security, it is from this direction that the issue of Terrorism and Internet Warfare will be addressed.

In recent times, particularly since the end of the Cold War, military and strategic analysts have taken broader views of security. Beyond sizes of military forces, their deployment and military deterrence, security planners are now considering other factors such as trade and economy, human rights and refugee movements, racial and religious tensions, environmental issues and sovereignty of natural resources, drug importation, intellectual piracy and the like. The rise of many of these issues is often attributed to factors such as the removal of east-west barriers, the globalisation of economies, and improvements in transportation and communication. The explosive deployment of the Internet is another factor that has the potential to influence security affairs both through its proper use for legitimate activities and as an avenue for terrorism and warfare. The Internet also poses some other unique problems that complicate consideration from a criminological and security viewpoint. The Internet, although physically implemented, creates a virtual rather than physical environment where actors are not constrained by physical location. This virtual environment cannot be readily delineated in accepted geographic or legislative taxonomies. However, military forces are accustomed to operating in four physically defined dimensions and in an international system that recognises nation states and other organisational groups. The military is not well practiced at dealing with entities that operate through a virtual realm and cannot readily apply military influence against objects that defy physical detection or description. Not only does that make it difficult for conventional military forces, but it also poses similar jurisdictional problems for law enforcement authorities.

Consequently, some questions that might have to be asked from time to time are: What is an Internet crime and what is an act of Internet war or a security threat? And noting that in Australia, terrorism is a civil matter for which police forces have responsibility and to which the Australian Defence Forces (ADF) may be called to assist.

Who did it and where? This isn't in jest as it is not only a criminal law issue but also an issue under the Law Of Armed Conflict (LOAC) which applies to military operations. To look at Internet Crime from the aspect of Terrorism and Internet Warfare, this paper will first look at a security framework against which to assess the subject. The paper will then address in turn, cyberterrorism, war against the Internet and war via the Internet. Before concluding, the paper will include a discussion on dealing with this virtually projected problem as a crime or security threat. Thus attacks against the Internet will only be considered from a logical perspective, the paper will not deal with attacks of a physical or electrical nature against the supporting infrastructure.

Changing Notions of Security

As mentioned in the introduction, security thinking is no longer dominated by the concern of defending our shores against the invading armies of another nation. Security thinking can be examined in a number of ways. Mostly they concern a nation's ability to pursue its national interests and to protect and improve the national powers used to pursue those interests. Commonly, national power comprises elements of social, political, diplomatic, economic, technological and military power. These elements, of course, inter-relate and are mutually supporting. A weakening of one element of national power will result in corresponding weaknesses in other elements and conversely, the strength of any one element of national power is dependent upon the strength and support from all the others.

In earlier times, when nations were more isolated, the defence of national boundaries had a significant part to play in the protection of the other elements of national power. However, as nations globalise in many different ways, national interests also tend to become globalised and are no longer cocooned by national boundaries. Consequently, the focus of national security is moving away from national boundaries toward national interests that are increasingly dispersed through the international market-place and economies, international trade routes and international institutions such as the United Nations.

Without suggesting that the role of military forces in national security is reducing, the national security problem is expanding beyond the bounds of traditional military involvement. The many globalising factors mentioned earlier impact upon all the elements of national power and no doubt the Internet is also having a pervasive influence on these elements. Via the Internet all elements of our national power are exposed and hence our national security is vulnerable to attack from the Internet. The elements of national power are exposed to the normal legitimate forces of the global community and market-place as well as those of crime, terrorism and conflict. All of which may use the Internet as a conduit for their activities where feasible.

Cyberterrorism

Until the Information Age, terrorism has been considered to comprise physical acts that have aimed at causing some threat of hurt in which to leverage a desired sanction. This may have involved hostage taking, bomb detonation, threat to the health of the populace or assassination of important personalities. The dawning of the Information Age unfortunately offers new possibilities for the terrorist, particularly in the range of vehicles that he can access to generate terror. Predominantly where a terrorist can access, via the Internet, dangerous forces that may be used to make threats and demands of a terrorist nature. A few examples illustrate the possibilities open to cyberterrorists. Consider where: a terrorist could access, via the Internet, systems which provide for the safety or the welfare of the public. Transport navigation and safety control systems could be malfunctioned to the peril of passengers and the public through collision or failure to operate properly.

Utilities could be interfered with to deny basic services, possibly where they are required in life supporting circumstances. Nationally significant manufacturing facilities could be sabotaged to cause destructive failure and subsequent economic impact. Public administration might be subjected to unrecoverable disruptions and national Financial institutions could be targeted to destitute the nation. All of these could possibly occur where connection to the Internet exists and inadequate protective measures are in place. Popular sentiment of the hacker community is that it is not a matter of what can be hacked but how long it takes to hack. It is through some of these latter examples that the cyberterrorist may now have at his disposal methods of terrorism which might be considered non-lethal if not non-violent, particularly where a cyberterrorist chooses to use economic terrorism methods. This form of terrorism could have insidious effects which cause significant strategic harm to a nation but only evoke insipid responses when life is not directly threatened. A lack of protection or swift response against this type of threat could have severe consequences.

In terms of the extent of cyberterrorism to date, the author is not aware of any reported instances of terrorism via the Internet. This may be because there have been no significant events or because the victims of such attacks do not wish to publicise that they have been subjected to this new form of terrorism. Concerns range from potentially encouraging other would-be cyberterrorists to attempt similar attacks, to alarming the public about the security of targeted institutions and their society. Some parallels to terrorism have been extortion attempts where, for instance, supposed demands have been placed on banks for money in turn Cobb, Dr. A., 'Australia's Vulnerability to

Information Attack', Strategic and Defence Studies Centre, Australian National University, Canberra, 1997.

For immunity from cyber-theft or where offenders have threatened to place compromising photos of super-models onto the Internet. Another aspect of cyberterrorism is the often publicised wealth of information on the Internet on how to construct bombs and the like, and for terrorist groups to recruit and organise themselves via the Internet. But this type of activity is peripheral to the real danger that terrorists could use the Internet to perpetrate their acts of terrorism, to make available to themselves, via the Internet, dangerous forces which could be used for terrorist activities. For Australia, the Sydney 2000 Olympics could provide a period of heightened sensitivity to cyberterrorism and any of the numerous issues of discontent in the domestic, regional or global communities could provide a motive.

Cyberterrorism can be dealt with by prevention and response. Obviously denying would-be terrorists opportunities to access dangerous forces via the Internet should be a priority. However, access denial can require restrictions which impact upon the advantages sought from connecting systems to the Internet in the first place. Dealing with terrorism by response requires an ability to be able to separate the terrorist from the dangerous force, which is the terror object. To do this is problematic both from aspects of time and being sure that the terrorist is properly isolated from the dangerous force. Part of the terrorists gaining access to the dangerous force may have included interference with security mechanisms to ensure future unhindered access.

Internet Warfare: When does the War Begin?

Before embarking upon the subject of Internet Warfare, I want to expand a little more on security as it relates to war. For many the notion of war would suggest the clashing of large military forces as was witnessed in the World Wars or more recently in the Gulf War, or in Guerilla style wars as have been fought in Afghanistan or by the Viet Cong. However, wars may be fought to conclusion with little if any military hostilities. For instance the Cold War, if you exclude the associated proxy wars. We often use the terms trade wars, propaganda wars or phoney wars, take for instance the recent confrontations in the Straits of Taiwan, all of these types of war can have strategic outcomes, if you like there can be winners and losers without bloodshed. The point being made is that the spectrum of war is very broad; it does not necessarily involve the absolute subjugation of one of the parties, but will conclude either when one of the parties is able to extract from the other certain conditions or concessions which were the objective of the conflict, or a stalemate is realised. Therefore, war could possibly take place upon or via the Internet, particularly for rather limited objectives.

However, for the time being large scale wars being fought purely via the Internet can be discounted. There are a variety of reasons for this. Firstly, to totally subjugate another nation would require an enormous undertaking. A nation would not likely cede its sovereignty unless its national power had been all but neutralised. To do this in the information realm would require such extensive domination of information systems that insufficient systems could be used or reclaimed to fight a defence. To achieve such a feat would require wide scale near-simultaneous penetration of national information systems, in turn requiring a massive logical assault backed by incredible intelligence resources. Therefore, any form of Internet Warfare is limited by available resources and by the victim's decision to remain exposed to attack, that his risk-benefit consideration is to remain connected via the Internet to the source of the attack. So with this in mind, any form of Internet Warfare must be necessarily limited, where it might have profound effect is where a belligerent is able to target a small set of information systems which are so critical in function that a small scale attack has such profound effect. When conducted in conjunction with potent military operations, such an attack may determine the outcome of a conflict.

The challenge for the criminology and security communities lies at the lower end of the conflict spectrum in differentiating when an Internet based attack is a crime and when is it an act of war. One theme raised in the introduction is the potential difficulty in recognising whether an act is criminally or politically motivated. There could be some disparity between the motive of the attacker and the perception of the attacked. Where the perpetrator chooses anonymity or covertness in his activities, his activities may, at least initially, be perceived quite differently than the way they were intended. For instance what may have been instigated as a theft for personal gain may have ramifications which evoke security responses, and what may have been intended to damage national power may be responded to as a criminal activity.

This has very similar hallmarks to the problems of handling Low Intensity Conflict where an adversary to a nation conducts destabilising harassment operations that are non-attributable or deniable and may appear to be criminal rather than military in nature. The object being disruption, distraction and difficulty for the attacked. In the case of some Internet based attacks, this will require determination of whether the attack was intended for criminal or strategic purposes, or indeed, whether the consequences of the attack have strategic implications or should be dealt with as an act of crime. To understand the nature of Internet based attacks will require the resources and cooperation of intelligence agencies assessing both criminal and strategic issues. Where attacks are occurring against private sector targets, the cooperation of those entities with each other and the national security architecture is essential. Without such cooperation attacks will go unreported and unnoticed, probably resulting in ineffective responses. As suggested in the introduction there are two ways to view the Internet in Internet Warfare, one is the Internet as a tool of war and the other is the target of a war which shall be dealt with first.

War upon the Internet: Attacking the Internet as a Medium

The Internet has become a very useful medium for a wide variety of activities, to such an extent that in some ways government, business and society may have become to a degree dependent upon it for continuity of function. In other words vulnerable to its failure should it become unavailable for them to use in the way that they have become accustomed.

The classic manner for the Internet to be attacked is to deny it as a service, to effectively shut it down to those over whom you wish to have influence. Now one strength of the Internet is its robustness as a network, that was the very reason for its original design, so how might it be effectively attacked? One such attack was the Internet Worm. Such an attack is not discriminatory, it potentially affects all users: friend, foe or those that may have been until that time neutral. Because of the routing technology and intermeshed nature of the Internet, any discriminatory attack upon the network at large can be circumvented unless a single point of failure can be isolated such as where the target connects to the network. There are a variety of methods of attack that can be used to disrupt a user's Internet services.

A direct penetration of the user's equipment can be undertaken to adversely influence the equipment's performance and such an attack may involve equipment reconfiguration or the installation of malicious code. Other forms of attack can involve saturation of the equipment with unwanted traffic such as ping attacks or mail bombing, otherwise known as spamming. One instance reported in 1997 was against an American Internet Service Provider (ISP) hosting the home page of a group supporting the Basque Separatists.8 The ISP was asked to remove the offending material by Spanish nationalists, but when snubbed the nationalists organised a mass mail bombing of the ISP. The result was that the ISP's equipment was saturated for several days affecting all its clients. Throughout the last year or two there has been a steady stream of publicly reported email bombings having similar consequences.

However, the motivation for these email bombings is rarely if ever reported, to claim that they were warlike or terrorist activities cannot be sustained. Alteration of web pages is another form of attack upon the Internet. Motives for doing so could be financial or to generate adverse publicity. Financially motivated attacks may result in disruption to flow of income to the target business or possibly theft of sales proceeds if the attack could force edirection of transactions away from the intended recipient. Attacks aimed at damaging the credibility or reputation of the target may have impact in a variety of areas. Against a commercial organisation the impact may be felt in the bottom line of the balance sheet but against other organisations the impact could be more political. Agencies of the Government of the United States of America have been the frequent targets of homepage graffiti. To some extent, these types of attack would be regarded as an example of the tall poppy syndrome however, the fact that these types of attack succeeded can be nonetheless very embarrassing. Others whose reputation and strength might be more tenuous could potentially suffer graver consequences. Take for example the attack by East Timorese sympathisers against the homepage of the Indonesian Foreign Affairs Ministry last year.

Although a seemingly trite example, such an attack might strike a chord either in the international diplomatic arena where the issue of East Timor is often raised, or internally in a society that some outsiders consider fragile and not blessed with the abundance of media enjoyed by western nations. The purposes of warfare upon the Internet must by their very nature be limited, causing for the most part inconvenience rather than substantial damage unless the target is very exposed. In any event there are means of avoidance to the problem. These means include various forms of logical security, reducing dependency upon the Internet, having available alternatives and the ability to isolate sensitive business from the Internet. Where Internet Warfare might be more of a concern is when the Internet is used as the avenue of attack against other more sensitive targets and for more far reaching effects.

The Internet for War: The Internet as a Medium for War

When considering the use of the Internet for war, it is worth first considering war in terms of military conflict and how Internet warfare can affect military forces. As many using the Internet could attest, the military forces of the world make significant use of the Internet. Apparently none more so than the armed forces of the United States. The Internet can be used by the military for communications between its units, communications with other government agencies and commercial support organisations. The military can also use the Internet as an information resource. In doing so, military forces may also provide connections between the Internet and their own Intranets. Aside from providing the military forces with access to a very useful tool, it can also leave the military exposed to threats from the Internet.

The military forces can be attacked via the Internet in a number of ways. Firstly, penetration attacks can be launched against their Intranets. These methods can be used to conduct denial of service attacks, to undermine the confidentiality of sensitive data processed via their Intranets and to damage the integrity of the data and processes. The worst types of attack are those, which are not recognised, when intelligence is unknowingly collected, when corruption of data is undetected and where loss of service is attributed to ystem management problems rather than external interference. During such attacks an opponent steals the initiative and gains opportunities to use that initiative with a minimum of resistance. This is the most dangerous situation in any form of competition. Otherwise attacks from the Internet can take the form of war against the military's use of the Internet as discussed in the previous section.

For a military force making heavy use of the Internet, attacks upon military usage can still have a significant impact. Simply observing a military's use of the Internet can provide valuable intelligence. This intelligence can be derived from aggregating and analysing information presented in web pages, public mailing lists and newsgroups. Intelligence can also be gained from interception of email and observing other aspects of military usage. Regardless of the way in which a military force may be attacked from the Internet, a military should not expose itself to such an extent that it would suffer severely if attacked. Military forces should remain capable of operating effectively without access to the Internet and should be capable of protecting their military capabilities from damage from Internet attacks. However, a significant danger is that the military's use of the Internet can be based on business decisions and not those of warfighting, consequently risks of attack may be underestimated and the protection of warfighting capability may be inadequately addressed. In a time of conflict, the risk assessments of peacetime may prove to be totally invalidated, leaving the military inadequately defended from an attacker that is not constrained by accepted peacetime practices.

Actual instances of Internet Warfare against military forces will no doubt be highly classified, therefore, access to details is strictly controlled, public comment is simply not possible. However, the United States armed force's introduction of Computer Emergency Response Teams (CERT) to respond to intrusion of military networks from the Internet have been publicly reported.They experience large numbers of attempts to access their networks, though most are nothing more than attempts to map their networks and gather network information. These 'attacks' fall within the first, preparatory phase of a penetration or hacking attack and do not cause any damage on their own. Reputedly, these attacks are detected and responded to in such a way that they cannot proceed any further. In conventional military analogy they amount to relatively benign intelligence, surveillance and reconnaissance activities, provided they are detected and countered before actual penetration attacks are attempted.

Where military forces are probably more at risk to serious attack from the Internet is through indirect attack upon non-military targets for which the military is highly dependent upon support. Recent trends in the downsising of military forces, the commercialisation of their support and their interaction with other elements of government make military forces part of a larger security collective from which they have less independence of action. Attacks upon other parts of that collective potentially impact upon the military's ability to pursue security objectives. Military forces are highly dependent upon civil communications industries, industrial support and transportation. Military forces are also an instrument of government.

Their employment is influenced by political circumstances, the support of the nation's society and the economic strength of the nation to support the cost of a military force. Recalling the earlier discussion of national power, all the elements of national power are interdependent and attacks upon other elements of national power can affect a nation's military power. However, it should also be remembered that national power can be attacked without having to attack the military power element. As all the elements of national power can be accessed via the Internet, all can be subjected to warfare via the Internet. Possibly the greatest danger to a nation is where it exposes itself widely to attack via the Internet; exposed in such a way that the nation's interests can be attacked directly via the Internet where defences may be totally inadequate. One commonly used term to describe this type of attack is Infrastructure Warfare or Iwar.

This includes attacks upon vital national interests and infrastructure accessible via networks like the Internet. The types of national interests that may be the target of Iwar include: energy, utilities, communications, transportation, government, finance and significant wealth producing industries. The networks binding these national interests and connecting them to their business environment and the society they serve is known as the National Information Infrastructure (NII). The objectives of attack upon the NII and the national interests could be the wholesale disintegration of a society or be limited to economic and trade warfare or some issue of limited strategic interest. A fictional example is the stock exchange attack in Tom Clancy's novel 'Debt of Honour'.

An example is contained in 'Army Stands Up Computer Security Coordination Center'. Both the Defense Information Systems Agency (DISA) and United States Air Force have had CERTs for some time, the latter often refereed to as AFCERT. While seemingly far-fetched, the principle of Clancy's example remains relevant. A welltargeted attack against a nationally sensitive information target could perceivably cause some strategic imbalance that may be used to leverage some other form of conflict. While the ADF, the Australian Federal Police, Customs and Immigration are defending our coast, ports of entry and territories, who is protecting the data highways into and within Australia?

Strategies for the Internet in Conflict

It would not be feasible or desired for government to provide a security organisation solely responsible for the defence of the NII. Much of the NII is not owned by the government and legislative controls limit government activity in that area. Certainly the information realm is not the domain of the traditional security agencies. However, I suggest there are some parallels with traditional security that might point to some options for dealing with Internet warfare. Warning mechanisms are required to understand the range of threats that might be used for attack. Warning mechanisms are also required to detect activity in the approaches if an attack is launched. A range of credible defences is required to discourage any would be attackers or to thwart any attacks that could be launched.

Those that are potential targets of Cyberterrorism and Internet Warfare ought to make themselves immune to, or resilient to such attacks. They should understand their vulnerabilities, respect the problem and develop information assurance plans for the protection of their information assets from attack via the Internet. Simple disconnection from the Internet upon attack may not be an effective countermeasure and may be the outright objective of the attack. Business continuity planning should also be undertaken to deal with the eventualities that the Internet cannot be reliably used or in the event that information assets have been damaged from Internet attack. These potential targets should also monitor their usage of the Internet to understand if they are being, or are to be, subjected to an attack whether criminally, politically or strategically motivated.

As the government cannot monitor the entire NII itself, it must be the responsibility of those operating the NII to defend it appropriately. This of course involves a diverse range of industries and organisations with a variety of capabilities and skills. Some, by the very nature of their business are very conscious of certain classes of threat and protect themselves accordingly. However, would many have addressed the possibility of facing an aggressor with political or strategic objectives rather than criminal? In the United States the problem has been sufficient for President Clinton to issue a decree to establish a Presidential Commission for Critical Infrastructure Protection (PCCIP). Similar, yet less grandiose, initiatives are afoot in Australia to establish a framework for dealing with threats to the Australian NII. Enthusiastic participation by the various sectors involved in the Australian NII will no doubt assist Australia in defence against Cyberterrorism and Internet Warfare. The benefits of broad participation include wider scale monitoring of threats against the NII, cooperative development of defences and an extended forum for the exchange of information and ideas for cyber-defences. Through the proper organisation of NII participants, reasonable defences against Cyberterrorism and Internet Warfare can be attained.

The deployment of the Internet is affecting society in a wide variety of ways including proliferation of new issues in crime and security. As a result of the Internet's influence upon globalisation of nations in the international community, national security is taking on new dimensions. National interests are becoming extra-territorial and all elements of national power are being subjected to influence via the Internet, potentially including influences of crime, terrorism and warfare. As more and more infrastructure becomes dependent upon, or accessible via, the Internet, the possibilities for unwelcome interference in that infrastructure are increasing. Cyberterrorists no longer need to gain physical access to dangerous forces in order to generate a terrorist threat. Protagonists in a conflict can deny the use of the Internet to their opponent thereby putting them at a comparative is advantage, or of more concern they can use the Internet to attack their opponent directly. From a national perspective the military's use of the Internet can be attacked, it can be used as a source of intelligence or it can be used to penetrate and damage military networks. But as the Internet is globalising society and exposing all elements of national power, attacks upon a nation can bypass the military. To defeat a military force an opponent may attack other elements of national power upon which the military is vitally dependent, hence leaving the nation's military forces impotent. However, an attack may be directed at elements of the National Information Infrastructure (NII) directly in pursuit of particular strategic objectives, effectively bypassing the military all together. The key to countering cyberterrorism and Internet Warfare is to curtail dependency upon the Internet, to respect the problem of cyberterrorism and Internet Warfare, plan accordingly and to adequately protect the NII.

The NII, however, does not belong solely within the purview of any one organisation. To attempt to defend the NII in its component parts will be ineffective. Those responsible for operating those parts will not be aware of all the various threats, weaknesses and possible solutions. Another emerging issue is the concern over determining whether an Internet attack is a criminal event or an act of war and responding appropriately. As the two potentially overlap, considerable cooperation will be required between law enforcement and security agencies to determine the extent of the problems and appropriate responses. The problem of protecting the NII was so concerning in the United States of America that President Clinton established the Presidential Commission for Critical Infrastructure Protection. A similar initiative has been established by the Australian Government. Broad participation by those responsible for operating and protecting Australia's NII will ensure the nation has an appropriate response for the emerging threat of cyberterrorism and Internet Warfare.

Nuisance or Crime?

Hacking has multiple meanings and is commonly used to refer to forms of trespass against a computer belonging to another. This brief examines the motives for hacking, in the sense of trespassing against another person's computer. However, this does not match the general criminal definition of hacking-type offences. An intention to commit a serious offence, or to cause harm or inconvenience, lies at the heart of the definition of the more serious computer offences under Australian laws modelled on the *Cybercrime Act 2001* (Cwlth). Accessing data alone is an offence where there is an intent to commit a serious offence. The modification or impairment of data is an offence if accompanied by an intention to cause (or recklessness as to causing) harm or inconvenience. Other offences under this model are based on breach of access restrictions in relation to data. Only in Tasmania is the law framed without reference either to the intention of the hacker, or to access restrictions on the computer being hacked.

Criminal Intent

The requirement in Australian anti-hacking laws for an intent to commit a serious offence, or cause harm or inconvenience, creates a high barrier for the prosecution to prove that a specific hacking incident is criminal. On the other hand, the category of recklessness as to harm or inconvenience caused by hacking invokes a standard of reasonably foreseeable consequences. Those who hack should be aware that, whatever their own intention, the convergence of technology and criminal activity heightens the risk that any hacking activity could become the platform for serious damage over the internet. Some hackers clearly intend to cause serious damage; for others, how far the law extends liability for hacking activity that is taken up and used maliciously by others remains to be seen.

2004 Victim Survey

The 2004 AusCERT computer crime and security survey asked respondents what they thought was the motive for any hacking attack experienced in the survey period. Fifty-one per cent of respondents attributed at least one attack to indiscriminate action. Such attacks occurred simply because they were connected to the internet, making them vulnerable to hackers anywhere, or to automated hacking tools. Forty-one per cent thought that hackers were utilising system resources for personal use. The respondents attributed different motives for various hacking attacks: to demonstrate skill (40%), malicious damage (34%), to anonymise further attacks (26%), financial gain (18%), unknown reason (18%), personal grievance (14%), political hacktivism (9%) and competitor commercial attack (4%).

Motives

The motives for hacking are varied and offenders form a heterogenous group. Grabosky and Smith (1998: 52-53) catalogue possible motives of hackers. They define hacking as unauthorised access to computer systems (hindering the operation or performance of a system or damaging its contents being referred to as vandalism). As they point out, the reasons given by hackers for their actions are likely to be self-serving and should therefore be treated with scepticism. In order to make sense then of the actions of hackers and begin to evaluate their explanations for hacking we must consider the full range of motives that underlie behaviour of this type. These authors cite a number of explanations for hacking that can be divided between those that are more likely and those that are less likely to indicate an intention to commit a serious offence, or to cause harm or inconvenience in accordance with Australian law based on the *Cybercrime Act 2001* (Cwlth) model.

The Act's test of intention for criminal hacking is less readily inferred where the motive is:

- Monetary gain;
- Intellectual challenge;
- Power;
- Self-expression and peer recognition (often focusing on military and other secure targets); and
- Youth, frivolity, mischief or curiosity (unleashing unknown consequences).
- The test of intention for criminal hacking is more readily inferred where the motive is:

- Vengeance and vindictiveness;
- Sttacking the 'system';
- Terrorism;
- Self-justification through minimisation of harm (often ignoring remedial costs, inconvenience, collateral damage and resource waste); and
- 'Testing' computer security.

Kilger et al. (2004) summarise the motivations of hackers (in a general sense) using the acronym MEECES, which is a play on the FBI acronym of MICE (money, ideology, compromise and ego) representing the motives for the commission of espionage offences. MEECES stands for money, entertainment, ego, cause, entrance to social groups and status. While this provides an easy to remember outline of the motivations of hackers, the analysis is constrained to fit the acronym. For example, intellectual curiosity is not given the prominence it should be. Combining the work of Kilger and Grabosky and Smith provides six generic headings that describe the various motivations for hacking. While the motives of money, entertainment, ego, entrance to social groups and justification may be less likely to involve the required specific intent, criminal liability may arise on the basis of recklessness regarding any harm or inconvenience caused. Cause or malice is the final motive in this list and is more inherently criminal. It encompasses the ideas of vengeance, 'attacking the system' and terrorism.

Money

The ways in which money can be raised include: transferring funds electronically (credit card skimming, ATM card and password scams), stealing valuable data, stealing valuable services or capacity (such as for communications or data storage), stealing intellectual property (piracy), extortion, diversion to premium telephone services, fraud and marketing schemes (client lists, email lists, free, linked and subscription site payments). There is increasing evidence of organised criminal activity involving, for example, persons in Russia, Romania and Ukraine.

There has been a convergence of hacking activity performed for monetary gain: in July 2004, employees of an IT service company contracted by the Commonwealth Bank, were alleged to have used bank computing capacity to download, save and reproduce pirated adult pornography; hackers sell email lists to spammers who create backdoors using Trojan horses - infected computers may then be made available as part of a 'bot army' to launch denial of service attacks enabling extortion (online betting services); and in the US, an employee of AOL has been charged with stealing the email subscriber list and selling it to a spammer who then sold it to others (The smoking gun 2004).

Entertainment: Youthful Frivolity, Mischief or Curiosity

In this category are those who hack for personal pleasure. This form of diversion may often be an offshoot of involvement in gaming and code writing. Grabosky and Smith (1998) cite the launching of the Morris worm, which partially disabled the internet, as an example of the result of curiosity leading to unexpected consequences.

Ego: Intellectual Challenge

This category includes those who hack to meet an intellectual challenge. These persons are not necessarily interested in any outside recognition. For hackers with this motivation there is a special challenge to be met in hacking into secure or high profile sites. Simon Vallor, who wrote the ResediB, Admirer and Gokar viruses, claimed he did so 'to see whether I could do it' (Leyden 2003). Vallor was convicted under the *Computer Offences Act* (UK) and sentenced to two years imprisonment. The intellectual challenge is often the motivation of those who create viruses or worms that work on a vulnerability to create a new exploit. In so doing, these hackers provide a platform for others to make malicious use of the exploit. An example is the creation of backdoors in systems that can then be used by spammers and others such as with the Bagle.B worm (Sydney morning herald 2004).

Entrance to Social Groups/status

The stereotypical image of the hacker as a lonely computer geek belies the fact that hackers constitute a well developed but heterogenous community. Some hackers may be motivated by this sense of community obtained through sharing their experiences with others and may hack computers simply to stay in touch with the hacking community. Online communities can be extremely absorbing and not only provide peer recognition, but also the tools to hack through the sharing of knowledge, skills, techniques and technology. Sometimes there is a division among subgroups of hackers and hacking becomes, in itself, a way for these groups to express their rivalry and to compete for supremacy. This has been seen with messages embedded in the code of worms (Kotadia 2004b). The case of David Smith is illustrative of the use of hacking to gain enhanced status in mainstream society. Smith wrote the Melissa worm and later submitted a version for a college thesis (Fuquay 2004). Adrian Lamo broke into the computer systems of major corporations so that he could then offer to fix them for free (Hulme 2003).

Justifications: Minimising Harm, Testing Computer Security, Claim of Right, Vigilantes

Hackers may operate out of a sense of self-justification. They may do this by downplaying the damage caused or their own awareness of the potential for damage to be caused. Others may argue that they were testing a network or computer. A case of this type involved students accessing privileged information in the computer network of Oxford University and then writing up the results in the student magazine. Other cases may involve genuine disputes over ownership of data particularly where a person is moving from one business to another. There are also vigilantes who take it upon themselves to investigate the illegal activities of others. In one example a hacker in Turkey provided information to law enforcement and this was then used to obtain a warrant to search the computer in the United States of a person accessing child pornography (*US v Steiger* 2003 WL 115261 (11th Cir. 2003); *US v Jarrett* 338 F. 3d 339 (Va., 2003)).

Cause/malice: Attacking the System, Vengeance and Vindictiveness, Power, Terrorism

Hackers may be motivated to commit widely distributed attacks on large targets such as have been experienced by Microsoft involving the MSBlast worm which carried an embedded message critical of Microsoft's founder Bill Gates (Kotadia 2004a). Another widely distributed attack targeted the SCO corporation, following its claim to part of the source code for Linux operating software (Moore and Shannon 2003).

Some hackers are motivated by individual grievances leading to attacks on individuals or companies. An example of an individualised attack that lead to widespread harm in the physical world was the hacking of the sewage treatment system in Queensland, which caused raw sewage to be pumped into waterways. The offender was convicted and sentenced to two years imprisonment (Smith et al. 2004). It is increasingly being recognised that web-based illegal activity may be used to finance terrorism. While computer hacking may in the future be used directly to further terrorist aims, this does not appear to have occurred to date. Hacking has the capacity to cause damage, or aggravate damage from other forms of attack. Items that are critical to the national information infrastructure or key utilities involving energy, communication, health and hazardous materials provide obvious targets for malicious hacking.

Importantly, hacking remains a contested concept incorporating, for example, the inherently contradictory values of the so-called 'white hat' and 'black hat' communities, which simplistically equate to 'good' and 'bad' hackers. Sometimes malicious hacking is separately labelled as 'cracking' in order to differentiate it from benign or good hacking. Ultimately, these labels give way to the legal tests laid out for hacking offences, which include recklessness as to the harm or inconvenience that a hacker may cause, thus potentially capturing the well-meaning hacker. It is important to understand the many possible motives for hacking in a general sense because issues of intent and recklessness are at the heart of criminal liability. With this knowledge we can better detect and deal with offending behaviour.

High Tech Crime

The Nature of Hacking

The term 'hacker' has multiple meanings and variously describes a person who explores programmable systems, who is obsessive about programming, who is able to program quickly, or is an expert in a particular program. More generally, it refers to an expert enthusiast, one who enjoys creatively overcoming limitations, or a malicious meddler seeking confidential information (Reymond 1996). Levy (1984) described three generations of hackers, beginning with the programming pioneers of the 1950s and 1960s, followed by those who developed the earliest PCs and then those programmers who developed computer games. Taylor (2000) added a fourth generation - those who illicitly access other people's computers. This is now the common meaning given to computer hacking (PJC 2004). However, because of these overlays of meaning, it is difficult to match the common understanding of what constitutes computer hacking with anti-hacking laws.

Perhaps in view of the ambiguity attached to the term hacking, it is not used in the substantive offence provisions (however, the heading of the Queensland provision does refer to computer hacking and misuse). Relevant offences do not rely on or define the term hacking. In each jurisdiction except Tasmania anti-hacking laws criminalise hacker behaviour by reference to the intention (or recklessness) of the hacker, or instances where restrictions on data access are breached by a hacker.

The Cybercrime Act Model

In 2001, state and Commonwealth laws dealing with computer crime were described as diverse in policy and partial in their application (MCCOC 2001). Since then, greater uniformity has been achieved as New South Wales, Victoria, the Australian Capital Territory and South Australia have implemented laws in terms similar to the Commonwealth Criminal Code provisions inserted by the *Cybercrime Act 2001* (Cwlth). The Northern Territory law is also loosely based on this model.

Importantly, access in itself is not prohibited. and an intention to obtain a benefit or advantage is not sufficient to constitute an offence, except for section 276B in the Northern Territory. In this scheme there has been a deliberate choice to peg criminal liability at four levels based on the defendant's intent or the way access to data is secured on a computer. It should be noted that the standard of criminal responsibility for the creators of viruses and worms under the *Cybercrime Act* model is set quite high and that this in itself reflects the tension inherent in seeking to adequately deal with malicious applications while allowing for the lawful use of the internet. The four levels are:

Level 1

Accessing data or impairing an electronic communication if this is done with the intention to commit a serious offence (defined as an offence with a maximum penalty of at least five years). In the Northern Territory the intention required is to cause loss or damage or to gain a benefit or advantage.

Level 2

Impairing or modifying data, or impairing electronic communications, if done with the intent to cause (or with recklessness to) harm or inconvenience.

Level 3

Possession, control, production or supply of data with the intent to commit any of the above computer offences. Recklessness is not sufficient. This type of offence may be very difficult to prove in relation to the unexpected consequences of the release of a virus, such as occurred with the Melissa virus (Ling 2000).

Level 4

Accessing data that is subject to an access control restriction (Commonwealth, ACT, NSW, Victoria).

Other Laws

The remaining three jurisdictions of Western Australia, Queensland and Tasmania have quite different laws to regulate hacking offences.

Western Australia

In Western Australia, section 440A of the *Criminal Code* was introduced in 1990 under the heading 'unlawful operation of a computer system'. The section refers to a person who 'without authorisation' accesses 'information stored in a restricted access system' or who 'operates' such a system 'in some other way'. A restricted access system is defined as a computer system or a part or application of a computer system that is accessible only through the use of a code that is withheld by the person in control of the computer system or made available on a restricted basis. This provision is particularly suited to the situation of someone hacking a computer from outside but leaves considerable difficulty in determining when initially authorised access becomes unauthorised either by exceeding initial permissions or by the subsequent use of data or information accessed.

Queensland

The Queensland law introduced in 1997 uses the heading 'computer hacking and misuse' but the offence is defined as the use of a restricted computer without the consent of the computer's controller. A restricted computer is defined as one that requires a 'device, code or sequence of electronic impulses' to gain access. There is a penalty scale of two, five or 10 years maximum term of imprisonment depending on whether (1) an offender simply uses a computer, (2) causes detriment or damage, or gains or intends to gain a benefit, or (3) the detriment, damage or gain is valued at more than $5,000.

Tasmania

The Tasmanian law follows the recommendations of Gibbs (1988). MCCOC (2001) noted that Gibbs addressed the protection of data stored on Commonwealth computers. The Tasmanian law requires intention and a lack of 'lawful excuse', in relation to damaging (or destroying, erasing or altering) computer data or simply accessing a computer or system of computers without authority. This formulation gives rise to uncertainty whether a person has a 'lawful excuse', which is not further defined. MCCOC (2001) argued that this formulation over-criminalises behaviour because of the breadth of the concepts of 'lawful use', 'access' and what constitutes a 'computer'. It is suggested, for example, that for one student to borrow the calculator of another student without permission would constitute unlawful use.

General Issues

Hacking incorporates two quite distinct concepts of acting 'without authorisation' and of acting 'illegally'.

Access

An initial problem is that of defining 'access'. As Kerr (2003) puts it, no one knows what it means to 'access' a computer.

'Unauthorised'

Determining whether a hack is authorised or not is not straightforward and may involve detailed consideration of whether a computer owner has any data access policy, whether and how that policy is communicated to others, how accessible a computer is, and how accessible are the files, directories and other information on that computer. There may be questions of contractual or moral rights, or of implied consent, or the limits of a consent once given. A dominant characteristic of modern computing is the interconnection of devices via local area networks (LANs) and global connectivity via the world wide web. Sorting out legitimate from illegitimate use of encryption, trademarks in metatags, bulk spam, anonymity and disguised identity has been seen as particularly problematic (MCCOC 2001).

The use of 'cookies' is an example of how the internet is itself based on the free exchange of data between computers and where the vagueness of standards for internet behaviour can be exploited. A cookie is a piece of data inserted by one computer on another so that the first computer can 'recognise' that other computer on a subsequent occasion. However, cookies can also be used to track, monitor and report on other internet activity conducted on the second computer. A cookie with this capacity is sometimes referred to as spyware. Spyware is relatively common and someone surfing the net may not realise, in agreeing to the terms of a download, that they are agreeing to such a cookie being placed on their computer (Barrett 2002). In the US and Australia it has been proposed to require consent for the insertion of such software (BBC 2004).

Privacy

In the Northern Territory there is an offence of unlawfully obtaining confidential information. Otherwise, Australian anti-computer hacking laws are concerned with computer security rather than issues of privacy. Where unauthorised access to data that are subject to access control is prohibited, but the relaying of confidential information gained through authorised access is not.

Computer

The laws in Queensland, Tasmania and Western Australia specifically refer to systems or networks of computers within the definition of computer. While the other jurisdictions refer to a computer, under the *Cybercrime Act* model, 'computer' is not defined. The use of digital technology in everyday machines and appliances is ubiquitous and the ordinary meaning of computer must be applied. An individual computer may or may not be connected to other computers and an increasing array of devices are capable of being connected either physically or using wireless technology. Interconnected computers can be hacked internally or externally and the world wide web itself might be considered to be a single computer (MCCOC 2001). Computers that are not connected to other computers nevertheless can be 'hacked' by someone directly accessing that computer.

Given the interconnectivity of the internet and the jurisdictional complications that flow from different laws in relation to this type of offending, there is a clear need to continue the process of harmonising anti-hacking laws in Australia. The *Cybercrime Act* model has now been adopted in the majority of states and territories and should be considered for adoption in the remaining three states.

Hacking Techniques

Criminal Hacking

Hacking has a number of meanings and in common use refers to gaining access to another person's computer. Australia's cybercrime model legislation prohibits causing unauthorised access to data on a computer, where this is done with the intent to either commit a serious crime, or to cause harm or inconvenience. Special meaning is given to the word 'access' which is defined as 'execution of a function of a computer'. This captures direct or remote use without any physical contact with an individual computer or its components. It includes viewing files, as the computer is required to execute a function to make data viewable. Associated offences are: impairing electronic communications; possessing data with intent; impairing data; and accessing restricted data.

This section examines the nature of hacking techniques, not to inform potential offenders, but to assist in law enforcement and preventive activities by alerting computer users to the security measures they need to employ to resist the intrusions of hackers. Not even a fraction of hacking incidents can be investigated, let alone prosecuted. Computer security therefore depends on all users being aware of the risks and taking responsible action to avoid these risks. Some of the distinct ways in which a computer may come to be under attack are: from within, by a person with physical access to a computer; from outside, by a person targeting a specific computer or any vulnerable computers on an intranet or across the internet; and from outside, in an automated process spread from computer to computer.

The Hacker's Target: Networked or not

The level of connectivity of a computer determines the ways in which a hacker can gain access to that computer. A hacker may use an input device for a specific computer (such as a keyboard). If a computer is connected to other computers by a local area network (LAN) or to the internet, then the hacker may be able to gain access to that computer over the LAN or via the internet. New technology creates new opportunities for hacking and hackers can also gain access to wireless computers or networks by intercepting the signals used to communicate between one device and another. At present this involves interception of telecommunications, which may be illegal if carried out without authorisation.

The Hacker's Base

A hacker may operate from more than one computer, using a personal home computer, publicly accessible internet cafes, large computer networks accessed through work or study, or remotely infected computers. For the hacker, a degree of anonymity can be secured through the use of encryption, by the use of email accounts that do not require user identification, and by routeing messages through proxy servers.

In a recent US case an AOL employee was charged with using the identification codes of a colleague to steal the AOL subscriber list of 92?million screen names in 2003. The list is alleged to have initially been sold to a spammer who resold a version for US$52,000 (The smoking gun 2004). In the 2004 AusCERT computer crime and security survey, 67?per cent of respondents said they had experienced at least one electronic attack that 'harmed the confidentiality, integrity or availability of network data or systems'. When asked about the source of attacks, 88 per cent of respondents identified at least one attack as coming from an external source and 36 per cent of respondents identified at least one attack as coming from an internal source.

Sometimes vital information about a system can be obtained from people with privileged access using 'social engineering'. For example, a hacker pretends to be another person with privileged access and rings up the IT help desk or another privileged user to obtain information in a 'crisis' or 'as a favour'. In some circumstances, a computer may not be physically secured from use by members of the public and portable items such as laptops are easily targeted. In some cases the privileged user becomes a hacker.

Vulnerabilities and Exploits

Most computer programs balance functionality with security and contain vulnerable points. A vulnerability can be used by a hacker to enter, damage or control an affected computer. The software created to make use of a vulnerability is called an exploit. When a vulnerability is discovered it may be reported publicly. A software developer or an anti-virus company may not report it until a patch has been prepared so that the fix is available at the same time the vulnerability is announced. There is an opportunity for the vulnerability to be exploited using malicious code between the announcement of a vulnerability and when individual computer users update their own computer operating system or anti-viral software. Hackers may also reverse engineer a patch to make new exploits that work around the patch (Ward 2004). The time in which malicious code can be written and distributed to exploit a vulnerability appears to be decreasing dramatically.

Schneier (2004) reports that the 'Witty worm' infected and destroyed the worldwide population of some 12,000 vulnerable machines within 45 minutes of its launch, which took place within about 36 hours of the announcement of the vulnerability. An attack of this nature leaves too little time for the development of a patch, let alone its installation on vulnerable machines. The situation is complicated further if the software developer restricts the availability of patches to those who can show that they are running authorised versions of the software product. In such instances a population of vulnerable machines will remain unprotected.

The Hacker's Toolkit

The hacker has available a range of digital tools, not all of which are illegal and many of which are automated. These tools can be loosely categorised in terms of the degree to which they intrude into the operation of another computer. Put simply, software may be used by a hacker to enter, damage or control another computer. The range of tools, from the least intrusive to the most, are used to scan, spy, insert data, manipulate data and cause a computer to launch an attack on another computer.

The following are examples of possible techniques: probing computers and systems by 'pinging' or sending out messages that identify computers that are online, and then scanning these computers for open portals; infringing security by using password sniffer programs, password cracking programs, or keyboard logging programs to reveal passwords and other information; creating backdoors once an open portal is found and then using software to keep it open and to make it accessible to other computers over a network or the internet; inserting code into computers such as spyware programs, which report activity on the target computer; malware is used to execute malicious code such as worms (self-replicating pieces of code that transmit themselves once released without requiring any further human intervention) or viruses (self-replicating pieces of code that are disguised as, or attached to, another application and that become activated when a person tries to open what typically appears to be an email attachment); remotely controlling other computers to affect internal data or operations:

'Trojan horses' are a form of code that once activated on a target computer, enable that computer to be commandeered to perform a pre-determined operation or to be actively controlled to perform operations in real time; remotely controlling a computer to affect other computers, such as in a distributed denial of service attack where literally thousands of remotely controlled computers (bot armies) are made to bombard another computer or service causing it to be overloaded and degrade or fail; and intercepting wireless data transmissions.

Establishing Liability

Given the definition of hacking offences, a number of the activities of hackers will not be captured. A key question is whether or not the entry into another computer was authorised (Kerr 2003). In addition, the attack needs to be properly characterised as being on data rather than, say, a server, while the capacity of a computer to handle high volume traffic may be at issue. There may also be the problem of proving a successful exploit attack, which by its very definition causes failure (Barrett 2004). Accessing a computer remotely involves a gap in time from when the hacker launched an application to the point that it executes a function on the computer of another and in the virtual world of computing it is often difficult to pinpoint where and when a particular action occurs.

Despite these problems, evidence of intent may be shown by the hacker's actions overall. Snooping around inside someone's computer (either by directly accessing it, or remotely accessing it, or by using automated spyware) may or may not be accompanied by malicious intent. Such intent is more readily identified in cases involving vandalising or corrupting data, stealing data, remotely controlling a computer to effect commands on that computer, remotely controlling a computer to launch attacks on other computers, or launching malware such as viruses, worms or Trojan horses over a network. The intent element may also prove difficult in relation to a virus or other code that is created by one person but launched by another, or in relation to unintended recipients of code that is self-replicating. Launching a so-called 'good' virus which patched a vulnerability could be classed as illegal in WA, Tasmania and Queensland. In the other Australian jurisdictions this would not be an offence unless it could be shown that there was, in fact, an intent to cau se harm or inconvenience, or the hacker was reckless as to that occurring. Where a person is engaged in testing a system to discover any vulnerability, this would not be a defence unless the testing was specifically authorised by a person responsible for the computer network being tested. If the testing is unauthorised, then while the prosecution might not be able to prove the intent to commit a serious offence, or to cause harm or inconvenience, the hacker is likely to be liable on the basis of recklessness to the possibility of causing harm or inconvenience.

Many of the sophisticated tools used in hacking are now widely available as easy to use tools. In addition, the authors of worms and viruses may post their work on the internet without necessarily intending to release harmful code themselves. The code may, however, be taken up by others (sometimes referred to as 'script kiddies') who, although unable to write the worm or virus, are able to create a vehicle to launch it to attack other computers.

Target Hardening

Hacking is an intractable problem of the internet. While governments need to address this problem through law enforcement agencies, perhaps the best form of protection is prevention. Computer users should be aware that they have a common responsibility to maintain the security of their own computer and make sure that it is not hacked or becomes a vehicle for hacking attacks on other computers. All legitimate users of the internet must share in the effort in target hardening. The security of all computers depends on a combination of measures: considering the physical security of a computer, isolating strategic components from internet connections, using internal firewalls, maintaining and updating anti-virus software, updating operating system components, treating all suspicious or unsolicited email with caution and remembering the human element in the overall maintenance of security.

The Future of CyberTerrorism

The definition of "terrorism" has been well studied, defined, and documented. There is also a degree of understanding of the meanings of *CyberTerrorism*, either from the popular media, other secondary sources, or personal experience. This paper examines the future of CyberTerrorism - a term the author coined a decade ago, as the indicia of technological dependence and frailty were forming in our New World disOrder. Indeed, that future has come to fruition, today. The face of terrorism is changing. While the motivations remain the same, we are now facing new and unfamiliar weapons. The intelligence systems, tactics, security procedures and equipment that were once expected to protect people, systems, and nations, are powerless against this new, and very devastating weapon. Moreover, the methods of counter-terrorism that our world's specialists have honed over the years are ineffectual against this enemy. Because, this enemy does not attack us with truckloads of explosives, nor with briefcases of Sarin gas, nor with dynamite strapped to the bodies of fanatics. This enemy attacks us with one's and zero's, at a place we are most vulnerable: the point at which the *physical* and *virtual* worlds converge. Let us first define theses two domains.

The Physical World

The physical world is matter and energy - light, dark, hot and cold, all physical matter - that place in which we live and function.

The Virtual World

The virtual world is symbolic - true, false, binary, metaphoric representations of information - that place in which computer programs function and data moves. The physical and virtual worlds are inherently disparate worlds. It is now the intersection, the convergence, of these two worlds that forms the vehicle of CyberTerrorism, the new weapon that we face.

Reliance and Dependence

This convergence of the physical and virtual worlds, this lattice, is growing larger and more complex as we venture further into technological dependence. Each day, we move ahead with blinding speed into the computerisation of every task and process that we face. We are becoming ever more inextricably reliant and dependent on the convergence of these two worlds.

Points of Convergence What are some of the more obvious points of convergence?

- A garage door opener.
- A heart pacemaker.
- The computer chip in a late model car.
- A microwave oven.

These are all things taken for granted. Yet, as we progress into a far more technological world, what other points of convergence are taken for granted?

- Food processing plants
- Pharmaceutical processing plants
- Electric and natural gas utilities
- Train crossings and traffic control systems
- Next generation air traffic control systems
- Virtually all modern military equipment
- Military and public safety communications
- Civilian communications

Convergence Drivers

What is driving the convergence of these two worlds? There are three goals:

1. **Access**: the goal of universal, ubiquitous interface;
2. **Control**: the goal of remote administration; and
3. **Mining**: the goal of knowledge acquisition.

Convergence Vehicles

To achieve these goals, there are four vehicles:

- **Transmission**: longer lines across land and through space;
- **Connections**: more links to more points;

- **Aggregation**: more information centralised, and disconnected information linked; and
- **Retrieval**: more ways of retrieving information, and more importantly, knowledge.

Achieving CyberTerrorist Goals

So how does a CyberTerrorist achieve his mission? Like any terrorist, a CyberTerrorist actively exploits the goals of the target population in areas in which they take for granted. There are three potential acts in CyberTerrorism at the point of convergence:

- Destruction;
- Alteration; and
- Acquisition and retransmission (these are a unit).

As we will see, these three types of acts are most heinous at the point where the physical and virtual worlds converge. To achieve a true terrorist goal, as we know, we must have *scale* and *publicity*. So how does the CyberTerrorist approach a new age - an age of convergence of the physical and virtual worlds? An age where, thanks to our goals, he can perform his CyberTerrorist acts from his living room, undetected, from 8,000 kilometers away?

Cracker or Cyber Terrorist?

A great deal of "cracks" are committed for the purposes of anarchy, humor, or as often stated by the perpetrators, "to be annoying." However, is this the mindset of a CyberTerrorist? Does the CyberTerrorist make a garage door go up and down? Does he change an Internet web site to say a country's government is evil? Does he hack into a major corporation's voice mail system to make long distance calls?

No - that is not the domain of the CyberTerrorist - that is the domain of the amateur cracker community that exists worldwide. A CyberTerrorist's mindset is quite different. A CyberTerrorist would not alter a voice mail, or even abuse credit cards.

Potential CyberTerrorist Acts

Let us examine some example CyberTerrorist acts. Based on the definitions of terrorism, a determination can be made if they in fact constitute terrorism:

- A CyberTerrorist will remotely access the processing control systems of a cereal manufacturer, change the levels of iron supplement, and sicken and kill the children of a nation enjoying their food. That CyberTerrorist will then perform similar remote alterations at a processor of infant formula. The key: the CyberTerrorist does not have to be at the factory to execute these acts.
- A CyberTerrorist will place a number of computerised bombs around a city, all simultaneously transmitting unique numeric patterns, each bomb receiving each other's pattern. If bomb one stops transmitting, all the bombs detonate simultaneously. The keys: 1) the CyberTerrorist does not have to be strapped to any of these bombs; 2) no large truck is required; 3) the number of bombs and urban dispersion are extensive; 4) the encrypted patterns cannot be predicted and matched through alternate transmission; and 5) the number of bombs prevents disarming them all simultaneously. The bombs *will* detonate.
- A CyberTerrorist will disrupt the banks, the international financial transactions, the stock exchanges. The key: the people of a country will lose all confidence in the economic system. Would a CyberTerrorist attempt to gain entry to the Federal Reserve building or equivalent? Unlikely, since arrest would be immediate. Furthermore, a large truck pulling along side the building would be noticed. However, in the case of the CyberTerrorist, the perpetrator is sitting on another continent while a nation's economic systems grind to a halt. Desta-bilisation *will* be achieved.
- A CyberTerrorist will attack the next generation of air traffic control systems, and collide two large civilian aircraft. This is a realistic scenario, since the CyberTerrorist will also crack the aircraft's in-cockpit sensors. Much of the same can be done to the rail lines.
- A CyberTerrorist will remotely alter the formulas of medication at pharmaceutical manufacturers. The potential loss of life is unfathomable.

- The CyberTerrorist may then decide to remotely change the pressure in the gas lines, causing a valve failure, and a block of a sleepy suburb detonates and burns. Likewise, the electrical grid is becoming steadily more vulnerable.

In effect, the CyberTerrorist will make certain that the population of a nation will not be able to eat, to drink, to move, or to live. In addition, the people charged with the protection of their nation will not have warning, and will not be able to shut down the terrorist, since that CyberTerrorist is most likely on the other side of the world. Sadly, these examples are not science fiction. All of these scenarios can be executed today. As you may know, some of these incidents already have occurred in various nations. More of such acts will take place tomorrow. Are you prepared?

CyberTerrorists: Who, Where, and Why?

The purpose of this paper is to help you understand the threats that exist, and hopefully, to help you prevent these types of atrocities. But know this - there are people out there with very different goals, who are our real threats, and who are, or will be, attacking us. Make no mistake, *the threats are real, today.* Who are the Cyber Terrorists? There a great many poor movies and too many works of fiction about the hacker and cracker communities. In the popular media, there recently was the Kevin Mitnick incident, where one cracker broke into another cracker's systems. This spawned endless press and at least two best selling books. While this incident received much attention, the events amounted to meaningless children's games.

By and large, the cracker community, based primarily in the United States, Europe, the Middle East, Asia, and in the nations of the former Soviet Union, is composed of individuals who see the cracking process merely as a challenge, a brain teaser, a puzzle. They view themselves as not only being innocent of any crime, but perhaps even doing something righteous, something to counter the dark monoliths of the corporate and government worlds. They believe they are being persecuted. These individuals believe that what they are doing is not doing any true damage. At its least harmful, these crackers just look at information. However, privacy issues and military secrecy can render such infiltrations acts of terror. Sometimes crackers make minor changes, just for fun, to be annoying, or to make a statement. The potential for damage here is enormous.

Crackers as Facilitators

Individuals with a background in intelligence are aware that a frequent element of case execution is enlisting the indigenous, sometimes called "facilitators," to assist in a campaign. At the convergence of the physical and virtual worlds, the indigenous are the crackers. There is the incorrect assumption in the cracking community that they, the crackers, are so sophisticated or so knowledgeable as to know when they are being approached for a truly illicit reason (*e.g.*, to be enlisted as a facilitator to commit an act of terrorism). However, despite cracker arrogance, these individuals are easy targets for enlistment.

What about those crackers who actively *wish* to cross the line, or more basically, need money? To a teenager, a $1,000 U.S. can purchase a good many compact disks, a new modem, and a great deal of libation. Beyond youths, there are professionals in this arena as well. Historically, individuals engaged in the practice of terror tended not to be people working upon a computer 20 hours per day. Terrorists have not been in the business of tracking the latest holes found in UNIX or an obscure government telnet opportunity. There *are* people, however, who are in that business - for illicit as well as good cause. As stated, just as indigenous people may be turned into soldiers, so can crackers be turned into CyberTerrorists. Sometimes such a transition may be motivated by money or prestige. Usually, this transition will occur without the cracker's cognizance. The potential threat from such transitions is mind boggling, considering the damage even one mis-directed cracker can cause.

Further, as young, educated people are brought into the folds of terrorist groups, this new generation will have the talent to execute the acts of CyberTerrorism of which we have spoken. We are going to see increasing levels of in-house expertise, and concomitant exponential increases CyberTerrorism. Unlike other methods of terrorism, CyberTerrorism is safe and profitable, and difficult to counter without the right expertise and understanding of the CyberTerrorist's mind. Combine our increasing vulnerability, with the explosive increases in the level of violence, and increasing expertise available inside terrorist organisations through new blood and outside through facilitators, and we can see that at the point where the physical and virtual worlds converge, the old models of managing terrorism are obsolete.

Methods of Protection: No Easy Answers

We must consider the following elements when building a counter-CyberTerrorist program:

- We must accept that while the theories of terrorism stand true, the way in which we approach counter-terrorism, in this case, counter-CyberTerrorism, must change.
- We must cooperate and share intelligence in ways we have never have before.
- We must enlist the assistance of those individuals who understand the weapons we are facing and have experienced fighting these wars.
- We must learn the new rules, the new technologies, and the new players.

Unfortunately, one cannot learn how to fight this very unconventional warfare from someone who hasn't been there, nor from someone whose experience is in the old ways and old technologies. The old data processing, auditing, and computer security models in use today are obsolete. On this battlefield, against this weapon, the terrorist is already far ahead. The building of a counter-CyberTerrorist team *must* be real-time and dynamic, as the weapons will continually change, to morph, in an attempt to beat you, your systems, and your people. There is no re-machining, and unlike other terrorists, if the Cyberterrorist loses today, he does not die - he learns what did not work, and will use that information against you tomorrow.

If a computer security advisor states that you, your organisation, and your country are safe behind firewalls, behind a system put into place by people who have never fought cyberbattles, behind audit trails, passwords, and encryption, then a great and dangerous fallacy (or fantasy) is being perpetrated upon you. The only solution is the quick deployment of a counter-CyberTerrorist - someone who knows what you are up against today, someone who lives in the world of the people who are, and will be, attacking - someone who can train the people who must fight the battles.

Ex Post Facto

An effective auditing system will only inform the target manager that they have taken a hit; perhaps a fatal hit. By that point, it is too late. *Now* is the time to take action. Unfortunately, due to this open nature of this document, specific counter-CyberTerrorism measures cannot be discussed. Those discussions must be reserved for secured facilities. Counter-terrorists of all backgrounds are duty-bound to save property, and more importantly, save lives. However, we are not isolated. We are all increasingly connected, dependent, and vulnerable. The very basic things we take for granted (*e.g.*, food, medicine, energy, air, freedom of movement, communications, freedom from violence) are being threatened by the new weapon of CyberTerrorism. If we do not work together, *we* will be responsible for the outcome. If we fail to be ready when and where the virtual and physical worlds converge, then all that will be left is terror in one's and zero's.

CYBER TERRORISM AND ITS SOLUTIONS: AN INDIAN PERSPECTIVE

Cyber terrorism is a catastrophic phenomenon that has not yet attracted the attention of the Indian Legislature. The law in this regard is not sufficient and the problem of cyber terrorism can be tackled properly either by making a separate law in this regard or by making suitable amendments in the already existing Information Technology Act, 2000. In the absence of the political and legislative will to fill in this lacuna, the judiciary has to play a proactive role and construe the provisions of existing laws in a liberal and purposive manner.

The traditional concepts and methods of terrorism have taken new dimensions, which are more destructive and deadly in nature. In the age of information technology the terrorists have acquired an expertise to produce the most deadly combination of weapons and technology, which if not properly safeguarded in due course of time, will take its own toll. The damage so produced would be almost irreversible and most catastrophic in nature. In short, we are facing the worst form of terrorism popularly known as "Cyber Terrorism". The expression "cyber terrorism" includes an intentional negative and harmful use of the information technology for producing destructive and harmful effects to the property, whether tangible or intangible, of others. For instance, hacking of a computer system and then deleting the useful and valuable business information of the rival competitor is a part and parcel of cyber terrorism.

The definition of "cyber terrorism" cannot be made exhaustive as the nature of crime is such that it must be left to be inclusive in nature. The nature of "cyberspace" is such that new methods and technologies are invented regularly; hence it is not advisable to put the definition in a straightjacket formula or pigeons hole. In fact, the first effort of the Courts should be to interpret the definition as liberally as possible so that the menace of cyber terrorism can be tackled stringently and with a punitive hand. The law dealing with cyber terrorism is, however, not adequate to meet the precarious intentions of these cyber terrorists and requires a rejuvenation in the light and context of the latest developments all over the world.

The laws of India have to take care of the problems originating at the international level because the Internet, through which these terrorist activities are carried out, recognises no boundaries. Thus, a cyber terrorist can collapse the economic structure of a country from a place with which India may not have any reciprocal arrangements, including an "extradition treaty". The only safeguard in such a situation is to use the latest technology to counter these problems. Thus, a good combination of the latest security technology and a law dealing with cyber terrorism is the need of the hour.

Forms of Cyberterrorism

It is very difficult to exhaustively specify the forms of cyber terrorism. In fact, it would not be a fruitful exercise to do the same. The nature of cyber terrorism requires it to remain inclusive and open ended in nature, so that new variations and forms of it can be accommodated in the future. The following can be safely regarded as the forms of cyber terrorism applying the definition and the concepts discussed above:

Privacy Violation

The law of privacy is the recognition of the individual's right to be let alone and to have his personal space inviolate. The right to privacy as an independent and distinctive concept originated in the field of Tort law, under which a new cause of action for damages resulting from unlawful invasion of privacy was recognised. In recent times, however, this right has acquired a constitutional status, the violation of which attracts both civil as well as criminal consequences under the respective laws. The intensity and complexity of life have rendered necessary some retreat from the world. Man under the refining influence of culture, has become sensitive to publicity, so that solitude and privacy have become essential to the individual. Modern enterprise and invention have, through invasions upon his privacy, subjected him to mental pain and distress, far greater than could be inflicted by mere bodily injury. Right to privacy is a part of the right to life and personal liberty enshrined under Article 21 of the Constitution of India. With the advent of information technology the traditional concept of right to privacy has taken new dimensions, which require a different legal outlook.

The various provisions of the Act aptly protect the online privacy rights of the netizens. Certain acts have been categorised as offences and contraventions, which have tendency to intrude with the privacy rights of the netizens. These rights are available against private individuals as well as against cyber terrorists. Section 1 (2) read with Section 75 of the Act provides for an extra-territorial application of the provisions of the Act. Thus, if a person (including a foreign national) contravenes the privacy of an individual by means of computer, computer system or computer network located in India, he would be liable under the provisions of the Act. This makes it clear that the long arm jurisdiction is equally available against a cyber terrorist, whose act has resulted in the damage of the property, whether tangible or intangible.

Secret Information Appropriation and Data Theft

The information technology can be misused for appropriating the valuable Government secrets and data of private individuals and the Government and its agencies. A computer network owned by the

Government may contain valuable information concerning defence and other top secrets, which the Government will not wish to share otherwise. The same can be targeted by the terrorists to facilitate their activities, including destruction of property. It must be noted that the definition of property is not restricted to moveables or immoveables alone. In R.K. Dalmia v Delhi Administration the Supreme Court held that the word "property" is used in the I.P.C in a much wider sense than the expression "movable property". There is no good reason to restrict the meaning of the word "property" to moveable property only, when it is used without any qualification.

Whether the offence defined in a particular section of IPC can be committed in respect of any particular kind of property, will depend not on the interpretation of the word "property" but on the fact whether that particular kind of property can be subject to the acts covered by that section. Thus, if any person without permission of the owner or any other person who is incharge of a computer, computer system or computer network:

(a) Accesses or secures access to such computer, computer system or computer network.

(b) Downloads, copies or extracts any data, computer data base or information from such computer, computer system or computer network including information or data held or stored in any removable storage medium;

(c) Damages or causes to be damaged any computer, computer system or computer network, data, computer data base or any other programmes residing in such computer, computer system or computer network; he shall be liable to pay damages by way of compensation not exceeding one crore rupees to the person so affected. The expression "Computer Database" means a representation of information, knowledge, facts, concepts or instructions in text, image, audio, video that are being prepared or have been prepared in a formalised manner or have been produced by a computer, computer system or computer network and are intended for use in a computer, computer system or computer network. The expression "Damage" means to destroy, alter, delete, add, modify or re-arrange any computer resource by any means. These provisions make it clear that secret information appropriation and data theft by the cyber terrorists will be dealt with punitive sting and monetary impositions.

Demolition of E-governance Base

The aim of e-governance is to make the interaction of the citizens with the government offices hassle free and to share information in a free and transparent manner. It further makes the right to information a meaningful reality. In a democracy, people govern themselves and they cannot govern themselves properly unless they are aware of social, political, economic and other issues confronting them. To enable them to make a proper judgment on those issues, they must have the benefit of a range of opinions on those issues. Right to receive and impart information is implicit in free speech. This, right to receive information is, however, not absolute but is subject to reasonable restrictions which may be imposed by the Government in public interest. In P.U.C.L. V U.O. the Supreme Court specified the grounds on which the government can withhold information relating to various matters, including trade secrets. The Supreme Court observed: " Every right- legal or moral- carries with it a corresponding objection. It is subject to several exemptions/ exceptions indicated in broad terms. Generally, the exemptions/ exceptions under those laws entitle the Govt to with hold information relating to the following matters:

(1) International relations;

(2) National security (including defiance) and public safety;

(3) Investigation, detection and prevention of crime;

(4) Internal deliberations of the Govt;

(5) Information received in confidence from a source outside the Govt;

(6) Information, which, if disclosed, would violate the privacy of the individual;

(7) Information of an economic nature (including Trade Secrets) which, if disclosed, would confer an unfair advantage on some person or concern, or, subject some person or Govt, to an unfair disadvantage;

(8) Information, which is subject to a claim of legal professional privilege, *e.g.* communication between a legal adviser and the client; between a physician and the patient;

(9) Information About Scientific Discoveries"

It must be noted that the primary aim of all cyber terrorist activities is to collapse a sound communication system, which includes an e-governance base. Thus, by a combination of virus attacks and hacking techniques, the e-governance base of the government can be caused to be collapsed. This would be more deleterious and disastrous as compared to other tangible damages, which were caused by the traditional terrorist activities. Similarly, the terrorists to the common detriment of the nation at large can illegally obtain information legitimately protected from public scrutiny by the government in the interest of security of the nation. Thus, a strong e-governance base with the latest security methods and systems is the need of the hour.

Distributed Denial of Services Attack

The cyber terrorists may also use the method of distributed denial of services (DDOS) to overburden the Government and its agencies electronic bases. This is made possible by first infecting several unprotected computers by way of virus attacks and then taking control of them. Once control is obtained, they can be manipulated from any locality by the terrorists. These infected computers are then made to send information or demand in such a large number that the server of the victim collapses. Further, due to this unnecessary Internet traffic the legitimate traffic is prohibited from reaching the Government or its agencies computers. This results in immense pecuniary and strategic loss to the government and its agencies. It must be noted that thousands of compromised computers can be used to simultaneously attack a single host, thus making its electronic existence invisible to the genuine and legitimate netizens and end users. The law in this regard is crystal clear. If any person without permission of the owner or any other person who is incharge of a computer, computer system or computer network:

(a) Introduces or causes to be introduced any computer contaminant or computer virus into any computer, computer system or computer network;

(b) Disrupts or causes disruption of any computer, computer system or computer network;

(c) Denies or causes the denial of access to any person authorised to access any computer, computer system or computer network by any means; he shall be liable to pay damages by way of compensation not exceeding one crore rupees to the person so affected. The expression "Computer Contaminant" means any set of computer instructions that are designed–

(a) To modify, destroy, record, transmit data or programme residing within a computer, computer system or computer network; or

(b) By any means to usurp the normal operation of the computer, computer system, or computer network. Thus, distribute denial of services by the cyber terrorists will be tackled by invoking the provisions of sections 43,65 and 66 collectively.

Network Damage and Disruptions

The main aim of cyber terrorist activities is to cause networks damage and their disruptions. This activity may divert the attention of the security agencies for the time being thus giving the terrorists extra time and makes their task comparatively easier. This process may involve a combination of computer tampering, virus attacks, hacking, *etc.* The law in this regard provides that if any person without permission of the owner or any other person who is incharge of a computer, computer system or computer network:

(a) Accesses or secures access to such computer, computer system or computer network

(b) Introduces or causes to be introduced any computer contaminant or computer virus into any computer, computer system or computer network;

(c) Damages or causes to be damaged any computer, computer system or computer network, data, computer data base or any other programmes residing in such computer, computer system or computer network;

(d) Disrupts or causes disruption of any computer, computer system or computer network;

(e) Denies or causes the denial of access to any person authorised to access any computer, computer system or computer network by any means; he shall be liable to pay damages by way of compensation not exceeding one crore rupees to the person so affected. The expression "Computer Virus" means any computer instruction, information, data or programme that destroys, damages, degrades or adversely affects the performance of a computer resource or attaches itself to another computer resource and operates when a programme, data or instruction is executed or some other event takes place in that computer resource. The person tampering with such computer source documents shall be punishable with imprisonment up to 3 years or with fine, which may extend up to Rs.2 lakhs, or with both. Further, if a person causes wrongful loss or damage to any person, by destroying, deleting or altering any information residing in his (owner's) compute resource or diminishes its value or utility or affects it injuriously by any means, he commits hacking and thus, violates the privacy of the owner. The person hacking shall be punishable with imprisonment up to 3 years or with fine, which may extend up to Rs.2 lakhs, or with both. However, an innocent infringer will not be liable if he proves that he committed the act without any intention or knowledge. A network service provider will be liable for various violations and contraventions mentioned under the Act if he makes available any third party information or data to a person for the commission of an offence or contravention. However, a network service provider will not be liable if he proves that the offence or contravention was committed without his knowledge or he had exercised all due diligence to prevent such commission. Thus, these provisions can be safely invoked for meeting challenges posed by network damage and disruptions caused by cyber terrorists.

BIBLIOGRAPHY

Arquilla, John, and David Ronfeldt, "Cyberwar Is Coming!" *Compara-tive Strategy,* Vol. 12, No. 2, Summer 1993

Arquilla, John, and David Ronfeldt, eds., *In Athena's Camp: Preparing for Conflict in the Information Age,* Santa Monica, Calif.: RAND, MR-880-OSD/RC, 1997

Arquilla, John, and David Ronfeldt, *Swarming and the Future of Conflict,* Santa Monica, Calif.: RAND, DB-311-OSD, 2000

Arquilla, John, and David Ronfeldt, *The Advent of Netwar,* Santa Mon-ica, Calif.: RAND, MR-789-OSD, 1996

Arquilla, John, and David Ronfeldt, *The Emergence of Noopolitik: To-ward an American Information Strategy,* Santa Monica, Calif.: RAND, MR-1033-OSD, 1999

Arquilla, John, and Theodore Karasik, "Chechnya: A Glimpse of Future Conflict?" *Studies in Conflict and Terrorism,* Vol. 22, No. 3, 1999

Arquilla, John, David Ronfeldt, and Michele Zanini, "Information-Age Terrorism," *Current History,* Vol. 99, No. 636, April 2000, pp. 179–185

Bonabeau, Eric, and Christopher Meyer, "*Swarm Intelligence,*" *Harvard Business Review,* pp. 107–114, 2001

Bosch, O. *Cyber Terrorism and Private Sector Efforts for Information Infrastructure Protection. Creating Trust in Critical Networks Workshop of the ITU Strategy and Policy Unit,* 2002

Center for Strategic and International Studies, *Cybercrime, Cyberterrorism, Cyberwarfare, Averting an Electronic Waterloo,* 1998

CERT Coordination Center. International *Coordination for Cyber Crime and Terrorism in the 21st Century,* 2005

Cohn, Norman, *The Pursuit of the Millennium: Revolutionary Messi*anism *in Medieval and Reformation Europe and Its Bearing on Modern Totalitarian Movements,* New York: Harper Torch Books, 1961.

Colarik, A. *Cyber Terrorism: Political and Economic Implications. Idea* Group Publishing, 2006

David, M. and Sakurai, K. *Combating Cyber Terrorism: Countering Cyber Terrorist Advantages of Surprise and Anonymity.* Proceedings of the 17th International Conference on Advanced Information Networking and Applications, 2003

Denning, D. *Cyberterrorism, Testimony before the Special Oversight Panel on Terrorism Committee on Armed Services* U.S. House of Representatives, 2000

Denning, D. Activism, *Hacktivism, and Cyberterrorism: The Internet as a tool for Influencing Foreign Policy. Internet and International Systems: Information Technology and American Foreign Policy Decisionmaking Workshop*, 2001

Denning, D. Chapter Eight, *Activism, Hacktivism, and Cyberterrorism: The Internet as a Tool for Influencing* Foreign Policy. Networks and Netwars: The Future of Terror, Crime, and Militancy, 2001

Denning, D. Cyberwarriors: *Activists and terrorists turn to cyberspace.* Harvard International Review. 23(2), 2001

Flemming, P. and Stohl, M. *Myths and Realities of Cyberterrorism* International Conference on Countering Terrorism through Enhanced Cooperation, 2000

Hoffer, Eric, *The True Believer: Thoughts on the Nature of Mass Movements,* New York: Harper and Row, 1951

Institute for Security Technology Studies at Dartmouth College. *Cyber Security of the Electric Power Industry*, 2002

Jachowicz, L. *How to prevent and fight international and domestic Cyberterrorism and Cyberhooliganism*, 2003

Janczewski, L. and Colarik, A. *Managerial Guide for Handling Cyber-Terrorism and Information Warfare*. Idea Group Publishing, 2005

Janczewski, L. and Colarik, A. *Cyber Warfare and Cyber Terrorism.* Information Science Reference, 2007

Johnson, Steven, *Emergence: The Connected Lives of Ants, Brains, Cities, and Software,* New York: Scribner, 2001

Kalathil, Shanthi, and Taylor C. Boas, "*The Internet and State Control in Authoritarian* Regimes: China, Cuba, and the Counter revolution," *First Monday,* August, Vol. 6, No. 8, 2001

Kapstein, Ethan B., "*The Corporate Ethics Crusade,*" *Foreign Affairs,* Vol. 80, No. 5, September/October, pp. 105–119, 2001

Lawson, S. *Information Warfare: An Analysis of the Threat of Cyber Terrorism Towards the US Critical Infrastructure.* SANS GSEC, 2005

Lesser, Ian O., Bruce Hoffman, John Arquilla, David Ronfeldt, Michele Zanini, and Brian Jenkins, *Countering the New Terrorism,* Santa Monica, Calif.: RAND, MR-989-AF, 1999

Lewis, J. *Assessing the Risks of Cyber Terrorism, Cyber War and Other Cyber Threats.* Center for Strategic and International Studies, 2002

Lourdeau, K. Testimony of Keith Lourdeau, Deputy Assistant Director, Cyber Division, FBI Before the Senate Judiciary Subcommittee on Terrorism, Technology, and Homeland Security, Cyber Terrorism, 2005

Metzl, Jamie F., "*Network Diplomacy,*" *Georgetown Journal of Interna-tional Affairs,* Winter/Spring, p. 796, 2001

Nagpal, R. *Cyber Terrorism in the Context of Globalisation.* Proceedings of the 2nd World Congress on Informatics and Law, 2002

Nisbet, C. *Cybercrime and cyber terrorism. Securing Electronic Business Processes* – Highlights of the Information Security Solutions Conference 2003. Vieweg, 2004

Oram, Andy, ed., *Peer-to-Peer: Harnessing the Power of DisruptiveTechnologies,* O'Reilly and Associates, 2001

Pollitt, M. Cyberterrorism – Fact or Fancy?, 2005

Raghavan, T. *In Fear of Cyberterrorism: An Analysis of the Congressional Response.* Journal of Law, Technology and Policy. 1, 2003

Rifkin, Jeremy, *Time Wars: The Primary Conflict in Human History,* New York: Simon and Schuster, 1987

Rogerson, S. (August) *Cyber terrorism and the threat to democracy.* IMIS Journal. 13(4), 2003

Sofaer, A. and Goodman, S. (August) *A Proposal for an International Convention on Cyber Crime and Terrorism*, 2000

Tan, K. *Confronting Cyberterrorism with Cyber Deception.* Master's Thesis. Naval Postgraduate School, 2003

Tyrer, H. Chapter 16: *Cyber-terrorism. Science and Technology of Terrorism and Counterterrorism.* Marcel Dekker, Inc., 2002

United States Department of Energy *21 Steps to improve Cyber Security of SCADA Networks.* President's Critical Infrastructure Protection Board, 2005

United States House of Representatives Committee on Science Hearing Charter: *Cyber Terrorism – A View From The Gilmore Commission*, 2005

Verton, D. Black Ice: *The Invisible Threat of Cyber-Terrorism.* McGraw-Hill, 2003

Warren, M. and Furnell, S. Cyber-Terrorism–*Political Evolution of the Computer* Hacker, 2005

Yurcik, W. *Adaptive Multi-Layer Network Survivability: A Unified Framework for Countering Cyber-Terrorism.* Proceedings of the Workshop on Countering Cyber-Terrorism, 1999